the Georgian Kitchen

About the Author

Emma Kay is a historian and writer. She has worked as
a museum professional for over fifteen years in major
institutions such as the National Maritime Museum, the
British Museum and the University of Bath. She has a
degree in History, a postgraduate certificate in Roman
Archaeology, an MA in Heritage Interpretation and a
diploma in Cultural Heritage Management. She has spoken
and written about the history of kitchenalia to a variety
of different audiences. Emma founded her own mobile
education service in 2012, the Museum of Kitchenalia. This
is the culmination of over seven years spent collecting
vintage and antique kitchen apparatus.

the Georgian Kitchen

EMMA KAY

AMBERLEY

First published 2014
This edition first published 2015

Amberley Publishing
The Hill, Stroud
Gloucestershire, GL5 4EP

www.amberley-books.com

British Library Cataloguing in Publication Data.
A catalogue record for this book is available from the British Library.

ISBN 978 1 4456 5056 2 (paperback)
ISBN 978 1 4456 3656 6 (ebook)

Typeset in 10.5pt on 13pt Celeste.
Typesetting and Origination by Amberley Publishing.
Printed in the UK.

CONTENTS

Acknowledgements

Thank you to all at Amberley Publishing, particularly Christian for inspiring me to write the book.

A special thank you to my husband Nick for photographing my collection for inclusion in the book, with such professionalism and creativity – continued gratitude for tolerating my absence throughout this project. To my lovely son, thank you for being so patient and good.

Most of all I give thanks to my father. The inspiration for me embarking on a career in history and museums, from a stimulating childhood visiting museums all over the UK and overseas, to an endless repertoire of exciting stories recounting Roman and Victorian Britain. You fired my passion and always gave me the confidence to succeed.

Preface

Just over twenty years ago I was embarking on my career as a museum practitioner, which began in a volunteer capacity working in small depository for local collections located by the sea. My journey would take me all the way to a senior position at the British Museum following a lengthy and enjoyable seven years at the National Maritime Museum.

From a Masters in Heritage Interpretation, a Postgraduate Diploma in Archaeology and a Diploma in Conservation I used my knowledge and skills to create a collection of my own to maintain and interpret for the benefit of wider audiences.

Many academics are concerned with preserving and maintaining the past behind doors and writing about the political and economic historical value of objects and archives that have been left behind. The most important observation I have made in my career is that people like stories. Stories about everyday people. There is no better way to tell these stories than through the very objects that were used, and from learning more about the individuals from whom they were inherited.

As someone who has always been passionate about food and cooking it seemed natural to collect items that were concerned with the preparation, cooking and serving of food. My initial interest grew from a gift of a 1950s Denby dinner service given to me ten years ago. From this I began to read about the various eras of development in kitchenware and started to trawl charity shops, antique stalls and online auction houses for objects that best represented these eras. Over these ten years I have built a collection of some eighty objects spanning the eighteenth century to the 1960s. This collection has now evolved into a mobile museum, an online blog and an ongoing archive of collected stories, recipes and objects that it is hoped will evolve into a broader resource for the public over the next few years. The objects pictured within the book are of individual items from the collection itself.

This book is inspired by my collection and the research that I have carried out on one particular era of history and is representative of just one nation during this period – Britain.

The Georgian period in Britain is one that I find particularly fascinating. It represents the transcending shift out of medieval naivety into an era of modernisation and materialism, not dissimilar to the one that we all live in today.

A word to the reader regarding the language in this book – many of the recipes, citations or direct quotes from the time have been translated verbatim. The English language of the eighteenth and nineteenth centuries is very different to what readers are familiar with today.

Introduction

*Some people have a foolish way of not minding, or pretending
not to mind, what they eat. For my part, I mind my belly very
studiously, and very carefully; for I look upon it, that he who
does not mind his belly, will hardly mind anything else.*

Samuel Johnson

The year in which this book was written marks the three
hundredth anniversary of the accession of George I, the
start of a period that would evolve into one of the most
revolutionary and defining times in Britain's history. It
was a time of British imperial expansion, the slave trade
(and its subsequent abolition), the Jacobite Risings and
the Act of Union. It was not, however, only revolutionary
in a political sense. It was also a time of great revolution
in food and eating. Our everyday worship of coffee shops
and fast food commenced in the 1700s, and we bought ice
cream from early Italian settlers establishing corner-shop
confectionery. People of the Georgian age ate macaroni and
parmesan cheese, cooked scotch eggs, made sandwiches,
drank Schweppes fizzy water and gorged on French and
other continental delicacies that were almost as available as
those to be found in an Aldi supermarket today.

The narrative within is concerned with investigating the
way in which people ate and their attitudes and responses to

food. It explores the developing nature of how ingredients evolved and were utilised in new ways for both domestic and commercial consumption.

In contrast to the limitations of the dark ages and the domestically destructive and superstitious Stuart and Tudor dynasties, politically, economically and socially the country was shifting and transcending into a regenerated, informed and intelligent nation. The French dominated Britain's kitchens; the streets were crowded with traders, markets, coffee shops, eating houses and opportunistic thieves. Never had class been so clearly defined, as the new hopeful and confident middle classes elevated themselves out of poverty into commercial trades, while the poor were patronised but left to wallow in the horrors of squalid shanties with next to nothing to eat. The wealthy looked on, gorging themselves on the delights of imported luxury produce, and formed the groups, societies, networks and industries that remain integral to Britain in the twenty-first century.

This period marks the start of globalisation. It is representative of an aspiring society and a divergence of communities. The Georgian age was built on the foundations of foreign influence and materialism, with its passion for scientific and aesthetic discourse. Within this context, food and food consumption in all its disciplines rendered a significant role. This book focuses on a range of culinary topics related to the period in order to present an overall definitive narrative of Georgian cooking, dining and eating.

Carrying the legacy of the Civil War and still recovering from the Plague of the century before, the political and economic turmoil of the eighteenth century combined with the early infrastructures of the Industrial Revolution were beginning to impact on the lives and quality of people living across the country. The population was increasing rapidly. According to Deane and Cole the population for England and Wales in 1701 was estimated at 5.826 million. By 1801 this figure had almost doubled to 9.156 million.[1] Britain was acquiring a wealth of foreign influences as a consequence of its trade and growing Empire. More than ever, class played a fundamental role in defining the political mood and cultural influences, particularly those associated with the French situation, which dramatically enhanced upper- and middle-class attitudes towards food and methods of cooking. The eighteenth and early nineteenth centuries were also known for taxation. Legislative limitations were placed on all basic items from bread to tea. Taxes were often collected from coffee houses up to twice a day every day.

While medieval and Tudor households were almost entirely staffed by men, it has been argued that this began to change significantly during the late eighteenth century, in part as a consequence of the tax imposed by the British government in 1777 on male servants, secured to help fund the war with America.[2]

By examining both the female and male servant tax rolls for Edinburgh in Scotland between 1785 and 1786 it is certainly apparent that the total paid in domestic servant duty is seven times greater for male servants as it is for female servants. There continues to be more men in employment in domestic service, some fifty-four male to forty-six female servants, between these two years.[3] Interestingly this figure differs considerably in Dumfries where in the same time period sixty-one female servants are recorded as working in houses in this district, while only nineteen male servants were employed.[4] However, by 1791 the number of women employed in this same district drops considerably to just forty-two. As of January 2013 the transcriptions of the male servant tax rolls for this same year had yet to be completed by the National Records of Scotland, so it is difficult to gauge whether the same decrease occurred for male domestic workers. Female servants had replaced male servants by the end of the eighteenth century, with the exception of the great rural and urban households of the wealthy, who only recruited eminent male cooks to manage their kitchens. Male

French cooks were the most in demand and as such would be rewarded some of the largest salaries of all domestic staff.

Increased social awareness and social theory was a motivating factor for collating population statistics and demographics. As the people of the Georgian age began to understand and empathise more with social and moral responsibilities, they began to theorise, openly debate and write about these subjects, from the need to resolve issues around immigration and trade to the politics of war and governance. This included an overriding desire to find a solution for poverty and illness, along with many other issues that dominated the headlines and lives of those living in this new age of enlightenment and technological and scientific advancement. Infant mortality rates were staggeringly high. If children of the poor did not die at birth, then they would often be left to the mercy of the streets, or the wrath of their gin-soaked mothers. Health was a subject broadly communicated in the media. An article that appeared in the *Chester Chronicle* on Friday 31 July, 1829, titled 'Dinner for Invalids', offers a solution to the nutritional needs of people who are sick, advising that roast beef or roast mutton are the most suitable of foods, preferably to be served no later than two o'clock in the afternoon. It is also suggested that veal and lamb are too indigestible, based on the widely unfounded idea that meat from young animals is detrimental to health, owing to the fact that it has 'not yet arrived to perfection [it is] unwholesome and ... very hurtful'. Fish is also considered an unwise option if a person is unwell, due to the fact that it can cause an 'exciting disturbance in the alimentary canal' as well as proving to be 'less nutritive than the flesh of warm-blooded animals'. Before the advent of the travel networks or proper refrigeration fish would have become rancid very quickly. If money was tight, the time to purchase fish in the markets would have been at the end of the day, when the real stench of early decay began to set in.

There is a significant amount of documented material

throughout the early eighteenth and into the late nineteenth century that offers advice relating to food, drink and eating practices of the day across all aspects of society. Despite the poorer and less-educated classes not having a voice, a great deal was recorded about their living conditions, health and diet by social commentators and observers, who provide some insight into the disparity across Georgian society. Similarly it was a period of documenting statistics and recording detailed accounts of events and day-to-day activities. The *Berkshire Chronicle* of Saturday 31 December 1825 gives the following calculations for consumption of food in London, based on London market sales: in 1822, 149,885 beasts, 24,602 calves, 1,507,096 sheep and 20,020 pigs were bought at market. On average 200,000 pigs were slaughtered each week in the UK in 2013, so around 10.4 million annually; 104,000 calves and 13 million sheep were also slaughtered the same year. Taking into consideration that the figures for 1822 are for London only, as well as the fact that the population has increased considerably in the last 150–200 years, these figures are not widely disproportionate to today's.[5]

Developments in medical science from the eighteenth century instigated the discovery of the relationship between dirt and disease that prompted the large-scale social changes of the following century. Preventative inventions, including vaccination for immunity from smallpox, perfected by Edward Jenner in 1796, prompted the trend for eradicating diseases, and new health and social legislations were implemented by the middle of the nineteenth century. During the Georgian period, hospitals were under scrutiny and midwifery became a taught subject in specialist maternity units.[6] Groups of wealthy men, forged together in the many coffee houses and clubs of the day, were driven to improve the existing medieval systems of medical care and treatment. By 1860 the theories of Louis Pasteur, confirming the germ theory linking contamination through micro-organisms, stimulated an already growing awareness of the relationship between keeping things clean and stopping infection spreading, a notion that the Hungarian physician Semmelweiss had suggested around ten years earlier.[7] The discourse around these theories and their emerging conclusions began to influence the way in which people were running their kitchens, and eating and preparing their food. As a consequence utensils and cooking apparatus that offered both smarter and more hygienic alternatives were in development as early as the late eighteenth century.

General advancements in kitchen technology were significant by the mid-eighteenth century. Once again it is worth emphasising the extent to which these changes were largely only pertinent to the wealthier strands of society, a distinction evident in this reference made to repairs on a Smoking Jack, one of the latest gadgets of the time, recorded in the private papers of a Mr John Webb in 1756. The Jack is described as 'an apparatus for turning a roasting spit, fixed in a chimney and set in motion by (a) current of air passing up (the) chimney'.[8] The cost to these repairs amounts to ten shillings and sixpence, which equates to over forty or fifty pounds in today's currency. The average domestic servant would have had to work in excess of five years to earn that sort of money. An inventory of household items listed in the estate of Revd John Forth and Mrs Elizabeth Forth between 1791 and 1806 provides further insight into the more upper-middle-class kitchenalia of this period. Items include: a mahogany coffee mill, brass mortar and iron pestle, a pair of steelyards (weights), a wooden horse to brush clothes on, an iron salamander (to brown meat) and butter prints.[9] Finally, extracts relating to the Earl of Ancaster's private household records denote the contrasting aristocratic luxuries acquired just thirty to forty years on: five stoves, as well as a kitchen range and cheeks (adjustable fire widths) with a Portland sink connected to a water supply carried by lead pipes, a large jack, two chains, a multiplying wheel and weight.[10] Brass fittings are also listed in abundance, possibly in relation to the modern plumbing systems.

In the last seven hundred years the kitchen has evolved from a fire in the middle of the home where the cooking took place, to a room now considered to be the hub of our modern dwellings. By the sixteenth century mechanical inventions were emerging, such as the turn-spit operated by a small dog to roast meat continuously over an open fire.[11] Writing mostly about the century before, Peter Earle confirms that during the 1600s as far as the middle classes were concerned the kitchen remained the least altered room. These were multi-functional spaces for cooking, serving and preparing food as well for washing, ironing and mending clothes and laundry. Kitchens also served as a refuge for domestic servants in which to eat their meals and relax. Ovens were a rare commodity, with baking taking place off site by local providers. Spit roasting and boiling were the predominant methods for cooking. In addition pewter had replaced wood for serving plates, dishes and basins. Innovations in the kitchen were uncommon, if not non-existent, during the seventeenth century.[12]

Prior to 1760, very little was being achieved in relation to enhancing the efficiency of kitchens or kitchen apparatus in Britain. However by the sixteenth and seventeenth centuries the European and Renaissance continental chefs of the time, such as the Italian Bartolomeo Scappi, as recorded in his manual *L'arte et prudenza d'un maestro Cuoco* (The Art and Craft of a Master Cook), negate this theory where other European countries are concerned. Scappi's list of essential items for the kitchen included brass pestle and mortars, tripods for frying pans, flasks, cauldrons, an array of copper pans and dishes, colanders, stew pots, baking sheets, rolling pins, dough cutters, cheese graters, flour sifters, moulds, horse-hair brushes, filters for filtering spices, strainers for straining jelly, special cloths to keep prepared dishes covered, serviettes and various weights and measures in order to meticulously weigh ingredients according to the recipe.[13]

The list goes on and includes descriptions of about six

different types of oven. Incredibly, Scappi's manuscript dates
to 1570. From this complicated list of inspiring culinary
objects, it becomes easier to determine how Britain's
relationship with Europe through increased trade and
immigration would have significantly influenced the way
in which cooking and eating evolved during the Georgian
age, considering Europe's level of advancement compared to
Britain's at that time. Cookery books were prolific and were
copied and reprinted in a variety of languages, depending on
their popularity. Just as recipe books written by well-known
chefs to accompany a series of cookery programmes today
gain tremendous commercial success and media attention, so
too did the cookery writers of the eighteenth and nineteenth
centuries. It is arguably easy to estimate that every middle-
class household would have owned at least one cookery
book of some sort. Throughout the early 1700s dinner rarely
consisted of more than two courses, but by the close of the
century, soup, fish and game courses had been introduced.[14]
This is also the time when 'Afternoon tea' became a popular
pastime, for those seeking refreshment between meals. New
raw materials entering the market and the cultural exchange
of ideas largely provided by the French had a diverse
impact on Georgian culinary society which was integral to
eighteenth- and early nineteenth-century attitudes towards
food and cooking.[15]

The French not only enlightened the British with their
cuisine and artful suggestions on preparation, presentation
and technical proficiency. They also provided them with the
incentive to develop more appropriate kitchen utensils and
tools. In France the three-pronged fork was in general use for
many years before it came to England during the eighteenth
century, despite the fact that many inns kept to their old
customs, enabling the two-pronged fork to continue to be
used as late as the nineteenth century.[16]

As people were travelling more, particularly throughout
Europe, the Georgian era captured a great deal of social

commentary relating to different cultural customs, from both the British and foreign perspectives. As French immigrants began to dominate traditional British culinary attitudes, mixed feelings of loyalty towards customary dishes and the new techniques and recipes introduced by the French generated a great deal of public debate and discourse. This is apparent in the written media of the time, the letters, personal travel journals and diaries. Joseph Addison, writing in the Tatler magazine in 1709, is critical of those in British society who abandon their own cultural culinary identities in favour of the fashionable French style, noting,

> They admit of nothing to their tables in its natural form, or without some disguise ...
>
> They are not to approve any thing that is agreeable to ordinary palates; and nothing is to gratify their sense, but what would offend those of their inferiors.
>
> I remember I was last summer invited to a friend's house, who is a great admirer of the French cookery, and (as the phrase is), at our sitting down, I found the table covered with a great variety of unknown dishes. I was mightily at a loss to learn what they were, and therefore did not know where to help myself. That which stood before me I took to be a roasted Porcupine, however did not care for asking questions; and have since been informed, that it was only a larded Turkey.[17]

Despite the fact that for many, the process of cooking and eating involved congregating around the only fireplace in the centre of the house, and that few dwellings afforded the luxury of a kitchen as a room for this central purpose, Dean et al.'s study of Kent dwellings between 1600 and 1749 provides some enlightening information on the evolution of activities and objects in domestic kitchens over a 150-year period. Throughout the early part of the 1600s most cooking utensils were stored in people's hallways. By the early to mid-1700s these objects had moved into the kitchen area. Similarly the act of eating also moved from hall to kitchen, and pictures, which had never been placed in kitchen areas, began to appear in this space by 1749. Interestingly the number of items made of pewter stored in kitchens almost trebled between 1600 and 1749. Many of the activities that formerly took place in the hall of the house moved to the kitchen. This can be explained in part by the increase in new equipment being manufactured for the kitchen, and the introduction of more diverse ranges of food and drink.[18]

The discourse on cooking and eating during the eighteenth and early nineteenth centuries is not limited to domestic activities. People ate in their homes, out in society, at work, as guests or in the myriad of inns, taverns, cook shops, clubs and coffee houses. Just as they do today, people also had to eat in schools, hospitals, prisons, or anywhere they were residing at the time. It is possible to glean from Clement Dukes' published report of 1803 that the provision available to some children was substandard, as he reveals that 'the cooking of food at school seems to be one of the chief grievances, the complaints in this respects being incessant and reasonable'. The children clearly needed more variety, being opposed to the bland 'plain and wholesome' dishes that were served up and prepared in the same way every day. Later in the report, this is attributed to the lack of good cooking staff, whom schools seemed unable to recruit. Whether this was due to poor pay, difficult hours or something else is indeterminable given the lack of detail offered in the report.[19] It is also a stark reminder of how little the situation of food in schools in Britain has changed since the early nineteenth century, if we are to understand the campaigns in the media led by the celebrity chef Jamie Oliver and the ongoing debates in Parliament on how to address the current situation.

Sir Frederick Morton Eden's 'The State of the Poor' describes the activities of a workhouse around 1797 in Halifax, Yorkshire, where eighty-nine of the town's paupers resided. Tragically, twenty of those eighty-nine were under six years old. Those granted the liberty of working 'out of doors', particularly in the kitchens, were provided with a dinner every day of butcher's meat. Others had rationed meat dinners on Sundays and Thursdays. Eden informs us that children received no meat at all. Instead they were given pudding, probably made from some sort of cereal or bread product. During the remaining days of the week meals consisted of potatoes, butter, milk or beer with a slice of bread. Breakfast, which was served at seven in the morning, was either boiled milk or broth and bread or a dish known in the Georgian period as 'Hasty pudding'.[20] This was a sort of cheap wheat-flour porridge, which later became popular in America and is now associated with a particular honorary status among theatricals.[21] Workers received a pint of beer at ten in the morning and another at four in the afternoon.[22]

By 1821 wheat prices were still high, due in part to prolonged bad weather, but other key items began to fall in price. For example bacon 'by the side', usually around a shilling or more, was now four pence, or half a penny for a pound of dried and smoked bacon. There was a push generally to promote local butchers and encourage people to start spending money on the lower-priced meats of the time, which also included lamb.[23] This was also a period where it was as important for food to look as good as it tasted. Consequently there were numerous cases in the media relating to the adulteration of food and incidents of poisonings. An edition of *The Bath Chronicle*, 1820, highlights opinions of the time on this subject, quoting from a recently published book by a well-known chemist – Mr Accum – who emphasises,

> Of all the strands (says he in his preliminary observations) practised by mercenary dealers, there is none more reprehensible, and at the same time more prevalent, than the sophistication of the various articles of food. This

unprincipled and nefarious practice, increasing in degree as it has been found difficult of detection, is now applied to almost every commodity which can be classed among either the necessaries or the luxuries of life; and is carried on to a most alarming extent in every part of the United Kingdom.

Artisans were fighting against the rise of industrialisation, which sparked the Luddite uprising in the early part of the nineteenth century, accounting in part for the high food prices of 1811. Britain was also plagued by famine, food riots and poor harvests. The country was constantly at war during the Georgian period but in exploration and trade the age was a golden one, making this a period of huge contrasts, disparity, change and progression. The following list provides a summary of some of these fluctuating prices:

1785
Wheat 28s to 38s
Barley 18s to 22s
Oats 14s to 17s 6d
Peas 28s to 33s
Flour, fine 33s to 40s

1792
Wheat 32s 8d to 39s 6d
Barley 22s to 25s 6d
Oats 15s 17s to 29s 6d
Peas 26s to 32s
Beef 3s 8d per stone of lb
Mutton 4s per stone of lb
Lamb 5s per stone of lb
Pork 3s 6d per stone of lb

1799
Wheat 46s to 53s

Barley 30s to 37s 6d
Oats 29s to 35s 6d
Peas 43s to 46s
Flour, fine 56s to 60s
Beef 2s 10d to 3s and 10d
Mutton 3s to 4s 4d
Lamb 3s to 4s 8d
Pork 3s and 8d to 4s and 4d

1811
Wheat 95s to 110s
Barley 40s to 46s
White peas 80s
Flour, fine 114s to 117s
Beef 4s 4d to 5s 6d
Mutton 4s 4d to 5s 4d
Lamb [none available]
Pork 5s to 7s

1815
Wheat 46s to 56s
Barley 23s to 27s
Oats 19s to 21s
White pease 36s to 38s
Flour, fine 60s to 65s
Beef 4s 8d to 5s 8d
Mutton 5s to 6s 4d
Lamb [none available]
Pork 4s 8d to 6s 8d[24]

Significant fluctuations in food prices are not only apparent chronologically. Frederick Morton Eden provides a weekly account of expenses for families working in agricultural labour across eleven counties in England. These expenses were recorded across different years and for different-sized families. By cross-referencing and analysing Eden's figures it is possible to provide a useful geographical overview of the sort of comparative prices the labouring classes were being paid. It is also possible to determine exactly what types of food they were buying and in what quantity between 1794 and 1795.

Typical weekly earnings for a family of four working in agricultural labour by county, 1794–5:

County	£	s	d
Leicestershire	0	12	10½
Lincolnshire	0	12	6
Hertfordshire	0	12	4
Oxfordshire	0	12	0
Suffolk	0	11	2¼
Northamptonshire	0	10	0
Somerset	0	9	10
Norfolk	0	9	8
Cumberland	0	9	4
Bedfordshire	0	9	0
Huntingdonshire	0	8	7

The mean weekly earnings, then, for a typical family of four working in farm labour between 1794 and 1795 equates to about ten shillings, or thirty-five to forty-five pounds in today's currency. Leicestershire is by far the wealthiest of counties, with Huntingdonshire representing the lowest paid area. From the same sample of population as that used above,[25] we learn that typically the largest amount of money was spent on bread, flour and oats. This is perhaps not so surprising, considering these food staples were comparatively cheap and enabled people to feel fuller for longer. The figures also reveal how much meat the labouring classes were consuming, perpetuating all of the long-standing evidence that this was the era of substantial carnivorous eating. Interestingly no meat is cited as being purchased in Norfolk; this could be a reflection of their largely arable farming identity.

Despite the fairly high proportion of dairy consumption, a number of counties show no cheese or milk was factored into the weekly expenses, in particular, Bedfordshire, Cumberland, Huntingdonshire, Lincolnshire, Northamptonshire, Oxfordshire and Somersetshire. Suffolk denotes that milk was very scarce, yet it demonstrates the highest consumption of cheese. It should be emphasised that the figures indicate the funds allocated to the purchase of specific items of food. Counties such as Suffolk grew their own potatoes, which is why they do not appear on the overall weekly list. Without exception all the counties allocated a substantial proportion of their weekly wage towards tea, sugar and butter. This emphasises the extent to which tea was rapidly becoming a mass consumer product in England as early as the late 1700s. Geography would have had a significant impact on the diet of populations; diet would depend on their travelling distance to markets, ports and available access to good trade routes. The type of land, the climate and the infrastructure would also have influenced the types of food communities were able to produce for themselves.

A great deal can be learned about the eighteenth and nineteenth centuries from writers and diarists. While the philanthropic statisticians relayed the issues and problems of the poor, novelists such as Jane Austen provided essential information relating to social dining of the middle classes. In particular the differences in rural and urban living, and how farmers and agriculturists made the most of the land and the animals on it. Farmer's wives were skilled in the ways of preserving, brewing, cheese-making and curing among other activities, and passed this knowledge down to their own daughters. Austen herself kept poultry. Rural lifestyles were almost totally self-sufficient, with the only bought necessities being fish, tea, coffee, sugar or other luxury imports available to this growing echelon of society. In stark contrast with the towns and cities, bought produce in rural areas, in particular meat, was both less available and more expensive. The journals of James Woodforde (1758–1802), a simple country parson and bachelor whose humble life in Somerset and then Norfolk is documented across almost forty years, provide a detailed and intimate knowledge of his daily routines. We learn how he attends regular country dances, often into the early hours of the morning, feasting on roasted shoulder of mutton and plum pudding, followed by veal cutlets, frill'd potatoes, cold tongue, ham, cold roast beef and eggs in their shells. All washed down with punch, wine, beer and cider. Food is a regular theme throughout Woodforde's diary. It is a stark reflection of the importance placed upon culinary satisfaction and excess at this time. He describes one dinner he hosts for three acquaintances, which consisted of a couple of boiled chickens, a tongue, a boiled leg of mutton with capers and a batter pudding. This is just the first course. The second course provided roasted ducks, green peas, artichokes, tarts and blancmange. It continues still with almonds and raisins, oranges and strawberries, naturally ending with port wine. The whole process of this rather unexceptional, yet hugely extravagant one meal commenced in the afternoon and continued until eight o'clock in the evening.

In the larger towns and cities street food had been enjoyed in Britain since medieval times, when it was common to purchase items such as ribs of beef, hot peas-cod and hot sheep's feet, trends incidentally that continued into the Victorian era. By the end of the 1700s, cook shops were evolving more into the type of restaurant model that is seen today. These had developed as early as the 1600s, alongside the coffee shops, as venues for men and some women across all social ranks to come together and discuss trade and politics, congregating in an environment conducive to discussion over a good cheap snack.

In 1698 M. Misson described one such venue in England

that is reminiscent of many of the contemporary up-scale grill houses to be found in major cities today, where the raw meats are brought to table for the customer to select prior to cooking.

> Generally four spits, one over another, carry round each five or six pieces of butcher-meat, beef, mutton, veal, pork, and lamb; you have what quantity you please cut off, fat, lean, much or little done; with this, a little salt and mustard upon the side of a plate, a bottle of beer and a roll; and there is your whole feast.[26]

By the 1850s the streets were crowded with food vendors. These vendors had either evolved from the Georgian age, or provided some contemporary alternative as trends and tastes changed. The streets would have echoed with the touting shouts of the vendors selling their cheap off-cuts and stolen wares, exposed to the filthy and putrid elements. A far cry from the food standards agencies and health-and-safety measures of today. During the earlier years of the Georgian age food was still predominantly sold in the markets, often open from five or six in the morning until seven or eight in the evening, and fresh produce would be sold six days a week. There are some accounts stating that as the seventeenth century progressed, that retailers were already pushing for Sunday trading hours in the larger towns and cities. Lists of bills of fare, similar to that outlined in Maria Rundell's 1808 edition of *A New System of Domestic Cookery*, provide us with a greater understanding of what types of food were eaten at particular times of year. Ingredients were still seasonal during the Georgian period, despite the introduction of new imports and a growing network of transportation.

The following extract is a summary of what key food items were available on a monthly basis, based on the notes made by Maria Rundell.

	Poultry & Game	Fish	Meat	Fruit	Vegetables
January	Pheasants, partridges, hares, rabbits, woodcocks, snipes, turkeys, capons, pullets, fowls, chickens, capons, tame pigeons	Carp, tench, perch, lampreys, eels, crayfish, cod, sole, flounders, plaice, turbot, thornback, skate, sturgeon, whitings, smelts, lobsters, crabs, prawns, oysters		Apples, pears, nuts, medlars, grapes	Cabbage, colewort, sprouts, leeks, onions, beet, sorrel, chervil, endive, spinach, celery, garlic, scorzonera, potatoes, parsnips, turnips, broccoli, shallots, lettuces, cress, mustard, rape, salsify, cucumbers, asparagus and some mushrooms
February & March	As above including ducklings	As above		Apples, pears, forced strawberries	As above including kidney beans
April	Pullets, fowls, chickens, ducklings, pigeons, rabbits, leverets	Carp, tench, soles, smelts, eels, trout, turbot, lobsters, chub, salmon, herrings, crayfish, mackerel, crabs, prawn, shrimp	Beef, mutton, veal, lamb		As above
May	Pullets, fowls, chickens, ducklings, pigeons, rabbits, leverets	Carp, tench, soles, smelts, eels, trout, turbot, lobsters, chub, salmon, herrings, crayfish, mackerel, crabs, prawn, shrimp	Beef, mutton, veal, lamb	As above	As above including peas, radishes, carrots, turnips, cabbages, cauliflowers, asparagus, artichokes and various 'forced' salads

June			Beef, mutton, veal, lamb, venison	Strawberries, cherries, melons, green apricots, currants and gooseberries	
July	Pullets, fowls, chickens, rabbits, pigeons, green geese, leverets, turkey poults, plovers, wheatears	Cod, haddock, flounders, plaice, skate, thornback, mullets, pike, carp, eels, shellfish except oysters, mackerel	As above	Cherries, strawberries, pears, melons, gooseberries, currants, apricots, grapes, nectarines, peaches, raspberries, pineapples, plums	
August	As above	Cod, haddock, flounders, plaice, skate, thornback, mullets, pike, carp, eels, shell-fish except oysters.	As above	Peaches, plums, figs, filberts, mulberries, cherries, apples, pears, nectarines, grapes, melons, strawberries, medlars and quinces, damsons	
September	As above. including geese, partridge (non-poached)	As above	As above	As above	Beans, peas, French beans

October	Partridge, larks, hares, wild ducks, teals, snipes, widgeon, grouse	Dories, smelts, pikes, perch, halibuts, brills, carp, salmon, trout, barbel, gudgeons, tench, shellfish	As above including doe venison	Peaches, pears, figs, bullace (wild plum), grapes, apples, medlars, damsons, filberts, walnuts, quinces	As in January including French beans
November	As above	As above	Beef, mutton, veal, pork, doe-venison, poultry and game, 'house-lamb'	Pears, apples, nuts, medlars, grapes, bullace	Carrots, turnips, parsnips, potatoes, skirrets, scorzonera, onions, leeks, shallots, cabbages, colewort, spinach, chardoons, cresses, celery, herbs
December	Geese, turkeys, pullets, pigeons, capons, fowls, chickens, rabbits, hares, snipes, woodcocks, larks, pheasants, partridges, sea-fowls, guinea-fowls, wild ducks, teal, widgeon, dotterels, dun-birds, grouse	Cod, turbot, halibuts, soles, gurnets, sturgeon, carp, gudgeons, codlings, eels, dories, shellfish	Beef, mutton, veal, 'house-lamb', pork, venison	As above, excluding bullace	As above including forced asparagus

We are so accustomed to sourcing the types of ingredients we want to use all year round from the supermarkets or online that it is difficult to comprehend a time when access to food was totally determined by the seasons. What is also interesting from this list is the number of items of food that are no longer consumed with any popularity in Britain. Neither snipes – a long-billed wading bird notoriously difficult to hunt – nor hares are eaten in Britain in any abundance. Domestic pigeons were regularly bred and kept in dove coups in more well-to-do households; they provided a source of meat for much of the year. Capons, or castrated cockerels, which were once considered superior fare to the chicken, are no longer fashionable to eat, along with sea-fowl, which may be a generic term for coastal birds. While most British people do not eat eels, lampreys (also a type of eel), or smelts, there is a national campaign to eat more line-caught fish and in particular types of lesser-known fish that are not at risk of overconsumption, as cod is. Many of the vegetables listed are still popular today. Scorzonera is an edible flower and not used domestically anymore. Similarly skirrets are like sweet nutty parsnips and were once a staple food in medieval Britain. What is surprising is the amount of fruit that was grown locally in Britain, much of which, for example nectarines, figs, melons and grapes, are nearly all entirely now sourced from overseas. Filberts are a type of hazelnut, no longer widely cultivated in Britain, but nonetheless possibly the only native edible nut in the country. Despite a trend for revival in some communities, mulberries, quinces, damsons and medlars are also fruits which are no longer as in demand as they once were. 'House Lamb' was the term given to ewes that were forced into season earlier in order to produce lamb meat beyond the spring.

Many academics writing about Georgian society tend to focus on the London-centric aspects of the overall narrative, but there is a much broader scope of information relating to the period from across the United Kingdom as a whole, including

Northern Ireland, Scotland and Wales. While the larger port cities and towns of England may have been benefiting from the early indulgences of a cultural and industrial revolution, most were still living as the generations before them had. The simple farm labourers, particularly those like the hardy Irish 'Cottars' who lived in mud-built cabins in remote and isolated regions, could only afford a kettle with which to boil potatoes in – their main staple diet. These communities would have had little experience of the culinary and domestic advantages that were taking place elsewhere in Britain.[27]

Nonetheless many of Britain's culinary consumers were thriving, growing and innovating in ways which are comparable with twenty-first century society, in part as a consequence of migration, globalisation, materialism and economic growth. The story of British food as we know it now is a complex and exciting one, with Georgian society at the heart of it.

The Georgians were the first to recognise the importance of diet. Despite frequently choosing not to practice what they preached, they understood the consequences of malnutrition and the ramifications of excess. They looked beyond the confines of their own food production to the wider markets to be found on the Continent and the subsequent benefits to be enjoyed from exploring new types of food and drink. This was the age in which the familiar world of modern Britain began, including the British love affair with tea; the emergence of the 'nation of shop keepers'; our understanding of the relationship between food, health and hygiene and Britain's determination to advance technologically while increasing its preoccupation with labour-saving gadgetry for the kitchen. As humans, food is fundamental to our existence. It is vital to the understanding of ourselves, our legacy and our future. If that long-anticipated meteor ever does hit earth and some are lucky enough to survive it, the first thing they will need to do is find food and drink, food and drink that may well need to be prepared, cooked, filtered and stored. That is how important our culinary heritage is and will remain.

1

Trade and Early Empire: Overseas Influence and New Ingredients

In the social state to which we have come today, it is hard to imagine a nation which would live solely on bread and vegetables.

Jean-Antheleme Brillat-Savarin, 1825

By the middle of the eighteenth century material growth and capitalism was expanding in Britain, in part due to improvements in education and communication. This era witnessed the rise of the middle classes and higher standards of living for many.[1] As the century progressed into the 1800s Britain entered the Industrial Revolution and began its ascendancy as a global force, reaping the benefits of early exploration and its usurpation of colonies across the Atlantic. The Age of Enlightenment elevated the Arts, Science and Philosophy, but this era was also a time of war with both France and America – wars that would significantly influence British political powers for years to come. British colonies in the Americas were beginning to become unstuck, and colonial legislation was being replaced by a new American set of rules and regulations. During the 1700s the country was tangled up in a series of victories and defeats with France, risk-managing a number of domestic Acts of Union and juggling an often ambiguous relationship with France during its revolutionary years. Relations with Britain's American colonies also deteriorated, culminating in the Revolutionary War and War of Independence. Throughout the 1700s and early 1800s Britain played a significant role within the transatlantic slave trade, up until its abolition in 1833.

As a consequence of Britain's worldwide trade and foreign conflict, the country underwent a number of cultural, social and economic shifts. This included exposure to new resources and materials as well as to diverse immigrant communities. A dominant world leader, Britain's imperial sovereignty during the Georgian age was expanding as it seized control of territories throughout the world. The total space in square miles occupied by the British Colonies by the end of the nineteenth century amounted to 13,012,000, including:

Canada	3,600,000
New South Wales	312,500
Cape Colony	230,000
Ceylon	25,500
British Guiana	76,000
Jamaica	4,250
Trinidad	1,880[2]

In terms of foreign trade, there was a huge increase in raw food materials being imported from Norway, Denmark, Iceland, Greenland, Germany, Holland, France, Flanders and the Baltics into England between 1699 and 1774. England imported £864,000 worth of foodstuffs from other European countries between 1699 and 1701. By 1774 this had increased dramatically to £1.141 million. But the most significant change is illustrated in the amount of imported foods acquired from Asia, Africa and America. Between 1699 and 1701 just over 18 per cent of all England's food imports derived from these countries. By 1774 this rose to just under 40 per cent. It is assumed that much of this can be attributed to the economic activity generated by the triangular slave trade.[3]

According to Laura Mason's food timeline appearing in her 2004 publication *Food Culture in Great Britain*, the first sugar refinery was built in England in 1544, the East India Company was established in 1600 and the first coffee house opened its doors in Oxford in 1650.[4] London's first coffee house was not far behind if the early newspapers are to be believed. A Turkish man is thought to have secured his coachman 'Bowman' in small premises in St Michael's Alley, Cornhill, in 1652, to sell what was then simply known as 'Kauphy'.[5] Caffeinated drinks such as tea, coffee and chocolate made the greatest impact, not just in terms of their replacement for alcohol, but for the immense social changes they brought to towns and cities with the growth of coffee shops and tea houses. Sugar and spices also impacted on the domestic economics and culture.

The table below provides an indication of the evolution of these products as they became more readily available to the mass markets of Georgian England. The contrast between the variety of goods typically sold by retailers during the seventeenth century and the provisions on offer in the eighteenth and nineteenth centuries is significant, and indicative of the growth of the import and export market during this period. Grocers typically stocked around thirty-four individual products during the late 1600s. A hundred years later this increased to around forty-two items.

Grocery stock held by shopkeepers 1660–1830 (mean number of varieties per shopkeeper)[6]

Product	1660–1699		1700–1729		1730–1779		1780–1830
	Grocers	Other Retailers	Grocers	Other Retailers	Grocers	Other Retailers	Combined
Caffeine drinks			2.0	1.7	3.7	3	3.1 3.3 7.2
Sugar	3.4	2.0	3.6	2.3	4.1	1.9	
Spices	5.6	5.1	6.1	3.1	7.8	3.4	

More specifically, this cultural shift and demand for greater quality and availability of key products can be analysed by observing the changes in the products themselves stocked by grocers trading in 1683, 1723 and 1730.

In 1683 Ralph Edge, whose shop was based in Cheshire, sold no caffeinated drinks and the only sugar he stocked was coarse brown molasses. His range of spices was, however, fairly broad, and included Jamaica pepper, long pepper, white pepper, aniseed, fenugreek, mace, coriander, nutmeg, cloves and cinnamon. Forty years later in 1723, Alexander Chorley, a grocer from Manchester, was recorded as selling coffee and bohea tea, together with refined sugars such as fine powdered sugar, fine bastard sugar, loaf sugar, white candy and brown candy as well as the coarser sugars and molasses. His range of spices was phenomenal and included nutmeg, cloves, mace, cinnamon, clove pepper, black pepper, long pepper, liquorice, ground ginger, white ginger, raw ginger, saffron, senna, bay berries, gauls, diapente, wormseed, aloes, aniseed, caraway, fennel, fenugreek and rice. Other items in his shop included luxury goods such as anchovies and capers, raisins from Malaga and figs.[7]

Parmesan cheese was consumed in England as early as 1511, and perhaps even earlier, as a gift (in a quantity of 100) to Henry VIII by the Pope.[8] Now Anglicised Italian favourites, macaroni and 'vermicella' manufacturers are recorded as trading in England from the mid-1700s. Sometime during this period the 'Macaroni Club' was formed in London, predominantly consisting of young men who had completed their Grand Tour of Italy and brought back the pasta of the same name which they had become so fond of during their travels. It is said that during their meetings a large dish of macaroni was placed on the table. The group members also became known for their leading fashion and eccentric sense of dress, wearing large, elaborate, curled and powdered wigs.[9] By the 1800s it seems that macaroni had become more popular generally, as advertisements for it, such as those appearing in the *Bath Chronicle* and *Weekly Gazette*, illustrate: 'Macaroni – the finest flour employed in making of.' *The London Gazette* of 16 September 1820 carries an article about the importance of tax to be paid on macaroni and vermicelli, stating it should be impounded if it enters the country unauthorised, without duty paid. The fact that these two products are singled out so individually suggests that a historical problem existed with the illegal importation of pasta, affirming its popularity at the time.

It wasn't just the food and drink that was becoming more diverse. Aside from the influx of well-known French cooks, a number of other immigrants, perhaps indentured slaves, ended up working as cooks in established venues, as this interesting obituary of the well-known 'coloured' chef, Anthony of the Antelope (formerly the White Hart) denotes:

> On Sunday died Anthony, the well-known Cook at the Antelope Inn (late at the White-Hart), aged 43 years, nearly the whole of which he had passed at the Antelope, having been fostered and supported by the late Mrs Best and family, when a helpless and nearly destitute child of colour. He had saved 110*l*. Mostly in guineas, which has been appropriated towards the support of his aged mother[10]

One of the major attractions of Tom and Moll King's notorious and salacious 'coffee house' in Covent Garden, London, was a beautiful black barmaid who went by the name of Tawny Betty. She was frequently satirised and can be found in a number of illustrations and visual references from the period.[11]

Undoubtedly sugar was the most lucrative of new imports during the Georgian era. It also influenced the diets of many people across the class system. The bleak truth of how sugar become much more accessible during the eighteenth century is by way of its integral relationship with the exploitative transatlantic slave trade. South American and the Caribbean colonies in particular suited the climate for sugar cane cultivation, which was carried out on a vast scale. Europeans consequently became more reliant on sugar in confection, preserves and generally for sweetening a variety of drinks and dishes.[12] England was not only benefiting from foreign culinary imports; improvements in domestic transport systems meant that fish was now more widely accessible to the whole population, as it could be directly transported to towns and cities in seawater containers. Oysters were also in abundance. Eliza Smith devotes an entire chapter to fish in *The Compleat Housewife*, 1727, later republished as *The Household Companion*. She noted that when selecting crab fish, they are likely to be stale if the shells are a 'dusky red colour' and if the claws are 'limber' and 'may be turned any way with the finger'. She also describes fresh prawns as those that are 'hard and stiff, with their tails turning inward'. In an age where technology still lacked the ability to ensure absolute quality, there were all manner of tests carried out on food to determine its freshness, from touching an egg with your tongue – if it was warm it was unspoilt – to testing the age of pork by pinching the flesh.[13]

Similarly England and Ireland traded in items such as oatmeal, which corporation minute book records highlight as an issue for the Irish in 1729, when a team of people were sent to 'Northern Britain' to purchase considerable supplies to trade in Irish markets.[14] The population of England and Wales had changed their diet from brown to white bread by 1800 according to the *Agricultural History Review*.[15] America began to provide Britain with wheat to produce a higher standard of bread, and liquorice was imported from Spain to enhance brewing. The Americas had developed flour milling technology to a greater extent than any other country during the 1800s and had subsequently become the 'breadbasket of Britain'. By 1800 some European countries were spending at least half their salaries just on bread consumption. Whereas Britain's climate was suitable for the cultivation of soft wheats, the harder wheats that were more suited to bread making were imported in considerable scales from America.[16]

Jamaica pepper is frequently quoted in recipes provided by Eliza Smith in her *Compleat Housewife.* This is what we now call All Spice and was introduced to England by Columbus from Jamaica during the sixteenth century. It originates from Pimento trees that grow in Jamaica and is a spice that makes foods slightly peppery, sometimes used as a substitution for bay leaves. It is to date the only popular spice incapable of being cultivated anywhere outside of the West Indies. Allspice is documented in English recipe books of the late 1700s and early 1800s and is still popular today in traditional dishes such as mincemeat and Christmas pudding. Cinnamon was a popular Georgian ingredient in both medicinal compounds and for fruit compotes, cakes and pastries. It was also used to flavour wines and ales.[17]

Curried food was also introduced to Britain during this period, and there were hundreds if not thousands of Lascars, or Bengali seamen, assisting on British ships who were living in London and other port cities across the country. An advertisement appeared in *The Times* newspaper on 27 March 1811 announcing that 'Indian dishes in the highest perfection' would be available at the newly established Hindostanee Coffee House in Portland Square, London.[18] This coffee house is mentioned in the writer Edward Nares' 1812 novel *I'll consider of it! A tale, in which 'Thinks I to myself'.* One of the heroes of the book is clearly of mixed race, and in the first person describes how the wealthy Indian merchants that frequented the Hindostanee Coffee House to partake in the smoking tradition of the Hookah did not accept him. Despite his racial background, he does not 'boast a tenth part of their riches'. He explains that as a consequence he is also unable to integrate with 'white faced Europeans', who think of him only as a slave.[19] This provides an interesting early example of attitudes to race, class and immigration. There was a possibility that regardless of colour, you could be accepted into English society during the Georgian period if you had money and status. William Kitchener's *Cook's Oracle* of 1817 includes a recipe for 'Cheap Curry Powder', which provides a good indication of the extent to which spices were available across Europe:

> Dry and reduce the following spices to a fine powder, in the same way as in the foregoing receipt.
> Coriander seed, four ounces
> Turmeric, three ounces
> Black pepper, one ounce
> Ginger, one ounce
> Cayenne pepper, quarter of an ounce
> Lesser cardamoms, one ounce
> Mix together, and keep them in a wide mouth bottle.[20]

The newspapers and periodicals of the time were also full of advertisements for curry-related products, including powders and pastes, like the one published in the *Western Times*, 30 August, 1828, by Cooke and Co., based at 99 Hatton Gardens, in which they announced that they have the pleasure of 'intimating [their Astirh and curry pastes] to East India families'. And 'Cooky's Indian Condiments', consisting of 'Indian Curry paste, Madras Mulligatawny paste and Madras Fish', appeared in the *Huntingdon, Bedford and Peterborough Gazette* of 16 May 1829.

One of the earliest spices to become established throughout Europe was ginger, being the most favoured of the Romans.[21] In Britain ginger became synonymous with gingerbread, a favourite of Queen Elizabeth I, and was used to enhance both wine and beer. Ginger appears in numerous recipes during the Georgian age, including one for gingerbread cake in Mrs Dalgairns' *The Practice of Cookery: Adapted to the business of every day life.*

Take two pounds of treacle, two and a quarter of
brown sugar and fresh butter three quarters of a pou
four ounces of caraway seeds, the same quantity o
orange-peel cut small, three ounces of finely pounde
four well-beaten eggs, and half an ounce of pearl ashes;
beat the butter to a cream, and mix it with the rest of the
ingredients. The next day work it well up, and bake it in a
buttered tin.[22]

Incidentally the pearl ashes would have referred to the ashes
scooped out of the fireplace, which was used as an early
precursor to baking powder.

Gingerbread sellers were a common appearance on the
streets of Britain during the eighteenth and nineteenth
centuries. *The True Briton, Volume III* records the murder
of a well-known gingerbread seller in London, known
affectionately as Tididol, or Tiddy-Doll as the *Gentlemen's
Magazine* named him, who was found in Chelsea Field,
mugged of the 20*l* he had in his possession.[23] This would
have been a considerable sum indeed, perhaps an indication
that gingerbread sales generated lucrative business at this
time. 'Tiddy-Doll' is once again remembered fondly in an
article in *The Gentlemen's Magazine* of 1816:

'Tiddy-Doll'. The celebrated vendor of gingerbread who, from
his eccentricity of character, and extensive dealings in his
way, was always hailed as the king of itinerant tradesmen. In
his person he was tall, well-made, and his features handsome.
He affected to dress like a person of rank; white gold lace suit
of cloaths, laced ruffled shirt; laced hat and feather, white silk
stockings, with the addition of a fine white apron.[24]

The article goes on to mention how Tiddy-Doll would always
sing to his customers in a speedy allegretto that included
the rhythm 'Ti-tid-dy, ti-ti, ti-tid-dy, ti-ti' and so on. Hence his
nickname. This recollection of a well-known and respected

London tradesman is evocative of the spirit of culinary street traders of the past. It provides us with an insight into their eccentricities and popularity, and is an example of the type of technique they may have used to engage with their audiences and prospective punters.

Nutmeg is probably the most widely written about of those spices that found their way to European shores. In America fraudulent traders were known to forge nutmegs by carving imitations out of wood. This earned the state of Connecticut the title of 'The Nutmeg State'. In Britain nutmeg was a spice in high demand, and cost in today's money about £400 per pound in weight. Pocket graters, similar to the one in the picture section, were both used in the kitchen and carried around so the flavour of nutmeg could simply be added to drinks or puddings wherever you were. In cooking it was added to desserts, puddings, cakes, drinks and lots of savoury dishes. It was still in wide use throughout the nineteenth century. Charles Dickens is said to have been quite addicted to nutmeg, and would carry a treen around with him wherever he went. Like so many other herbs and spices, the medicinal properties of nutmeg have been recorded for centuries, and people regularly used it in drinks and poultices to alleviate or even attempt to cure a variety of ailments.

Troutbeck is a small village in the Lake District, north-west England. An extract from the supplementary records for this village contains the following letter, dated 12 August 1708, from Elizabeth, Lady Otway, to Benjamin Browne:

I am very sorry to hear of Roland Brathwait sickness. If it be a jaundiceow penyworth off saffron into it and cover it with the top, and sett it to rost, and when rosted quez it into a pint of white wine and let the lemon infuse 24 hours, and take the fine powder of turmerick as much as will lye upon a crown piece and a nutmeg granted and a good sponnefull of aneseed bruised, and mix this in treacle and take the quantity of a nutmeg or more morning and afternoone and drink a little glas off the wine aforesaid after it. This is a very good medicine ifn get this done for him, if thee would give him 20 headlice mixed with nut-meg and sugar and powder of turmerick and drink a litle warm ale after it sweetened with treacle and nutmeg and a litle powder of turmerick in it and aneseede, it would perhaps doe him good.[25]

It is difficult to continue without commenting here on the suggested inclusion of head lice as a cure. The application of head lice to cure jaundice was a popular concept in eighteenth-century Britain. This may have originally transcended from Spanish folklore, a country which has always adhered to this type of treatment.[26]

There is a wonderful description of the presence and use of vanilla in Britain during the mid-1700s in *A History of the Materia Medica.* The writer informs us that during this time three varieties of vanilla were available in the shops. The thicker and shorter pods were known as Spaniards, Pompona and Bona. The second variety had longer, slender pods, and was referred to as 'genuine' or 'legitimate' vanilla. The final variety of vanilla was much stronger, with a somewhat unpleasant smell. This type of vanilla was 'apt to give People the Head-ach, and to throw weak women into the Vapours, only by smelling it'. This begs the question of why the latter was on sale at all, if it was so unpalatable?[27]

Turmeric was derived from the East Indies. It is possible that it was first used more prolifically to colour fabrics before being used in cooking during the Georgian period, as this process of using it to dye silk illustrates: '... aluming in the cold for twelve hours, a pound of silk in a solution of two ounces of alum, and dyeing it hot, but without boiling, in a bath composed of two ounces of turmeric and a quart (measure) of aceto-citric acid, mixed with three quarts of water'.[28]

Competition throughout Europe over the spice-producing

islands of South East Asia and Oceania raged from the
sixteenth century to the early nineteenth century, when the
East India Company was provided with a secure base to trade
in what was founded as Singapore in 1819. America also
joined the competitive spice race at the end of the 1700s as
the newly established New England ports competed for the
trade. Today the United States remains the chief importer of
spices, while India remains the main producer, exporting 70
million kilos a year.[29]

The way in which we consume coffee in the British home
today has a long and interesting narrative that is surprisingly
more British than might at first be thought. From fireplace
to cafetière, the British contribution to and association
with coffee making and grinding apparatus is worthy of
comparison with the French and the Italians. Early United
States statute books determine that coffee was first imported
to Britain in 1660. By 1801 total consumption of coffee from
the United States to Britain reached 930,141 lbs. Just seventy
years later this had escalated to a staggering 40 million lbs.[30]
This exemplifies the extent to which this popular drink had
become somewhat of an addiction for the British people. The
first definitive references for hand-operated coffee mills in
British newspapers start to appear around 1736,[31] sixty-two
years before the first United States patented coffee mill.[32]
References to coffee mills in personal family papers are
also evident in Britain from 1712.[33] One local Lancashire
newspaper reported in 1832 that the celebrated new domestic
wooden coffee mills were being manufactured at a high rate,
with one factory alone producing around 90,000 annually.[34]
In addition to Lancashire being recognised as an area
associated with coffee mill makers, Wolverhampton is also
considered to be of significance in this area of manufacture.
There are ninety coffee mill makers listed in the 1881 census
occupations for that year for Wolverhampton. A search of the
trade directories throughout the 1800s by county suggests
the main manufacturing regions appear to remain central to

London, the West and East Midlands and Lancashire, with a few located in Wiltshire. It is assumed that this was due to the presence of so many iron and brass foundries in these regions, the materials that most early coffee mills were cast in.[35]

The heightened popularity of coffee drinking in the home and in the coffee houses undoubtedly hit the traditional coffee mill maker hardest. According to the census, by 1901 there are just twenty-one coffee mill makers operating in Wolverhampton. After 1910 it is difficult to find reference to any coffee mill makers, suggesting that the consumption of coffee mills was already in decline. This can be attributed perhaps to the progressive advent of the new percolator and influence of the cafetière. Coffee percolators start to make an appearance as retail items in the British press from the beginning of the nineteenth century. It was an Englishman, George Biggin, who invented the first percolator as early as the 1780s, and this is when the filtered coffee movement began to emerge. Incidentally the National Archives also inform us that Biggin was one of the party of people to participate in the first balloon flight in Britain in 1785.[36] The concept of percolating coffee using coffee in a bag made of cheesecloth or muslin, which is then dipped in a pot or cup, similar to our teabags of today, was being explored in a variety of ways during the 1800s. A British patent was filed in 1899 for filtration bags distributed from 'coin-freed machines' to allow one cup of instant coffee to be produced. The idea that vending-machine coffee could have been available as early as 1899 is extraordinary.[37] It is also difficult not to wonder at the extent to which people were experimenting in Britain to refine the coffee-filtering process.

At what stage did the French iconic cafetière become invaluable to the British kitchen? We know that 'The Etzensberger Patent cafetière' was in public circulation by 1880 because one was presented to a Charles Bradlaugh at a banquet held at the Hall of Science on 19 May 1880, in honour of his election as MP for Northampton.[38] Further research into Etzensberger reveals that in 1878 he received a British patent for his 'improvements in apparatus for making infusions extracts from substances by steam pressure'.[39] Born in Zurich, Etzensberger took up permanent residence in the UK and became the manager of the Midland Grand Hotel in St Pancras in 1873. The well-known holiday travel entrepreneur Thomas Cook collaborated with Etzensberger when designing the appearance and layout of his international hotels, and we are informed that 'although the apparatus has been for many weeks in full and successful operation in Mr Cook's boarding-house for English tourists, in the Rue de la Faisanderie, Avenue du Bois de Boulogne, they look askance on an invention calculated to supersede their traditional and costly process of coffee-making.'[40] What this information determines is that there is an argument for crediting Britain as a leading competitor in the coffee apparatus market from as early as the 1700s.

Introduced initially from China and then cultivated for mass consumption by the English in India during the eighteenth century, tea has a long and complex narrative and history with Britain. It is believed to have first been served to the general public by Thomas Garraway as early as the seventeenth century, initially promoted as a medicinal remedy. An illustrated guide of London from 1890 describes Garraway's shop as having being situated in Change Alley in London and surviving two centuries. It finally closed in 1866. In its early days it was used as an auction house for wine, tea and later wood.[41] Although Garraway is frequently cited as the first tea dealer, an article appearing in an edition of *The Gentleman's Magazine* in 1794 states that during the mid-1600s there were in the region of 30,000 tea dealers trading in Great Britain. Tea dealers of this period are often to be found classified as grocers or grocers and tea dealers. Tea had a subtle flavour, easily tainted by the cargoes it was transported in during the eighteenth century. It was subsequently packaged in fine porcelain pots from China, pots that became as popular as the tea stored within them. 'China', as it was affectionately nicknamed, was imported as tea and dinner sets by the British throughout the 1700s, gracing the tables and dining rooms of many middle- and higher-class families. China would also become the inspiration for many of the newly established potteries of the time, who designed and crafted a variety of fine cups, saucers, plates and teapots in the image of these highly merchandisable Chinese products. Thomas Twining established the first tea shop in 1717, specifically marketed towards ladies, and a tea garden was erected in Vauxhall Gardens around the 1720s. Here ladies would be escorted in their sedans to sip tea, exchange gossip and keep an eye out for prospective beaus.[42] This was also supposedly the inspiration for a verse that appears in Edward Young's *Love of Fame, the Universal Passion*, published around 1728:

> Here two red lips affected zephyrs blow
> To cool the Bohea and inflame the beau;
> While one white finger and a thumb conspire
> To lift the cup, and make the world admire.
> Tea! How I tremble at thy fatal stream[43]

Twining's first business was a coffee shop in Devereux Court, just off the Strand in London, in 1707. It was simply called after his namesake, 'Tom's'. From here he sold tea as well as coffee. The tea sales became so popular that Twining decided to convert and expand his existing coffee shop into an establishment that specialised in tea. This first tea-only shop was called 'The Golden Lyon'.[44]

One very interesting story of an unlikely early tea merchant is that of Mary Tuke, a Quaker who overcame all the restrictions and laws that fought against her, due to her sex, her religion and because she was a commercial trader.

In 1725 Mary Tuke opened a grocer's shop in Walmgate, York. She achieved this by campaigning for the right to become a Freeman and member of the York Merchant Adventurers Company. She overcame the fact that she was an unmarried woman and therefore trading illegally through sheer determination and she escaped the legal hierarchy of the York Merchant Adventurers Company. She managed this because the expense of taking her to court outweighed the inconvenience of allowing a woman to trade. In 1752 she passed the business on to her nephew, William, a Quaker philanthropist. William was joined in the business by his son Henry in 1785, and from this time the Tukes manufactured cocoa and chocolate behind their Castlegate shop, as well as dealing in tea and coffee.

Tuke would not only become famous as the first woman and business owner to fight British trading legislation, she would also become a part of the legacy of the Rowntree dynasty. Henry Rowntree purchased the Tuke tea, coffee and chocolate business in 1862, adding to Tuke's legacy her contribution to one of the biggest chocolate manufacturers in the world.[45] The Tuke shop would also become famous for its Rock Cocoa, a mixture of sugar and cocoa formed into 'rock' shapes. Aside from a few standard references, much of the documentation on Mary Tuke does not appear to be readily available. Her succeeding nephew in the tea trade, William, also appears to be an interesting character, who established one of the first humane asylums for the mentally ill in York, an institution which was established in 1796. Primarily funded by Tuke, the Quakers and Friends of the Quaker society, it is cited in the historical directory for York for 1893.[46] Mary Tuke is also honoured in a slim publication written by R. O. Mennell, *Tea: An Historical Sketch*, which denotes,

This particular instance of a woman challenging and defeating
a powerful monopoly was of historic significance; as showing

how the old restrictions were thrown off as a result of the
determined courage of a few strong minded individuals ...
Mary Tuke not merely founded a firm which, handed down
through generations of the same family, still flourishes [and]
... helped to mould the character of the eighteenth century.[47]

Undoubtedly one of the most eccentric of all tea dealers of
the Georgian age must be Edward Davies, whose premises
were located in Philpot Lane, London. Davies was finally
acquitted of lunacy after a lengthy trial and temporary
confinement. The case became well documented in the
press and discussed widely in society. Davies was a shy,
solitary child of extraordinary intelligence. In particular
he grew to develop an amazing comprehension of tea
and how it could be mixed to produce the best flavours.
As a consequence he became so nervous when attending
tea auctions, in anticipation of not being able to acquire
the right teas for his mixes, that he often needed medical
attention after the proceedings. By the age of twenty-seven
Edward Davies had a thriving tea business, despite the
restraints of his controlling and dominant mother, who
would eventually instigate his trial for lunacy. She controlled
his money, blackmailed him into parting with large sums of
money to benefit other family members, and would often
lock him out of his own shop. Davies attempted on several
occasions to put a distance between himself and his mother
by offering her a final settlement or the opportunity to
inherit his shop premises, neither of which she accepted.
Davies became well known for his public outbursts of
paranoia and hatred towards his mother and family. At some
stage between 1829 and 1830 Davies' mother instigated the
process of having him certified insane by employing a doctor
who was well known for his abilities to validate lunacy
for the purposes of incarceration. Aware of his mother's
intentions, Edward Davies sought the consultation of other
doctors, many of who testified to him being a theatrical

personality, incoherent and prone to melodrama, but none could condemn him as a lunatic. Prior to his trial Davies is recorded by many witnesses as displaying a number of instances of madness, including forgetfulness, incoherence, paranoia, inappropriate public laughter, hallucinating and talking to himself. Nonetheless he was given his freedom and retained the right to continue trading.[48] Perhaps Davies is an early documented example of someone with paranoid schizophrenia or bipolar, as demonstrated by his incredible talents for creating specialist teas. Whether he was the victim of an illness or a breakdown, or merely some sort or eccentric, the case of Davies is indicative of late Georgian society's new growing awareness of mental health, and the need to take greater consideration of people's individual behaviours and personalities before condemning them to a life of incarceration. This case also highlights the corrupt nature of medical practitioners, who were often paid favourably by family members to unscrupulously condemn their relatives to a life of incarceration, in order that they might benefit from their absence in some way.[49]

Sadly Edward Davies became such a public phenomenon that despite usurping his mother from the premises, he was forced into eventually selling his shop in order to escape both the media and the constant attention from scrutinising visitors. Davies retired young, ironically having to sell his shop to his mother, which provided him with the means to buy a large estate in Wales where he lived out his years in relative obscurity.[50]

Used for storing tea in a domestic or coffee house setting in Britain during the eighteenth century, the English caddy evolved from the word *Kati*, which is a Malaysian term for weighing tea. It is believed that the earliest tea caddy was developed by Thomas Ash in 1708. From the middle of the 1700s these caddies were made in silver and had bottle necks. By the middle of the eighteenth century the tax imposed on tea was 119 per cent, and it therefore became a valuable asset. As a consequence, boxes that could be locked were designed to keep this prized commodity safe. Many tea boxes from this period also have three compartments. It has been argued that the third compartment was to enable the different teas to be mixed, while others suggest, perhaps more logically, that it was meant to store sugar. The introduction of different types of tea also meant that many caddies were engraved with the letters H and B, to denote Hyson, green tea from China, or Bohey, black tea from India. Teaspoons appeared towards the middle of the seventeenth century, but they were most probably caddy spoons, which then evolved into the teaspoon. Pre-packed tea was available in 1826, but it did not become popular until the 1880s, by which time it was sold in grocery stores. Tea caddies were popular throughout the nineteenth century, although a fashion for wooden boxes that were lined with zinc, to help preserve the tea, replaced the more opulent silver caddy of the previous century.[51]

Tea caddies were prized possessions. Richard Forester of Derby, a doctor of medicine, is cited as leaving his tea caddy, together with a set of silver teaspoons, to his sister Mary Jane French in 1843. This was the only item he left her.[52] Again in 1880 Jane Miles is recorded as bequeathing a Miss Jane Draper her 'best tea caddy' and her sister 'the best tea pot' only. All her other possessions are listed as saleable.[53]

According to the British Museum, the British physician and collector Hans Sloane, who had developed an interest in studying the medical properties of chocolate, was the first person to combine chocolate with milk, following a voyage to Jamaica in the late 1600s. Whether this is accurate or not remains conjecture. Chocolate was being experimented with from an early age and was typically mixed with other liquids such as wine and water. Humphrey Broadbent, writing in *The Domestick coffee-man. Shewing the true way of preparing and making of chocolate, coffee and tea*, refers to the combination of milk and chocolate as a key mixture, due to their chemical properties. He suggests that they are 'analogues to each other, and very proper to be united'.[54] Writing in 1722, he may have learnt about Sloane's amalgamation of these ingredients, although Sloane did not publish his journals relating to his Jamaican tour until 1725. Similarly, John Radcliffe mixes milk and chocolate together in a medicinal recipe of his dated as early as 1716.[55] The first person historically credited with adding hot milk to cocoa was Nicholas Sanders, who worked under the direction of Hans Sloane.[56] Humphrey Broadbent's book provides a whole section on recipes for popular chocolate drinks, particularly those served in the many coffee houses of the day:

Wine Chocolate

Water three quarters of a pint, good sherry, half a pint, sugar-chocolate; a quarter of a pound, Flower, a quarter of an ounce, and a little salt, mix dissolve and boil these about ten minutes, then Mill and brew it, and its done.[57]

As Broadbent refers to in the above recipe, with chocolate beverages came the art of milling. Just as the Georgians used tea pots and coffee pots, so too was the chocolate pot. This is best described from a quotation reproduced in Grivetti and Shapiro's exquisite *Chocolate: History, Culture and Heritage.*

[A cake of chocolate] must be scraped fine, added to a sufficient quantity of water, and simmered for a quarter of an hour; but milling is necessary to make it completely smooth. For this purposes [chocolate pots have] a circular wheel of wood or metal within, fixed to a stem that passes through the lid, and which, being whirled about rapidly by the palms of the hand, bruises and mixes the chocolate with the water. The chocolate must be milled off the fire, then put on again to simmer some time, then milled again until it is quite smooth.[58]

For a picture of what a chocolate milling stick looked like, see the accompanying images. This is not the small milling stick, muddler or stirrer, as referred to in Britain in the eighteenth century, that would typically have been fixed into the centre of chocolate pots. Rather this is an example of a Mexican Molinillo, which was held between the palms and rotated to generate froth. It may have been the inspiration behind the Georgian milling stick, although the Italians also had their own version called the *frullo*. The popularity of all the new caffeinated drinks – tea, coffee and chocolate – during the Georgian age gave rise to a whole market in pottery and metal wares such as specialist pots, cups and decorative accessories.

As a consumer product sugar was rapidly being stocked across grocers' shops throughout the country. In the main, grocers had the monopoly on its sales, which would have been considerable if we are to believe that by 1700, sugar consumption had risen to 10,000 tonnes, rising again just ten years later to some 14,000 tonnes.[59] This new luxury came at a price, a human price, with Britain's sordid lucrative investment in Jamaican crops supplying the country at large. The planters and merchants who served their white Jamaican plantation owners were also impacting on British politics, lobbying and influencing decisions on how and where sugar was imported. The English poet William Cowper, best known for his religious hymn compositions, was also an advocate for the abolition of the slave trade, and wrote a number of widely distributed, powerful poems such as 'Pity for Poor Africans' and emotive pamphlets including 'To Everyone Who Uses Sugar', remarking, 'Think how many backs have smarted, for the sweets your cane affords.' Not only was it an aid to sweeten beverages, but new confectionery and patisserie techniques relied heavily on sugar, as did the domestic distillation of alcohol, and there was a rising trend in home baking and entertaining.[60] Undoubtedly Britain was rich in new ingredients, which continue to dominate the culture of today's consumers. Problems with alcohol, obesity, sugar and caffeine addiction are not new to modern society. They herald from the Georgian age of excess and availability.

2

From the Streets to Fashionable Society

For what do we live, but to make sport for our neighbours,
and laugh at them in our turn?

Jane Austen, *Pride and Prejudice*

We are given to believe that all Georgians with the financial means to do so were considerable meat eaters, gorging themselves on as many different types of flesh as they could catch and slaughter, and as the previous chapter intimated, they were enjoying the consummate pleasures, variety and excess of new luxury items from overseas. Certainly the Georgians were beginning to analyse and consider their food more in relation to nutritional value, health benefits and economy. Drink in particular is something that radically changed during this period, with a shift away from alcohol: caffeinated drinks such as tea, coffee and chocolate were adopted as substitutes for gin, beer and wine.

However the records for Scotland throughout the eighteenth century are not consistent at all with this notion. This is where meat was eaten rarely and in very small quantities across all classes of people. When it was eaten it would be mixed with barley and vegetables in a broth. One account notes 'flesh meat they seldom or never taste'.[1] In 1729 this is echoed in James Mackintosh's 'An Essay on ways and means of enclosing': 'For half the year, in many towns of Scotland there is no beef or mutton to be seen in the shambles and, if any, it is like carrion meat, yet dearer than ever I saw in England.'[2] In fact the Scottish diet mostly consisted of oatmeal, which towards the end of the eighteenth century included the introduction of potatoes. Similarly, tea-drinking was non-existent in most parts of Scotland until the late nineteenth century.[3]

By 1827 potatoes were clearly used considerably in Scotland to bridge the gap between poor grain harvests and famine. However, an article in the *Caledonian Mercury* of that year reveals that the country's dependence on potatoes led to even greater food problems as the population were unable to manage annual crop rotation and the pressures of deficient crop yields every other year. The article also maintains the argument that since the introduction of potatoes as the main source of food, the rise in illness and in particular 'organ disease' across the Scottish population was notable, particularly where the labouring classes were concerned. A figure of six pounds of potatoes per meal for an average labourer is quoted as the typical intake. The difference in diet across Britain meant that different utensils would often be adopted for cooking and eating. In the North of England and Scotland porridge mixers, mostly crafted in wood, were used to stir, while scrapers made of iron ensured that any porridge stuck to the interior of the cooking pot was removed. Crochans and catels were cast-iron cooking pots only found in Wales. The word catel would eventually find its way into English vocabulary as kettle.

Traditionally the different classes throughout Britain would generally eat their meals at contrasting times of the day. This is exemplified in a poem composed by an unnamed member attending a controversial meeting of linen merchants in Londonderry, Ireland, during a general election. The verse is part of a much broader observation of the exploitation of the wealthy over the working classes:

How ganders will cackle when rain is at hand;
How (gooselike) the farmers the note understand;
How the poor dine at one, when rich are at lunch;
How the rectors drink port, and the curates drink punch.[4]

A letter between Messrs Shannon and Boyle, the former describing a visit to Castle Barnard, recounts, 'The hours are breakfast at 9, dinner 4, tea 7, supper half past 8, and bed 9.'[5] In reality, mealtimes were extremely changeable during the Georgian period. In the early 1700s, the middle and higher classes would breakfast between nine and ten in the morning. Dinner was then served between the hours of two and three. By the end of the century dinner had moved to six or seven in the evening, leaving a considerable gap between then and breakfast. It is as a result of this gap that afternoon tea evolved. It is understood that this new phenomenon was introduced by Anna Russell, the then Duchess of Bedford. Ms Russell would frequently complain of a 'slump' in her energy levels. She counteracted this 'sinking feeling' by instructing her servants to prepare a tray of tea, bread, butter and cake at around four in the afternoon. Her habit of eating at this time soon became fashionable, and was well-received in popular society.[6]

The remaining classes of society continued to eat dinner as a meal in the middle of the day, tea in the afternoon and supper in the evening.[7] To some extent this has remained in British culture today, where there is a different approach to mealtime names, with some families calling lunch dinner or referring to dinner as tea, and vice versa.

Undoubtedly food consumption varied from class to class and from town to town, depending on availability and affordability. There was also an overriding obsession during the Georgian period with recognising the responsibility to teach the poor and uneducated how to cook properly, which became a much more governing and legislative issue for the Victorians. The media of the 1800s is dominated by letters, articles and recipes submitted by well-meaning members of the public on this very subject, which was largely determined by the growing correlation between food, health and hygiene.

Despite the middle- and upper-class fascination and preoccupation with enhancing their kitchens and learning new elements of the craft of cookery, the poor of Georgian Britain remained desperate and disparate. The overcrowding, poor sanitation and poverty eventually gave rise to the need for greater statistical information, and one of the foremost reports of the time was published by the social reformer Edwin Chadwick. His 'Report on the sanitary condition of the labouring population of Great Britain' was a summary of a large-scale inquiry actioned in 1832, which culminated in a revision of the Poor Laws and established a firm relationship between disease and poverty. During his investigations Chadwick recalls visiting one house where a corpse had remained for 'twelve days in a small room not above ten feet by twelve feet square and a fire always in it ... the only one for sleeping, living and cooking in'.[8] Whether there is any direct relationship between late Georgian and early Victorian approaches to sanitation and hygiene and the development of general kitchen apparatus and utensils is difficult to determine, but few members of the poorer classes owned ovens and they relied on open-fire pan cooking in cramped, contaminated and stifling conditions.

Often poorer families possessed just one cooking pot, which was used for preparing and cooking as well as for washing and as a urinal.[9] Fuel must also have been a consideration when it came to the amount of cooking that was possible in the average household, due to the sheer expense. When early gas and heating stoves began to replace old open fireplaces or closed ranges, records held in the London Metropolitan Archives reveal that for those on lower incomes unable to purchase these new luxury items, gas companies would rent them out as an alternative. A law was in place to protect defaulting tenants, who would not be liable to have their stoves removed by any recovering bailiffs.[10] Whether this law was in place to protect the gas companies or to ensure the poorer classes were not left without cooking and heating apparatus is unclear. But these advances in technology and accessibility to safer, more convenient and cost-effective methods of cooking would doubtless come to influence the kitchen dramatically by the turn of the twentieth century. The recognition of poverty during the seventeenth and eighteenth centuries is complex and contradictory in many ways. There was a belief that cheap labour had to be maintained in order to keep the economic wheels of commerce turning. In order to achieve this goal, the suffering that poverty generated needed to be eradicated to ensure that labourers remained fit and healthy enough to undertake their work. The French situation also inspired a new attitude towards 'liberty, equality and fraternity', the essence of the Revolution and epitomising the moral responsibility of ensuring the poor were given equal opportunities. Similarly, while it was considered foolish to educate the poor and provide them with the means to excel beyond labouring, early industrialisation was recognising the benefits of mass education to the new work force.

As Britain pushed through into the nineteenth century, social reformers began to generate greater awareness of the vast divide between rich and poor. There is also cause to consider whether geographic locality as well as class could determine the type and nature of an individual kitchen. Food was clearly an issue in places like Northern Ireland, and there were policies in place to support the poor. Towards the end of 1782 it was ordered that a grant of £200 would be provided for the sole purpose of establishing a new committee in Londonderry with the authority to purchase meals for the city's poor.[11] Thousands of settlers left Ireland for the American colonies during the eighteenth century as a consequence of severe ongoing crop failures, cattle disease and the high price of food that perpetuated famine conditions.[12] The diaries of John Galt, a resident of Londonderry, Northern Ireland, notes the ongoing bad seasons, the lack of fresh provisions and the direct consequences this has on the poor. In 1800 he records, 'How easy it is for God to punish a world, provisions are now got to a melancholy price for the poor. Meal is 5/- to 5/6 per score of 20 1b and potatoes 3/3 to 3/6 a bushel and flesh meat is 8*d* to 9*d* per pound.'[13] In stark contrast, a description of a dinner served at Castle Ward in County Down in 1772 highlights the extreme disparity of wealth in this region.

> There was an excellent dinner, stewed trout at the head, chine of beef at the foot, soup in the middle, a little pie at each side and four trifling things at the corners ... The second course of nine dishes [was] made out much in the same way. The cloth was taken away, and then the fruit – a pineapple, not good; a small plate of peaches, grapes, and figs (but a few), and the rest, pears and apples. No plates or knives given about; we were served in queen ware ... During dinner two French horns of Lady Clanwilliam's [Lady Bangor's daughter by her previous marriage] played very fairly in the hall next to the parlour which had a good effect ...[14]

Soup kitchens for the poor were clearly operating in Northern Ireland during the early nineteenth century, as a letter from Sir John James Burgoyne from Strabane to the Marquess of Abercorn based in London suggests. He requests a charitable subscription of five pounds a week to fund a local soup kitchen in the small town of St Johnston.[15] There is often an association made between soup kitchens and Victorian London, or as part of twentieth century wartime austerity. However, as indicated above, Northern Ireland references these much earlier, as does England. William Hillyer's 'Extract from an account of a London soup shop' provides us with the following information on this early service, in this case, provided for the benefit of labourers working on the Foundling estate in 1796. The concept was to provide nourishing food at a much cheaper rate than that charged in the eating houses, cooks shops, inns and taverns. Hillyer established his soup shop using a 'Rumford roaster', sixteen and a half inches wide, twelve inches high and thirty-two inches deep, together with two 'Rumford boilers', one of thirty-five gallons the other forty-six gallons. The equipment was assembled in his back kitchen, where soup was made and sold to a maximum of 400 people a day. His menu was as follows: 'For a mess of boiled beef and vegetables three-pence; for half a pound of rice plum pudding one penny; and for a pint of pease soup one penny.' It should be noted that the prices charged by individual businesses such as Hillyer's would have been higher than the charitable soup shops.[16]

It was also customary for owners of large country houses and estates to ensure the poor of their parishes were provided with some sort of nourishment (usually soup) for the period that the owner was away from his estate. One account of an example from the north of England in 1797 details both the expense and total quantities made to provide for seventy families over a period of one month:

Four bushels of barley flour 12s
Two bushels of peas 13s
One stone of salt 2s 2d
One pound of pepper 2s 4d
In addition to this three bushels of potatoes, one and a half bushels of onions and other miscellaneous vegetables from the estate gardens (unfit for sale) were used to make 256 gallons of free soup.[17]

Benevolent public soup shops established during the Georgian period would also be scrutinised by those expected to use them as being too cheap to be of any good. In the city of Birmingham it was said that the poor would disdainfully chant, 'There goes meat for the soup shops,' when dead horses or carrion were dragged through the streets.[18] One such soup shop in Spitalfields, London, supplied the poor with meat soup at one penny per quart. The original recipe they used is detailed here, enough to make one hundred gallons of soup:

> 8 stone or 64 lbs of beef, consisting of fore-quarters, clods, & 16 stone, or 128 lbs of shins, 46 lbs of split peas, 36 lbs of Scotch barley, 24 lbs of onions, 8 lbs of salt, 10 oz of black pepper (ground).

It was calculated that the average expense of making this soup, exclusive of any overheads, amounted to 1¾d per quart (or two pints).[19] *The Times*, on 27 Aug 1795, published an article about a 'new mode of cookery' that would benefit the poor, the content of which reminds us that

> a pound of meat when boiled, roasted or baked, can go but a little way in a large family. But if this be well stewed with plenty of vegetables, thickened with rice or scotch barley, and the whole be well seasoned with a good slice of bacon and some pepper and salt, it will afford a hearty meal for half a dozen persons.

Articles such as these are representative of early social marketing, designed to appeal to the philanthropic nature of the 'country gentlemen', instructing them on the financial means with which to offer wholesome meals free of charge to their needy poorer neighbours. This is also on the more cynical proviso that once the free hand-outs ceased, the process will have provided the poor with a taste for the dish, one that they will then 'gladly purchase [for] themselves'. The concept of cooperative eating and cooking food in bulk was a typical one in Georgian Britain; there were even advertisements for wholesale commercially viable food mixes, like the one published in the *Chester Courant*, Tuesday 28 July 1795:

Cheap Food
For one hundred and twenty persons

50 lb. Lean beef cut in very small pieces, 10 lb. Of rice, 15 lb. Of potatoes, 10 lb. Of turnips, 15 lb. Of onions, mix therewith a proper quantity of parsley, thyme and salt; boil these ingredients in fifty gallons of water four hours, frequently stirring it. This quantity formerly cost 11s. 6d. It will feed 120 persons, and is very nourishing and savory – Smaller quantities may be provided in proportion, to accommodate single families or workhouses.

Reading through the high number of well-meaning, self-congratulatory attempts to offer advice and recommendations for what were fundamentally serious political and social issues of the day, one can't help but interpret them as patronising. More philanthropic members of the financially advantaged classes were donating to charitable causes, and offering their advice wherever possible to assist with the ever-burgeoning issue of poverty. This may have been because it was seen as both worthy and fashionable. An interesting announcement appears in the *Chester Chronicle* of Friday 3 January 1817, which simply addresses 'The Poor' and exclaims that a man of 'pious example' has printed and distributed a series of recipe cards for the benefit of poorer districts in the town, to produce economic soup dishes. It also appeals to other wealthy citizens with a view to doing the same or trialling the recipes themselves to serve up for general widespread consumption. These recipes are costed out and include:

	s	d
Sheep's Head and Pluck	1	0
Barley, 1 lb	0	4
Potatoes, 4 lb	0	2
Onions	0	½
Pepper and Salt	0	½
Water, 11 pints	0	0
Produce 6 quarts	1	7

The reality of how the poor were actually provided for was no doubt in stark contrast to what was preached in the media. Gordon Bradley Hindle's comparative study of two workhouses in Manchester and Shrewsbury, taken from *Provision for the Relief of the Poor in Manchester, 1754–1826*, is an interesting insight into the provisions that were afforded the inhabitants. Between 1788 and 1789 it seems on first reflection that both Shrewsbury and Manchester paupers were well fed. In Manchester this consisted of butcher's meat served four times a week, and a full half-pound of wheat bread issued to each person. On 'banyan days', traditionally the days when no meat was available, potato hash with bread, porridge and treacle or bread and milk were served at suppertime, while dinner consisted of greens or potatoes in fat. Each adult received a pint of beer. However, the personal accounts of Thomas Battye, a social observer and writer documenting the conditions of Manchester during the late eighteenth century and early nineteenth century, describes the meals provided for the 'spade-men', who worked in the grounds of one of these same workhouses. He notes that their meals consisted of 'soft sour oaten cakes, which are laid close together, from the time of baking until they are used, and with it sour butter milk ... scarcely food for a PIG'. In point of fact a closer inspection of the accounts for this same Manchester workhouse disclose discrepancies, including £395.4.0*d* allocated to butter and cheese, when Battye's dietary record for that period records no butter was consumed, together with almost no cheese. In contrast to the realities of what was actually being fed to the inhabitants, the bills for groceries reveal there was almost twenty times as many provisions listed as those recorded for Shrewsbury. Battye's writings cite high numbers of residents dying in Manchester, noting withheld information and ongoing incidents of sickness and ill treatment.[20] Undoubtedly these large supply orders were not being received by the residents. If these unaccounted groceries were not supporting the community they were supposed to be, one can only assume someone somewhere with authority was reaping the benefits and corrupting the accounts.

It became almost fashionable to extol the country's gross disproportionate wealth, and this is best illustrated from the literature and observations of the time. It was popular to publish manuals that would assist the poorer classes with learning to cook on a budget, despite the irony that many would neither be able to read nor afford to buy these books. Some examples include *Domestic Economy and Cookery for rich and poor*, compiled somewhat enigmatically by 'a lady' and offering a number of ideas for how key dishes could be substituted with cheaper ingredients. This particular 'lady' remarks passionately on the injustices suffered by the poor in terms of the cost of food, stating, 'It is a notorious fact, that the poor people pay much more than the rich,' and commenting that 'when the poor go to market, they are absolutely blackguarded into buying; and though they are forced to pay much more than the middling classes, they receive, as if it were a charitable contribution, the meat, that is absolutely thrown at them. In their coals, and in every thing else, they are in the same manner brow-beaten and cheated – cheated in the quality, price and measure.' The writer uses an example from personal experience, by describing an incident when her own servant was instructed to purchase tea, but rather than go herself to the tea house, sent in her place a lowly charwoman. Based on her appearance, the shopkeeper sold the charwoman a large quantity of 'undrinkable' substandard tea. The 'lady' in question returned the tea, this time sending her servant, who was assured that a mistake had been made, with many 'excuses and assurances' on the part of the shop, who quickly exchanged the product.[21]

Unquestionably one of the most prolific of writers and an advocate for improvements in cooking during the eighteenth century was Sir Benjamin Thompson, also known as Benjamin Graf von Rumford, or simply Count Rumford.

Confusingly, Thompson, although born in America, lived for some years in England before being honoured as a count for the pioneering work he achieved in Germany. He experimented with heat for the purposes of advancing ovens and improving the process of cooking generally. He wrote broadly on many subjects, from the principles of the fireplace to insulation and the measurement of heat, observations of the poor to invention. He was the pioneer of the kitchen range. Essentially he achieved this by suggesting that the top of the fire be covered with an iron plate, in order that the flame from the fire and the smoke itself transcend through bars, which would heat the sides and front of the enclosed oven area. The plate above also heated up, allowing for a hot surface that could be used to boil, fry and so on.[22]

Rumford had a number of theories relating to poor relief, and to feeding the poorer classes. He was a proponent of nutrition and recognised the need to explore new food types in order to establish improved healthy diets for the masses. Within this concept he promoted the importance attached to establishing public kitchens in all towns and cities throughout the known world of the eighteenth century. He campaigned for free food to be made available to all those without the means to purchase it, and at a reduced cost for all those struggling on a daily basis. He believed this was a more cost-effective approach to ensuring health, alleviating famine and stabilising the economy generally. In particular Rumford was convinced that soup was the ideal one-bowl meal source of nutrition. He also believed that Britain was not making more use of the potential to grow, harvest and utilise barley as a primary source of nutrition. In relation to his conviction over the contribution that soup could make towards alleviating the problems of poverty, Rumford also stipulated that it must not be boiled, as he believed this process removed all of the good qualities retained in the stock and vegetables – a notion that is widely adhered to generally today. Rumford insisted,

Causing any thing to boil violently in any culinary process is very ill-judged; for it not only does not expediate, even in the smallest degree, the process of cooking, but it occasions a most enormous waste of fuel, and by driving away with the steam many of the more volatile and more savoury particles of the ingredients renders the victuals less good and less palatable.

To those who are acquainted with the experimental philosophy of heat, and who know that water once brought to be boiling hot, however gently it may boil in fact, cannot be made any hotter, however large and intense the fire under it may be made.[23]

His foolproof recipe for economical soup and that which is the 'most savoury and nourishing' needed to be composed of Scotch barley, peas, potatoes, cuttings of bread, vinegar, salt and water – in certain proportions.[24] Rumford calculated a proposal for the government of Great Britain to implement across the country which would essentially ensure every person received three nourishing meals a day, consisting of:

For breakfast, 20 ounces of the soup No. 11, composed of pearl barley, peas, potatoes, and fine wheaten bread ...
For dinner, 20 ounces of the same soup and 7 ounces of rye bread ...
For supper, 20 ounces of the same soup ...
In all 4 lbs. 3 oz. of food, which would cost 2 3
Should it be thought necessary to give a little meat at dinner, this may best be done by mixing it, cut fine or minced, in bread dumplings; or when bacon or any kind of salted or smoked meat is given, to cut it fine and mix it with the bread which is eaten in the soup. If the bread be fried, the food will be much improved; but this will be attended with some additional expense. Rye-bread is as good, if not better, for frying than bread made of wheat-flour; and it is commonly not half so dear. Perhaps rye-bread fried might be furnished

almost as cheap as wheaten bread not fried; and if this could be done, it would certainly be a very great improvement.

There is another way by which these cheap soups may be made exceedingly palatable and savoury, which is by mixing with them a very small quantity of red herrings, minced very fine or pounded in a mortar. There is no kind of cheap food, I believe, that has so much taste as red herrings, or that communicates its flavour with so much liberality to other eatables; and to most palates it is remarkably agreeable.

This allowance is evidently much too large; but I was willing to show what the expense of feeding the poor would be at the highest calculation. I have estimated the 7 ounces of rye-bread mentioned above at what it ought to cost when rye is Jt. 6d. the bushel, its present price in London.[25]

Count Rumford's influence in Britain was significant and his revolutionary fireplaces, boilers and hot-water systems, in addition to his theories on feeding the poor, were instrumental in elevating the country's ailing antiquated systems in the kitchen.

The Foundling Hospital was a children's home for unwanted or deserted children, established in 1741. Now it is a museum, whose collections tell the story of the original Foundling Hospital. A report for the Society for Bettering the Condition and Increasing the Comforts of the Poor details the Foundling kitchen and its fittings that were modified in 1796 by Count Rumford. The kitchen was seventeen by twenty-one feet with two large Rumford iron boilers divided into economic double boilers, heated by one small fire and a five-foot 'roasting machine'. The benefits of this new system were groundbreaking, saving at least twenty-five chaldrons (an old English measure of volume equivalent to about three pounds in weight, so seventy-five pounds in total) of coal annually, the need for one cook instead of two. Very little smoke was discharged up the chimney; instead it was enhanced and used to heat the roaster. Similarly repairs were minimised from once every six weeks to just one in sixteen months. Rumford's revolutionary kitchen design was hailed as a great success and the kitchen at the Foundling became a benchmark for other public industrial kitchens for their ability to remain productive, safe, healthy and economical.[26] Rumford would succeed in becoming one of the founding protagonists and funders of the Royal Institution of Great Britain, to ensure that scientific research and progress would continue and be disseminated for the benefit of the wider public. His ideas to improve standards and reduce poverty were instrumental in evolving the kitchens we recognise today and advancing the philanthropic advocacy of the Victorian generation.

Certainly the communal preparation and sharing of food for the benefit of poorer communities was something Lanarkshire in Scotland decided to implement in 1821. Robert Owen was a Utopian, philanthropist and social reformer, an idealist who configured a newly established small industrial village, New Lanark, during the early 1800s. Now a World Heritage site, New Lanark reaped the benefits of Owen's investments and ideologies. The 1821 report for the county gives a detailed outline by Owen, who instructed that the new villages would benefit from food for all its inhabitants to 'be prepared in one establishment, where they will eat together as one family'. He envisioned that food would cost a great deal less and would be easier to prepare and cook en mass. He strongly believed that once the community adjusted to this way of life, they would have no inclination to eat in any other way. Land would also be provided to enable the community to cultivate and harvest their own produce.[27]

This was a new model of cooperative living that Owen believed would enhance the productivity of workers, by improving their quality of life and physical living conditions. In addition to the shared cooking and eating, healthcare was free of charge, housing was sanitary and practical and education was provided for all from the age of two. By 1820 the village was receiving around two thousand visitors a year from across Britain, Europe and America. It stood as a benchmark for idealised living and other pioneering entrepreneurs were persuaded to replicate its success.[28]

With the commencement of the Industrial Revolution came the rise of the middle classes. While traders and shop owners retained their positions in society among this group, equally elevated by the rise in retail consumption, it was the foremen, small factory owners and managers and investors who began dominating Britain's social transformation in the Georgian age. They were upwardly mobile, economically driven capitalists who, while remaining sympathetic to the poor, had little regard for socialist ideals. Their focus was built around sustaining domestic growth, determining this new stratum of society as both patriotic and anti-immigration.[29] The *Naval and Military Magazine*, volume three, of 1828 reminds the reader that in Britain during the early nineteenth century it was the middle classes that retained most of the power, as a consequence of 'the creation and distribution of capital made by commerce and manufacturers ... now rapidly advancing, from the increase of machinery'.[30] As more wealth circulated and greater choice entered the food market, there began to emerge what we now term a 'throw-away society'. Georgian middle- and higher-class society could indulge and therefore also over-consume to the detriment of those less fortunate. Thomas Gisbourne explains how 'in some houses as much provision is scandalously consumed in this manner, as would have sufficed for the support of several poor families. Sometimes too, piles of broken meats are thrown to be devoured by a number of useless dogs, instead of being distributed to relieve the wants of the necessitous. Or large portions of vegetable crops are suffered to decay on the beds of the kitchen-garden; while neighbouring cottagers, or labourers attached to the house, would have rejoiced to be permitted to receive them.'[31]

It was the middle classes who were financially supporting the growth of eating houses, confectioners and grocers across Britain and indulging in the pursuit of culinary social engagement and entertainment. They aspired to transcend the poorer generations from which they emerged. One of the ways in which they could tangibly flaunt this aspiration was through food, the ultimate consumerist product of the day. The distinction between the classes within the context of food is referred to frequently during the Georgian age. Louis Eustache Ude's iconic recipe book of the time, *The French Cook*, notes in his chapter on sauces, broths and consommés that while the veal gravy is best suited for the table of the great, 'the gravy of beef may do for private families of the middle classes'.[32] The middling classes were also criticised for their lack of culinary training, as Samuel Smiles notes quite satirically in 1800 that during the average dinner hour in a middle-class household tempers were frequently raised as men quarrelled with their wives due to the lack of a good meal, and as a consequence often turned to alcohol as a substitute.[33] This also suggests that while on the surface these newly gentrified ambitious glory seekers appeared to have everything society aspired to, they were descended from the darker underbelly of Georgian society. They emerged from an unrefined, uncultured and largely disadvantaged heritage, fighting for their right to be accepted by the hierarchy – more succinctly defined as 'the nouveau riche'.

Several hundred years shy of the period under discussion, this account of Archbishop of York Thomas Wolsey's kitchen exemplifies the status and value placed on the preparation, cooking and presentation of food. It also denotes the importance of spices within this context as early as the sixteenth century.

And now to note of our own time somewhat. Not omitting in this Place Thomas Woolsey [*sic*], Archbishop of York, and Cardinal: His Servants daily attending in his House were about 400, omitting his Servants Servants, which were many. You shall understand, that he had in his Hall continually three Tables or Boards, kept with three principal Officers; to wit, a Steward, who was always a Priest; a Treasurer, a Knight; and a Comptroller, a Squire. Also a Cofferer, being a Doctor; three Marshals, three Yeomen Ushers in the Hall, besides two Grooms and Almners. Then in the Hall Kitchen, two Clerks of the Kitchen, a Clerk Comptroller, a Surveyor of the Dresser, a Clerk of the Spicery; all which together kept also a continual Mess in the Hall. Also, in his Hall Kitchen he had of Master Cooks two, and of other Cooks, Labourers, and Children of the Kitchen, twelve Persons; four Yeomen of the ordinary Scullery, four Yeomen of the Silver Scullery, two Yeomen of the Pastry, with two other Pastelers under the Yeomen. In the Privy Kitchen, he had a Master Cook, who went daily in Velvet and Sattin, with a Chain of Gold about his Neck, and two other Yeomen, and a Groom. In the scalding House, a Yeoman and two Grooms. In the Pantry, two Yeomen. In the Buttery two Yeomen, two Grooms, and two Pages. In the Chandery, two Yeomen. In the Wafary, two Yeomen. In the Wardrobe of Beds, the Master of the Wardrobe, and ten other Persons attending. In the Laundery, a Yeoman, a Groom, thirty Pages, two Yeomen Purveyors, and one Groom. In the Bake House, a Yeoman and two Grooms. In the Wood Yard, a Yeoman and a Groom. In the Barn, one. In the Garden, a Yeoman and two Grooms: A Yeoman of his Stage; a Master of his Horse; a Clerk of the Stable; a Yeoman of the same; the Saddler; the Farrier; a Yeoman of his Chariot; a Sumpterman; a Yeoman of his Stirrop; a Muleter; and Sixteen Grooms of his Stable; every one of them keeping four Geldings; Porters at his Gate; two Yeomen, and two Grooms: In the Armoury a yeoman and a groom.

A clerk of the spicery was specifically in charge of deliveries of spices and other goods supplied by the grocer and Oylman. Clerks of the Spicery were employed in noble households right up until the mid-nineteenth century.[34]

In contrast, the list of all staff employed in King George III's household some 300 years later for 1801, as published in the Court and City Register for that year (excluding the pantry, buttery, spicery and confectionery cooks), included: the clerk controller, C. Ramus esq., paid 200*l*. Under him was the first clerk, paid 250*l*, the first under clerk, paid 150*l*, then the second under clerk, paid 150*l*. A third under clerk was paid 75*l* and then someone called the youngest clerk received just 65*l*. The kitchen porters were paid 30*l*. The first master cook, William Wybrow, was paid 237*l* (around £7,000 to £10,000 a year in today's money); a second master cook called Nath Gardiner esq. received 217*l*. Then there was a (fascinatingly appropriately titled) yeoman of the mouth, or king's food taster, who was paid 138*l*, followed by a yeoman of the kitchen on 130*l*, several grooms and 'children', two master scourers paid 80*l*, then a small group of assistant scourers paid just 30*l* each. Finally there are listed six turn-broches (to roast the meat – often a hard task as the large pieces of meat prepared in the royal kitchens would have weighed twice as much as a dog, and taken over three hours to cook), two door keepers and two soil carriers, paid just 25*l* a piece (about £900 a year). There was a separate Egg Office, run by Eliz. Dyer, who was paid 60*l* and was the only woman on the team of staff.[35]

These two accounts of illustrious household kitchens reveal that little had altered in terms of the elaborate staffing models and importance attached to food and dining for the privileged across several centuries. It also illustrates the differentiation of the division of labour, according to wage. The cooks were clearly highly valued and were rewarded as such, while the young, the less skilled and the women, as is consistent throughout history, were the most disadvantaged. Other diets relating to public institutions are worthy of greater analysis. The following daily menu, taken from the minutes recorded of a meeting of the governors in 1768, represents a typical account of the food offered to patients residing at County Down Infirmary.

Table of Diet
Flesh meat days shall be Sunday, Tuesday and Thursday.

For Breakfast:
Water-Oatmeal-pottage one pint with a pint of milk or small beer or a pint of milk pottage without sauce

For Dinner:
8 Ounces of beef or mutton or pork or veal weighed when raw for each patient: either of these to be boiled and broth made of it, thickened with cutlings or 'grotts', a pint of which to be served to each. Roots are to be used when to be procured, as potatoes turnips or parsnips. When there are roots six ounces of bread and eight ounces when otherwise. A pint of small beer when to be had conveniently.

For Supper:
Water pottage a pint, or a pint of flummery or potatoes: with either of these a pint of milk. Occasionally a pint of milk pottage or six ounces of bread and pint of milk.
'Meager' days shall be Monday Wednesday Friday and Saturday Breakfast and Supper the same as on Sunday Tuesday and Thursday.

For Dinner:
10 Ounces of bread and pint of milk or 12 ounces of plain pudding, one ounce of butter and pint of small beer or a sufficiency of potatoes and one pint of milk or ten ounces of bread, two ounces of butter and pint of small beer or three ounces of skimmed milk cheese, eight ounces of bread and a pint of small beer or one quarter of broth made the day before and four ounces of bread or a quarter of 'grott' gruel or barley or seasoned with salt and butter and four ounces of bread.

The chronological list concludes:

Resolved that the allowance of victuals here mentioned ...
we apprehend fully sufficient for any patient whatever and
larger than many can consume, particularly as to flesh meat
and bread, the housekeeper is to take care that what is left be
laid by for the use of the house and that no patient presume
to claim a property in any part thereof of attempt to convey
it away.[36]

Christ's Hospital School was established as a charitable
foundation for the education of poor children in the sixteenth
century, originally situated in London and now located in
Sussex. John Strype's 'Survey of the Cities of London and
Westminster', 1720, provides a detailed account of what the
children were fed:

And after this manner the Children fare daily. They have
every Morning for their Breakfast Bread and Beer, at Half
an Hour past Six in the Morning, in the Summer Time;
and at Half an Hour past Seven in the Winter. On Sundays,
they have boiled Beef and Pottage for their Dinners; and for
their Suppers, as good Legs and Shoulders of Mutton as can
be bought; as of 12, 13 or 14 Pounds apiece. On other Days,
their Fare, as it is thrify, so it is sufficient. On Tuesdays and
Thursdays, the same Dinners as on Sundays; that is, boiled
Beef and Pottage. On the other Days, no Flesh Meat: But
on Mondays, Milk Pottage; On Wednesdays, Furmity; On
Fridays, old Pease and Pottage; On Saturdays, Watergruel.
They have Rost Beef about Twelve Days in the Year, by the
Kindness of several Benefactors; who have left, some 3l. some
50s. per Annum, for that End and Purpose. Their Supper is
Bread and Cheese, or Butter for those that cannot eat Cheese.
Only Wednesdays and Fridays, they have Pudding-pies for
Supper. Their Bread formerly was very coarse and brown;
but by the Care and Order of Mr. Breerwood, a late Treasurer,
it was changed, and is very good wheaten Bread. And when
it first was brought into the Hall in the Bread-Baskets, the

poor Childrens Hearts rejoiced, and they gave a great Shout, praying God to bless their good Treasurer.[37]

In a very different type of school, an interesting reminiscence taken from a mid-nineteenth-century diary of a former Etonian and member of the then distinguished 'Evans family' provides some insight into how the male students at Eton were fed. According to this account, retold by Ernest Gambier-Parry, the boys were either encouraged to eat in their tutor's dining room or pay an additional ten guineas to use the matron's rooms. The matrons did not encourage dining in these rooms and we are told that there is 'no inducement' for the boys to eat in. Tablecloths were only changed once a week, 'common knives' and two-pronged forks were provided, along with tin cups. Supper consisted of bread and cheese. Instead the boys would frequent local cooks' shops, where they ran up considerable bills for their parents to subsidise together; one assumes their parents were mistakenly of the belief that the extra ten guineas would be contributing towards their child's regular meals.[38] In fact Giuseppe Pecchio's account of what the children of the higher classes are fed, taken from his observations of the English in 1833, are indicative of an almost frugal diet considering the period:

> Their food is simple, – milk, preserved fruits, bread and butter, and fresh meat, which is never allowanced out to them ... The large English loaves, piles of potatoes, and mountains of meat, seem made on purpose to prevent greediness, and to satiate little gluttons with the site of them alone ... The children abstain from wine, and until ten or twelve, even from tea and coffee.[39]

Inmates at the infamous Bethlehem Hospital (Bedlam) were fed very well indeed on a daily basis, according to John Strype's revised survey of London, with

Boiled Beef and Broth, and Bread for Dinner. And a Mess of
hot Broth and Bread for Supper served on Sundays, Bread,
Cheese, and Butter for Dinner. Milk Pottage, and other
Pottage, with Bread for Supper on Mondays, Boiled Mutton
or Veal, and Broth for Dinner. Hot Broth for Supper on
Tuesdays, Bread and Cheese, or Butter for Dinner. A Mess of
Milk Pottage, or other Pottage for Supper on Wednesday's,
Boiled Beef, Broth and Bread for Dinner. And a Mess of hot
Broth and Bread for supper on Thursday's, Bread and Cheese
and Butter for Dinner. Milk Pottage or other Pottage for
Supper on Friday and then on Saturday Pease Pottage, Rice
Milk, and Furmity. Or other Pottage and Bread for Dinner.
And Bread and Cheese and Butter for Supper.

Seasonal fruit was also apparently available as and when
required.[40] It is important to consider, as outlined in the
aforementioned Manchester workhouse accounts, the
likelihood of a discrepancy between what was officially
recorded in all these institutions and what was actually
available to inhabitants and inmates. The reality may have
varied considerably from the recorded. There are a number
of studies written about the history of Bedlam, which include
references to the lack of availability of good nutritional
food and cases of patients who would be denied food as
punishment, out of spite or simply neglect. There were also
correlations made between diet and health, which meant
some patients would receive food based on superstitious
conclusions made about their ailments in relation to what was
considered good or bad for them to eat. Up until around the
1770s the asylum was open to the public. Visitors could pay
to watch and taunt inmates. It is testament to the emerging
Georgian culture for gentrification and empathy that this
practice ceased and was seen as cruel and detrimental to the
wellbeing of the patients.

Perhaps one of the worst places to be unlucky enough to
eat during the eighteenth and early nineteenth centuries

would be in prison, and prisoners who were incarcerated for debt were not legally entitled to any food.[41] In Lancaster Castle prison inmates were allocated all of their daily food allowance in the morning, which provided them with the opportunity to barter items with local tradesmen that sold their wares at the prison. After it was reported locally that the prisoners had external access to bread products, outside trade of this kind was stopped and prisoners were only able to sell what bread they were given internally to the prison debtors. By 1812 Lancaster prison had a communal kitchen, but it proved to be unpopular with most prisoners, particularly the debtors, who cooked their own meals on the fireplace in their room.[42] A published report of Clerkenwell Prison, London, estimated that around ninety-five males and fifty-four females were imprisoned for crimes including 'bastardy', housebreaking and highway robbery. Each prisoner was provided with one pound of wheaten bread each day, with additional rations given to the sick and infirm. Fifty pounds of meat, together with vegetables and oatmeal, were boiled down every other day. Alternately meat was provided one day and soup the next.[43]

Finally, in the services, the Army provided each soldier with a pound of bread and a pound of meat per day and the Navy spent in the region of 9s 21/4d per sailor each week in 1811.[44] Beef broth and potatoes was the staple diet of most eighteenth-century British troops. Beer and rum were in good supply, but always watered down to prevent drunkenness, which was a problem in the Army. As shipping and transport systems were still evolving during the eighteenth century it is easy to determine that many soldiers would have suffered the detrimental effects of malnutrition through lack of supplies. There were a number of inventions designed to assist with the cooking and preparation of food for large and smaller scale armies, which was an issue during the Georgian period. These problems became of higher profile during the mid-nineteenth century, and the renowned cook Alexis

Soyer was commissioned by the government to develop a solution for catering for the Army during the Crimean War. The Soyer Stove was an enclosed cylindrical furnace that ran on any type of fuel available, from wood to camel dung. It was strong and lightweight; each one could feed up to fifty soldiers. Soyer's invention was extremely popular and was utilised through both world wars, and a number of other campaigns, until the whole stock of existing stoves was wiped out during a bomb attack on the Falkland Islands in the 1980s.

Next to the Army, accounts of life at sea during the eighteenth and nineteenth centuries offer conflicting messages. Samuel Johnson's recollections in Boswell's *Life of Johnson* remember a colleague who compared a ship to being worse than prison, in that prison provided 'better company, [and] better conveniency of every kind'; however, every captain worth his salt (pardon the pun) would have ensured that his crew received the best regular on-board diet possible, in order to remain healthy and manage the tough toil of working at sea for months at a time. Deficiencies in vitamins D and C as a consequence of limited fresh food resulted in rickets and scurvy respectively. Alcohol was in itself a necessary evil for life on board a ship, as a source of liquid and as a relaxant to combat the stresses and strains of the work involved.[45] A sailor's weekly diet in the eighteenth century would have resembled the following: one pound of salted pork or two pounds of salted beef, dried cod, a pound of biscuits (daily), two pounds of peas, three pints of oatmeal, eight pounds of butter, a pound of cheese and a gallon of beer (daily). Unquestionably the amount of alcohol consumed at sea would also have contributed to illnesses among the men, including long-term liver damage and gout. Long voyages would offer less choice, as it would have been more difficult to store provisions for any length of time. Beef or pork would have been substituted with flour, suet and raisins. An oatmeal diet became a rice diet and olive oil was substituted for butter. Similarly wine and brandy would have replaced beer.[46]

The eighteenth century was a time of tremendous contrast, and this is represented in the availability and consumption of food. The wealthy were getting fatter in every way on their diet of roast beef and French red wines; the newly gentrified and aspiring middle classes were lucratively trading in food, as well as feasting on the abundance of newly accessible exotic imports. Everyone was affected by the consistently high taxes, the riots, famines and widespread poverty. Trade, communication, transport and agriculture were all changing and evolving, and so too were the types and availability of food and drink.

3

Price, Profit, Pilfering and Probate: The Value of Kitchenalia

A kitchen properly supplied with utensils kept neat and clean,
is an ornament to a house, and a credit to the cook.

The Universal Cook, 1806

The Georgian era represents a period on the cusp of significant change. Domestic kitchens not only needed to be stocked with food and fuel, but they required the right services with which to maintain and operate them, as well as the repairs and refurbishing to the latest fashionable designs and specifications. More than ever, cooking utensils had an important function to perform.

Kitchen equipment has always been a valuable commodity. As early as the time of Edward I in the fourteenth century it was recorded that carts were hired to 'carry the kitchen' when the king travelled between residences, as kitchen utensils were regarded as valuable property. Iron pots and old gridirons were frequently recorded in the wills of nobility 'with ludicrous solemnity'. Indeed the 'pots, spits, and frying pans' of Edward III were classed among 'his Majesty's jewels'. Items of kitchenalia were also considered financially integral to some marriage dowries.[1] When James II fled England in the 1680s to escape a Protestant overthrow, he was forced to melt down, among other items, 'all sorts of kitchen utensils' which he had in his possession. The metal itself was rated by workmen at three pence or a groat a pound, which, when coined into sixpences, shillings and half-crowns, could turn a pound of weight into about five pounds of currency.[2]

In the eighteenth century, the acceleration of technology in the domestic kitchen did not just happen by chance. It was a combination of increasing demand and notions of necessity generated by the media, together with an opportunity for domestic households to connect directly with the novelty of invention and innovation. In 1800 the Royal Institution of Great Britain met to constitute the establishment of a number of new committees 'for the purpose of specific scientific investigation and improvement'. Among these was a committee for improving kitchen fireplaces and kitchen utensils of private families.[3] It was recognised that if invested in wisely, kitchen utensils could save both time and money by assisting with the quicker preparation and practice of cooking. This is exemplified in Margaret Dods' notes in *The Cook and Housewife's Manual*: 'Kitchen utensils – ought to be provided in proper quantity, as well as of suitable kinds – Rather numerous than otherwise, to save the distraction and waste of time occasioned by a scanty supply. A digester, meat-screen, salting-trough, meat safe, balnea maria & c.' These items will, Dods insists, pay for themselves over time by saving on 'fuel, labour and provisions'.[4]

Just as the consumption of kitchen goods increased, so too did their value and the potential for theft. The eighteenth and nineteenth centuries are dominated by criminal incidents, perpetuated by both poverty and aspiration. This ranged from the theft of entire kitchen ranges, as with the case of Richard Smith, tried for grand larceny on 22 February 1786 at the Old Bailey,[5] to frequent small incidents relating to stolen flat irons, tea caddies and copper goods. What these records also demonstrate is the real monetary value of these items. In the case of Ann Ford, 1761, among other items she was accused of stealing one copper stew pan, valued at one shilling, and a flat iron valued at sixpence.[6] In today's currency this would equate to around five or six pounds for the copper pan and about three pounds for the flat iron, making these relatively expensive items in eighteenth- and nineteenth-century Britain.

The values placed upon items of kitchenalia vary considerably from case to case. For example, a pair of steel sugar nippers in 1774 were valued at sixpence[7] while another pair of steel sugar nippers cited in an incident of theft just two years later is listed as five shillings.[8] This is over ten times the value, which suggests that the same items of kitchenalia either varied tremendously in terms of their style, design and quality or that their monetary value fluctuated according to the date at which they were stolen or manufactured. Sometimes the thefts would be opportunist, or would be committed internally by a member of staff or person familiar with the house and its contents.

Items that were used generally in the kitchen fluctuated significantly in fashion, usage and price. We tend to associate jelly or frozen ice shapes with the Georgian and Victorian eras. The copper mould is one of the most iconic of items displayed in large historic house kitchens. Until well into the second half of the nineteenth century moulds were in fact only used by the very wealthy. It wasn't until the Great Exhibition of 1851 was staged in the Crystal Palace that the jelly mould really became popular. This was entirely due to the availability of brightly coloured and shaped jellies available in the refreshment rooms that were set up to cater to visitors. Many people had never seen a jelly, let alone eaten one, and so began the trend for both making jellies and setting them in a variety of attractively designed moulds. Mass-market inexpensive moulds were set in tin or Britannia metal to resemble either pewter or silver. Indeed, it must have become more difficult in many ways for thieves to identify genuine products alongside reproduction copies cast in inferior metals. Given the variety of new metals being processed and the high levels of production for increasingly demanding markets, this must have impacted on the smaller traders with some significance.

One of the most familiar examples of a typical kitchen item of the eighteenth- and nineteenth-century kitchen is the rolling pin. Introduced in the Middle Ages, they would originally have represented little more than a small piece of wood, round enough in shape to roll back and forth. A fashion for crafting glass rolling pins in the eighteenth century became very popular and in Britain these were predominantly manufactured in Bristol, as 'Nailsea glass'. These objects became widely associated with sailors, being kept as superstitious trinkets out at sea. The opaque solid glass pins of the 1780s became hollow glass, then were replaced with ornately coloured and patterned glass by the middle of the 1800s. Visually, these items looked quite stunning and would have made particularly desirable swag for any industrious thief.

Pastry cutters, wheels or jaggers, as they were known by all these names, were designed to trim the crusts of pies or to cut decorative shapes or leave a crimped finish. Also medieval in origin, they were at the height of their use during the Georgian period. Cutters were cast in various metals and then later fashioned from material such as bone, scrimshaw (whale bone) or ivory, with wooden handles. Essentially a pastry cutter was a short item about twelve centimetres in length consisting of a wheel that turns and cuts at the end of a handle. Just as rolling pins have diversified, pastry cutters have been crafted in every material possible and in all manner of shapes. Again, like rolling pins, they have an association with the sea, as sailors would carve ornate, decorative pastry cutters out of scrimshaw.

Frying pans have altered little in purpose since the time of the ancient Greeks and Romans. But they have altered significantly in appearance, from long-handled pans for open fires to short-handled skillets on squat legs. The terminology for frying pans has varied frequently throughout the centuries and in America they were typically known as 'spiders' in the eighteenth century due to the little legs the actual pan rested on. They were also unpopular, and were considered unhygienic – a source of indigestion unless coated in a heavy grease prior to cooking. How this made the food more digestible is a mystery. The Americans were in many ways ahead of Britain in terms of kitchen utensil technology. This may be a consequence of the number of British manufacturers establishing their factories out there at the height of Georgian commercialism and consumerism. Nonetheless, not long after America gained its independence, it chose to cease trading for a time with England. This meant that imported copper was scarce for Americans. Consequently American copper utensils were a rare commodity prior to sometime in the mid-nineteenth century, when Americans discovered their own rich copper deposits to manufacture with. Marked American copper from pre-1850 is a rare and collectible find on today's market. Typically frying pans of the Georgian period (as we understand them today) were made of a combination of copper and iron, the handles secured with large rivets, similar to that depicted in the illustrations.

Toasting is a very English custom, practised since the Middle Ages. The three-pronged fork of the Victorian kitchen was very different in the preceding years. Toasters were either fixed or revolving devices. Fixed toasters consisted of wooden or iron slabs with feet and spikes to hold the bread for grilling in front of the fire. There were also more decorative eighteenth-century standing toasters, like the 'dog toaster'. This was a tripod stand with an upright rod down the centre, displaying iron or steel prongs. The nineteenth century had a variety of revolving, pivoting and swivelling prongs attached to frames, which were often very decorative. Toasters with swivelling hooks were called Trammels.

One of the most classic combinations in British food culture is tea and toast. The British tea kettle has become an iconic symbol in many ways – a metaphorical object that represents a nation of traditionally devoted tea drinkers, a fashion that commenced in the Georgian period. The Romans can be credited with the fundamental shape of the kettle as we recognise it today. Not for the purposes of drinking tea, but for boiling water for any number of tasks. The Roman aquamanile had a lid, a spout and one or more handles. By the late 1600s this had evolved into the round-shouldered, hoop-handled object that is most familiar as a tea kettle. During the eighteenth and nineteenth centuries kettles were predominantly made of brass, copper or cast iron. Some kettles of the eighteenth century had a flat frontage, for the purpose of faster boiling, as a stand-alone trivet-based kettle positioned directly in front of the fire. This period also provided tilters, tippers or lazy elbows. Known by other names as well, principally a kettle tilter was a wrought-iron contraption that hooked on to the handle of the kettle, enabling it to be both suspended and poured from without having to be removed from its position above the fire.

Mary Nichols from of the St Katherine's district of London was indicted for stealing a brass kettle to the value of five shillings, and other goods taken from the house of Mr Edward Blount, on the 19 October 1714. She very craftily tried to double her money by going to Mr Blount and telling him that she would advise on the whereabouts of the missing goods for a fee of one crown. On further investigation it came to light that Ms Nichols had sold the items to the very shop where she recommended Mr Blount to go to reclaim his goods. When questioned, Mary had no defence other than that she claimed she was given the items to sell by a sailor. Having no further proof and no one to vouch for her character in court, she was found guilty of felony and branded (burnt on the hand) as punishment.[9]

We learn that in April 1779 a Mr Naphthali Jacobs stole

'a quantity of kitchen furniture' from a house in Hoxton, London, belonging to Rowland Ridgley, and was subsequently executed for it at Newgate Prison.[10] In fact there are a total 371 indictments of crime and punishment relating to kitchen thefts recorded in the British newspaper archive between 1714 and 1830. These include a domestic kitchen in Tanner's Hill, Deptford, London, which was burgled, while the family were upstairs. A silver plate, silver mugs, silver ladle, silver spoons, a gravy dish and a sauce ladle were included in the raid.[11] A kitchen in a house in Hatton Garden, London, was robbed of eight silver tablespoons and twelve dessert spoons, teaspoons, salt spoons, sugar tongs and basin, as well as a gravy basin.[12]

Other crimes relating to kitchen items were pre-meditated and involved violence. One such was the case of John Barrett, who was described as a 'desperate character' and stole a tea-caddy from a shop in Oxford Street, London in 1828. He knocked the owner of the shop down by striking him twice, and then drew a knife on a bystander who tried to pursue him. It is not known what happened to Barrett, other than he was taken to Marylebone Police Station and committed for trial.[13] John Savil, William Tibbs and Nath Windsor, of the London Parish of St Giles-in-the-Fields, were indicted for breaking into the house of John Lee in 1714. They stole a brass kettle, a 'sawce-pan', and seven pounds in weight of cheese. Savil pleaded guilty while Tibbs was found guilty of burglary, and Windsor was somehow acquitted .[14] William Deveral, of the Parish of Holbourn, London, was indicted for breaking into the house of Eliz. Davis between the hours of three and five a.m. on 24 August 1716. He stole a porridge pot, valued at thirty shillings, a fish-kettle valued at forty shillings, two 'Stew-pans' at thirty shillings and other miscellaneous goods. A jury unanimously found Deveral guilty and he was sentenced to death for his crime on 6 September 1716.[15]

Other criminals of the day, like Ann Richardson in 1721,

were transported for their crimes. She was accused and tried for stealing a porridge pot worth five shillings, a brass kettle also worth five shillings and a skimmer valued at six old pence. The lengths Ann went to to acquire the goods is worthy of mention. She hid herself among the hay in a barn adjacent to the victim's house for seven days, before waiting for him to leave the property and steal the kitchen items.[16] Ann would have been transported to America during this period, whereas after 1787 the new destination for deported criminals became Australia. This was due to the war and breakdown of colonial power in America from 1776.

The following two stories are particularly emotive as they reveal the extent to which people in the eighteenth century could so easily lose respectability and their place in society as free, working civilians, due to circumstances that would be unlikely to occur today. The most curious of all these cases is that of Thomas Jenkins. It is a case so bizarre that it is difficult to determine whether he was lying all along, or whether he really was just an unfortunate victim of circumstances. In 1728 Thomas Jenkins, a man of about thirty years of age of St George's Hanover Square, London, was indicted for stealing from his then employer, John Wright, Esq. Among other things, he stole the following items of kitchenalia: a silver tea kettle, a 'Soop-ladle', the top of a cruet set, three silver forks, twelve silver spoons, a silver milk pot and five silver teaspoons. In total the value of goods stolen amounted to between around four hundred and eight hundred old pounds. Originally from Herefordshire, his parents had provided him with a good education and instructed him in Christianity. His schooling was cut short somewhat early when Thomas was sent to live in Bristol to work for his uncle. He then found employment as a butler in 'Houses of Noblemen of great Quality'. Thomas is described as an honest and respected man. When in court, he denied that he had ever stolen before and that he had a led a life devoid of violence, swearing, drinking and lechery. He is also described as a church-going man. Thomas had become acquainted with two vagrant men who had frequently goaded him into stealing from his master. Thomas insisted that after ignoring their suggestions over a period of some time, the two men decided to carry out the burglary themselves, after he had left his place of employment for the evening to go for a drink. The accused is said to have been accosted by the two vagrants in the street and handed the stolen goods, which he took. Arrested the next day, Thomas declared that he had been set up by the vagrants, who had taken advantage of the fact that he would have been an ideal scapegoat for the crime, having recently been so long out of work. When asked to identify the vagrants in question Thomas had refused, citing God and his honour as the reasons why he would not pass the blame on to anyone else. The records of the Old Bailey reveal that he was visited on several occasions in his cell and given the opportunity to be released if he provided the names of those involved in the crime. Thomas refused right up until the morning of his death, and was subsequently executed.[17]

In contrast, but with equal measures of tragedy, is the story of Richard Marshal. The same age as Thomas Jenkins, he too is described as originating from a good background and education. Marshal became an apprentice to a wig maker and progressed into his own business, eventually marrying and having children of his own. His downfall is described as idleness, which led to him neglecting his business and falling into bad company. These less salubrious acquaintances lured Richard into stealing hens and cocks, for which he was imprisoned and punished. His reputation now in jeopardy, Richard found it difficult to maintain his business and turned to burglary, which he continued to do for a few years until he was caught in 1733 for stealing one silver spoon, brass candlesticks, fourteen pewter plates costing ten shillings and another two valued at five shillings, a coffee pot, a tea kettle, a pestle and mortar, copper pots, a table cloth, a ham, six pounds of cheese and a number of other miscellaneous items. That same year he was also tried alongside his wife and another woman for a second crime committed some two years before, which came to light during the proceedings. The cache was once again mostly kitchen items, including: eighteen pewter plates, six brass candlesticks, two china teacups, one silver teaspoon, two copper tea kettles, one copper coffee pot, one copper chocolate pot, three saucepans, one porringer, one pair of snuffers, six knives, six forks, and one tablecloth. The Old Bailey records inform us that while imprisoned, Richard Marshal always 'behav'd very decently and christianly, profess'd a deep repentance, an unfeign'd faith in Christ, and that he dyed in peace with all the World.'[18]

With many of the crimes listed above, it seems difficult to imagine how desperate the poor of Georgian Britain had to be in order to literally risk their lives to commit such small crimes. It must have been an unbelievably hard struggle for many, with little relief from the government, and few options other than the workhouse if you found yourself in difficult circumstances. It also seems incomprehensible that the theft of three items of standard kitchen equipment could have seen you transported overseas forever, never seeing family, friends or loved ones again. From the perspective of the victims of the crimes, wealthy people would often issue public appeals for leads in identifying those who had stolen their property. For example, the *London Gazette* of 28 November 1734 published an appeal for witnesses to come forward regarding a burglary in an apartment next to the Old Crown Office in London's Temple district. The items taken are described as 'goods to a considerable value' including among other things 'a set of silver teaspoons, with tongs and strainer ... a china tea-pot with silver spout, some India tea cups ...'[19] A reward of fifty pounds was offered in exchange for any information regarding the theft.

The type of utensils that were used in the royal kitchens are indicated in an appeal published in a 1716 edition of the *London Gazette*, stating, 'Whereas there have been lately lost, mislaid or taken out of His Majesty's Kitchen in St James's, one silver sauce-pan, and 4 silver sauce-pan covers, having the late Queen's Arms with A.R. Engraven on each of the said pieces.'[20] A reward of twenty old pounds is offered in exchange for information on the missing items. The majority of saucepans during the Georgian period would be manufactured of cast iron; those in the higher-end luxury range were made of copper, so to have silver saucepans would have been the ultimate luxury kitchen item.

Inventories of kitchen contents during the eighteenth and nineteenth centuries provide an interesting insight into the comparative aspects of kitchen life and work during this period. David Humphrey was a Welsh farmer with debts amounting to twelve pounds in 1778. Unable to pay his debtors, his estate was seized and the contents of his kitchen is listed and valued as part payment. Many of the items are medieval in their origins and there is certainly no element of modernity or labour-saving devices present. Included in the list are noggins (usually old-fashioned wooden bowls or drinking vessels) and trenchers, which again are wooden boards used to serve or eat food off. The spoons were wooden and the candlesticks were made of a primitive clay, or 'rusk'. There are few metal items, no china and no kitchen gadgets. The entire contents of David Humphrey's kitchen and stables, including the family beds and other pieces of furniture, amounted to just four pounds, nineteen shillings and eleven pence. This equated to merely a quarter of what his debts amounted to.[21] In comparison, the Will and Testament of a Shropshire yeoman – a similar occupation to that of farmer – dated four years earlier, cites kitchen items including pewter plates, brass spoons and a tin broiler.[22] This may suggest that there are geographic as well as economic factors in the extent to which new types of kitchenalia were circulating on the market at this time. Perhaps farmers in Wales were residing in more primitive and less progressive locations in comparison to the southern areas of England, or perhaps demand was not as great in some areas as it was in others for these types of improvement.

There are many auctions advertised in the press during the eighteenth and early nineteenth centuries listing kitchen equipment as part of larger inventories. There are probably not many house clearances today that would focus on promoting this area of contents to be sold. Kitchenalia may have been the equivalent of how we value our small electrical products today. Examples of auction listings include a house in Eastwood, Hanley, in Staffordshire, belonging to the late Robert Wilson, selling off skewers, a sugar shovel, butter knife, 'every kitchen and cooking utensil', a Dutch oven and copper boilers.[23] Also premises at Court Lodge disposed of 'useful kitchen and cooking utensils.'[24]

Several prints held in the collections of the Science Museum suggest the importance attached to kitchen items during the 1800s. The 1830 lithograph 'Implements animated in the kitchen' personifies kitchen utensils as figures enjoying life, including dancing bellows and a washboard being used as a musical instrument, and plates balancing on a clothes line resembling a trapeze. The whole kitchen comes to life in a playful animated setting, illustrating a range of domestic kitchen implements of the time.[25] Similarly Thomas Tegg's earlier 1811 print 'Dedicated to the Housemaids and Cooks of the United Kingdoms' shows two figures composited of kitchen implements, including brushes, spoons, forks, skewers, cooking pots, pails and flour barrels.[26]

It is evident that the wealthy and middle classes valued their kitchens and made considerable efforts to follow fashion in cooking, and this extended to the equipment which they needed to create these dishes.

For the English living in India during the mid-1800s, items for the kitchen would have been a great luxury for many of the country's poorer indigenous population, and it would have been common in Anglo-Indian households for the house owners to bequeath some of the more luxury goods, including their freedom, to their faithful slaves, whom they thought more of as domestic servants. Elizabeth Clayton's Will, drawn up in Bengal in 1824, is one example: 'Harry my Male Servant I give and bequeath his liberty forever besides twenty Sicca Rupees ... with all my Cooking Utensils for his Family's use.'[27] It would be unlikely for people today to leave the contents of their kitchen in their Will, so we are reminded of the value of these items in the eighteenth and nineteenth centuries in comparison to today's throwaway culture.

The increasing number of advertisements for large public retail auctions began to emerge after around 1800. A trader by the name of Richard Clarke is cited as selling all of his kitchen stock in order to go 'into another line of business' in 1804, as his wares are advertised for auction, including 'tea and coffee urns, tea pots, tea trays ... brewing coppers ... saucepans, tea kettles, stewpans ... fish kettles ... fire irons,' and so on.[28] This could be indicative of progress or evolution in kitchen items and culinary fashions changing. The more traditional traders of kitchen ephemera may have been forced to update their stock or sell it on to start a new business.

To satisfy the new demand for innovation in cooking there were a significant number of ironmongers specialising in the manufacture of cooking apparatus that established themselves across Britain during the Georgian period. There were also brasiers (or braziers), who imported brass as well as working as brass founders. Henry Newhouse was a brasier advertising his wares in a 1755 edition of the *Derby Mercury*. He sold wholesale and retail goods including 'Pottages, Pots, Stew Pans, and Sauce Pans; Tea Boilers, Tea Kettles, and Coffee Pots ... Plate Warmers, Fowl Shapes, Lobster Shapes, Mellon, Whole or Halfs, Turks caps &c.' (The former items were probably decorative moulds.)[29] Similarly, tinmen worked in the same principle, making items from tin or 'tinning' existing metal items. Most of these independent traders have now disappeared from history. All of them were capitalising on the trend for better, more efficient and sleeker equipment for the kitchen. Shops would promote the fact that they had the latest patented items, like James Grant and Co. of Edinburgh, whose advertisement in the *Caledonian Mercury*, 1780, is headlined, as many were at the time, simply as 'Patent kitchen Utensils, &c.' and boasted 'an assortment of patent light cast iron goblets, sauce and stewing pans, tea-kettles, oval and round pots'.[30]

The Georgian age was also the age of tin and canning, which many traders would capitalise on, like Thomas Foster of Birmingham, who claimed his kitchen utensils were 'tinn'd' in his shop with TIN only'.[31] This suggests perhaps that less scrupulous traders were mixing the tin with other cheaper components to make a greater profit.

A stronger sense of civility was emerging in the way in which people ate from the seventeenth century onwards. With the introduction of the fork and mid- to late nineteenth-century discoveries relating to contamination and disease, eating became somewhat more contained. As 'civilised' societies developed, there also emerged a greater appreciation for manners and the consideration of others. This is a notion particularly associated with the Victorians, but its foundations are firmly rooted in the Georgian age. The combination of 'civility' and hygiene can be attributed to the evolution of the more elaborate process of eating at the table, surrounded by a number of attractive ceramic wares, silver eating and serving aids. The French writer Antoine de Courtin published his much-procured *Rules of Civility* as early as the seventeenth century. It was republished in a translated version for the benefit of the wider English market in the eighteenth century. A quote from Courtin's book summarises his theory perfectly. 'Having serv'd yourself with your spoon, you must remember to wipe it, and indeed as oft as you use it; for some are so nice, they will not eat Pottage, or any thing of that nature, in which you have put your spoon unwip'd, after you have put it into your own mouth.'[32]

The demand for attractive tableware and more sanitary methods of preparing, serving and eating food was at the heart of the powerful role played by the early ceramic factories that evolved during the 1700s. Names that we associate today with quality, collectability, beauty and decorative function in the house include Wedgwood, Spode, Royal Worcester, Royal Crown Derby, Royal Doulton, Mintons and so on. All of these originated during the 1700s. They manufactured cookware, dinnerware, glassware and luxury items that reflected the newly emerged social etiquette around dining. These factories were able to evolve due to the growth of transport systems across the country and the emergence of new manufacturing potential in the form of equipment, tools and materials. Most importantly the demand for their products was increasing at a good rate. The household account books of Sir Charles Stanley between 1772 and 1782 illustrate the extent to which wealthier households were purchasing goods of this type during this period. Stanley made a number of purchases from Wedgwood's London showroom, including teapots, mugs and double-handled cups. He also bought a china table service at auction costing two pounds, eighteen shillings and sixpence, along with a breakfast set for one pound and eighteen shillings in 1773.[33]

Some of the biggest names in British household kitchen goods emerged in the Georgian age. Addis Housewares was established in 1780, known simply as Addis today, and W & T Avery Ltd., a British manufacturer of weighing machines, was founded in the early eighteenth century and took the name W & T Avery in 1818. More popularly known as Avery, the company still exists today as Avery Berkel and continues to specialise in weighing equipment.

There were also emerging big stores, initially founded as fashionable bazaars or emporiums, like Browns of Chester, Fortnum and Mason in London, Kendal Milne and Faulkner (now House of Fraser) in Manchester, and Bainbridges (now John Lewis) in Newcastle. All of these built their foundations in the Georgian period. Perhaps the most renowned of these stores, and one of the few that originated from a grocer's shop rather than a draper's, was Harrod & Co. Grocers', originally established in East London's Clerkenwell district in 1832.

The streets of most Georgian towns and cities were overcrowded with Hucksters and Pedlars touting their wares, many of whom were pot sellers, cutlery sellers and other hawkers of kitchen-related items. The lowest of these in terms of financial status and integrity appears to be the pot seller, as numerous references are made to this occupation throughout the press in relation to insolvency, bankruptcy and crimes such as theft and fraud. There were cutlers and street cutlery sellers, all profiting from the boom in steel production and the variety of implements that were being created to cut and serve new ingredients such as luxury cheeses, exotic fruits and shellfish. The street sellers traded in items such as table and carving knives, forks and scissors. They would also sell more specialist oyster, fish, cheese and bread knives in areas close to the main food markets. The figures for 1851, although not of the Georgian period, provide an insight into the extent of their profits. For table knives and forks the street cutlery sellers would have paid no more than one shilling and three pence from local swag shops. These would then be sold in the street for around two shillings. Their rate of profit was typically around 50 per cent, but they would accept lower prices rather than miss out on a sale. An account relayed by a diarist of the time reveals that many street cutlery sellers by 1851 were struggling to keep their businesses, and reminisced of the years prior to this date when sales of cutlery were more lucrative.[34] This can be attributed to the mass consumption and cheaper production of these items, which continued to rise into the Victorian period. By this time production of kitchen ephemera had generally increased and therefore quality and price were reduced and these items became much more accessible.

Perhaps more interesting than the street sellers is the surprising list of breaches of ordinance for the more professional cutlers – the manufacturers of the cutlery itself – who are chronologically listed in the *History of the Company of Cutlers in Hallamshire, in the county of York,* from as early as 1657. In Sheffield it was forbidden to trade as a cutler unless you were formally initialised into the Company of Cutlers and each workshop was issued with their own trademark. Cutlers were only permitted to recruit local labour and every man hired was expected to serve a period of seven years as an apprentice before being allowed to trade themselves. Cutlers were also refused the right to hire out or lend their tools to anyone else.[35] It is unsurprising, then, that the list of breaches of these rules was so considerable. Several were for the exploitation of child labour, such as John Barber who was fined twenty shillings in 1735, and Joseph Hobson forty shillings in the same year. Many manufacturers were reprimanded for not issuing the correct markings on their cutlery, presumably because markings were a denotation of quality.[36] Incidentally Sheffield and the North developed at a much slower rate than Birmingham and the West Midlands during the Industrial Revolution, perhaps as a consequence of the antiquated regulations established by organisations like the Hallamshire (historic name for Sheffield) Company of Cutlers.[37]

As early as 1625, 'searchers' were new inspectors, recruited with the purpose of seeking out disreputable cutlers. By 1662 it was deemed unlawful for any cutler to sell their wares until they had undergone an official 'search'. During the 1600s searchers were paid one shilling for their work – around five or six pounds in today's money. Whether this was the rate per search, or as a one-off payment, is unclear. Searchers were ruthless and would seize tools, issue fines and essentially have the authoritative powers to destroy a cutler's career in one visit. By 1843 it appears that searchers had gradually declined.[38] Undoubtedly they would have been feared and avoided by any cutler attempting to earn a bit more money from forging their wares or using substandard metal production, such as 'pig iron' or cast iron, or engraving their cutlery with fabricated markings. By the mid-1700s there are references in the accounts of the Company of Cutlers in York to police constables accompanying searchers and being paid for their time. In 1748 in the case of Joseph Parkers this amounted to six old pence for assisting searchers. This payment to the police had increased to one shilling by 1769. Whether more payment was rewarded based on how complicated a case was is unknown.[39] Indirectly it illustrates how a variety of people were benefiting financially from the growing trade of early cutlery manufacturers. The other well-known organisation that regulated and oversaw the manufacture and retail of early cutlery was The Worshipful Company of Cutlers, which still exists today.

The disappearance of searchers by the mid-1800s is indicative of the more cost-effective methods of mass production and kitchenware and cutlery being produced using steel. From the early part of the nineteenth century more references can be found for the insolvency and debt of travelling and resident cutlers, such as William Dimaline of Yorkshire and Jane Storey, trading between Middlesex and Bath, listed in the Petitions of Insolvent Debtors in 1824 and 1831 respectively in the *London Gazette*. William Henry Woolhouse of Sheffield filed for bankruptcy as a cutler in 1828,[40] William Stratford of Tottenham Court Road, London, also filed for bankruptcy in January of 1829[41] and William Offord from Essex was listed as bankrupt in the July edition of the *Edinburgh Gazette*, 1830.[42]

By 1838 the Worshipful Company of Cutlers had established a fund and almshouses to provide some sort of welfare for pensioners and those finding themselves destitute from their trade. This was largely achieved by a number of considerable bequests left in trust to the company by both former cutlers and other members of society who shared an interest in honouring the trade for its contribution.[43]

While the small independent cutler and street vendor may have been floundering under the new competition, trade in cutlery on an industrial scale was about to explode. In 1816 the first illustrated catalogue of Sheffield tools and cutlery was published. Titled the *Explanation or key to the various manufactories of Sheffield: with engravings of each article designed for the utility of merchants, wholesale ironmongers and travelers*, it demonstrated all the different patterns that were made in Sheffield.[44] Joseph Smith's catalogue is a wonderful surviving example of detailed scaled drawings of, among other items, basic kitchenalia from this period, including table knives, bread knives, fruit knives and scissors. The purpose of this illustrative guide was to market items for the American export market. Many of the expanding established manufacturers of the time were beginning to capitalise on the new American market. Marsh Brothers, trading since 1631, opened a second overseas office and warehouse in Philadelphia in 1817, expanding even more during the 1830s and 40s with premises operating in both Boston and New York. Similarly William Greaves & Sons were able to open their renowned Sheaf Works in Sheffield on the back of their trading success with America. Sheaf Works was the first factory in Sheffield to combine all the stages of cutlery manufacture, from the conversion of Swedish iron into steel, through to its packaging and distribution.[45]

It is difficult to imagine nineteenth-century prisons overrun with criminals interred for stealing items of kitchenware. Or that people would offer substantial rewards for the return of these same stolen goods. In the 1700s and 1800s this was customary and indicative of the new value attached to this growing industry. Thieves would tout their cutlery and plate wares in the street stall markets, and independent metalworkers were mobilising themselves for entrepreneurial expansion. In 1800 a typical kitchen may have contained one or two pans; by 1899 there would undoubtedly have been a whole set to cook a variety of new dishes with. The fashion to craft beautifully manufactured items for the purposes of cooking and dining using new technology and creativity meant there would have been a significant range of good-quality items owned by the wealthier and aspiring middle classes. The advertising and retail of kitchenware was visible across the wider media throughout the Georgian age. The promotion of these items was aggressive and persuasive, based on the fact that they were newly patented, safer, quicker, smarter, or adhered to new techniques in metal and pottery manufacture. If they came endorsed by a well-known cookery writer or a fashionable craftsman, they were even more likely to generate sales. Undoubtedly this was the era of the dawn of mass consumerism.

4

The New Gastronomic Culture

Round and sound,
Two pence a pound,
Cherries, rare ripe cherries!
Cherries a ha'penny a stick
Come and pick! Come and pick!
Cherries big as plums!
Who comes, who comes?

'The London Barrow-Woman', William Shenstone, 1764

The trend to cook more technically and with greater exotic influences began to generate a new enthusiasm for cooking both domestically and in the wider public domain. Kitchen culture and the manufacture of food for the purposes of retail and leisure were changing and evolving. Coffee houses, inns and taverns were catering to a new middle-class mass market, with over 650 established eateries trading in London alone by 1834. Britain's aristocracy were committed to providing the very best in modern fashionable cuisine in their households.

Social codes of eating and entertaining were changing. Culinary literacy and French influence were pervading the higher echelons of society and Georgian Britain was at a turning point in the way it ate, drank and socialised, largely as a cumulative consequence of European influence, immigration and trade. While confectioners and patisseries sold elegant sweet and savoury fancies, ice creams and cold drinks, the country also retained its traditional inns, taverns and eating houses that dominated the streets of towns and cities, while the street sellers continued to hawk their hot and cold snacks. The well-known French gastronome Jean Brillat-Savarin defined gastronomy as a science, with the objective to

> watch over the preservation of man as a feeding animal ... by directing, according to certain principles, all those who procure, search for, or prepare things which may be converted into food ... This is what moves cultivators, vine-dressers, fishermen, huntsmen, and the immense family of cooks, whatever title or qualification they bear, to the preparation of food.[1]

It was not only in England that this revolution in new eating habits was emerging. There are eleven confectioners and one confectioner and pastry cook listed in the commercial street directories for Belfast alone in 1819.[2] In Scotland Charles Spalding, a retailer named in the 1787 shop tax roll for Edinburgh, left a ten-page inventory recorded in the Edinburgh Commissary Court Register of Testaments for his 'defunct shop'. This inventory provides a useful indication of the types of stock and equipment a typical confectioner of the day would have owned and used.

Seventy two bags unfinished sweet meats
Two pound liquorice Cakes
Small quantity of Jesuit bark
One pound St Catherines' prunes
Crushed almonds
Six cakes ginger bread
Plain almond biscuit
Two pounds mixed bisquit spunge

Five pound Barlie Sugar
One and one half pounds Cinamon Tablet
One and half pounds Sugar candy
Two pounds seed cake and plum cake
Two pounds orange peel
Twelve potts containing Jelly Jam and marmlade weighting
ten pounds
One half pound pepper mint dropps
A wooden pestle and mortar.[3]

There are a total of 6,976 pastry cooks and confectioners listed in the 1841 census for Great Britain.[4] This can be attributed to the continental and in particular the French influence for skilled fine pastry chefs, an influence that had steadily been increasing since the century before. By the time the 1881 census was conducted, the figure for both men and women employed in this same capacity had risen to a staggering 25,534.[5] This is indicative of cooking becoming a more widely recognised craft. It is clear that this trend was manifesting itself much earlier, as a quick scan of the Leeds Directory for 1817 determines. A total of nineteen confectioners were operating in the city. This directory of local businesses also lists a staggering 119 shops dealing in just groceries, tea and flour.[6] In contrast only twelve confectioners are listed as trading in the whole county of Cornwall in 1830.[7] The fashion for contemporary cuisine would have varied geographically, in terms of the extent to which European influences permeated different societies.

Up until the mid-eighteenth century the consumption of alcohol, principally gin, had had a lasting detrimental impact on society, particularly as many were able to brew their own concoctions at home. But new laws and the huge popularity of drinks such as tea, coffee and chocolate that offered natural mild stimulants of their own meant that these drinks began to replace harsh alcohols. As the 1736 publication *The Present State of Great Britain* recognises, 'It may be truly affirm'd, That at present there is generally less excess in drinking, especially about London since the use of coffee, tea and chocolate and less excess in diet than heretofore.'[8]

Fashionable society's desire for the latest imported culinary delicacies and the trend to engage the finest French cooks available had also become something of a mockery in some circles, particularly those intent on retaining English traditions and attitudes. This is best exemplified in artistic references of the time. A satirical and rather vulgar ballad published in 1790, printed by William Bailey, a printer and music seller, was titled 'T**d no tansey, or the disappointed pastry-cook'. (Tansy was a popular eighteenth-century dish served at Easter and undoubtedly T**d is a scatological reference.) It was composed at the height of the new cooking and food revolution, and is a sardonic cultural reference relating to popular fashions in food and dining. It reflects the slightly pretentious popularity of culinary excellence dominating the country at that time, with one verse reading,

Now out it comes (from the oven) and if it stunk before,
it stinks full twenty times as much, or more ...
In vain he twirls the pan; the more it fries,
the more the nauseous, fetid vapours rise.[9]

Similarly William Kitchiner's highly renowned bestselling recipe book *The Cook's Oracle*, first published in 1817, was satirised in the stage show of one of the leading comedy actors of the time, Charles Mathews, called 'Mr. Mathews Invitations' and performed at the Theatre Royal Opera House. The sketch transcript was as follows:

... a recipe for concocting a quadrille party, from the 'Cooks Oracle'.
Get all the ladies and gentlemen you can, put themselves together in a small room, over a slow fire – stir them well, have ready a piano, a harp, and four or five violins – throw

in some ices, jellies and oranges, when they are half done, add lobsters, sandwiches, negus, and bottled porter, sweeten it with politeness, but as that is hard to be got, use flattery, that will do as well; put in plenty of wine, the more wine the better; fill your rooms quite full and let the scum run off itself.[10]

The new food revolution came with a desire to learn how to achieve many of its innovative culinary techniques, and the teaching and learning of cookery became popular throughout the Georgian era. There are some references to those who taught cooking in the press of the time. It was typical to both write and teach on the subject.

A Mr James Mackay appears in an advertisement in the *Leeds Intelligencer* of 1777 as having just opened a school on the premises of a confectioner's shop with the intention of instructing 'Young Ladies' in the art of 'Pastry cookery and Confectionery, in all its branches'. Courses were available three days a week on Monday, Wednesday and Friday at a cost of two shillings per week and five shillings to apply.[11] The *Kentish Gazette* of 1768 provides an interesting description of what might have been sold in a typical pastry cook's shop, in addition to advertising the business's own in-house teaching provision:

Mrs Terry and Partner, beg Leave to acquaint the Public, that they have just opened a Pastry Cook's Shop in Prince of Orange Lane, and intend to have the said Shop constantly supplied with every Article in the Pastry, with Jellies, Pickles &c. N.B. Soups, Ragouts, and all sorts of Made Dishes, with rich Puddings, Cakes, &c. Alamode Beef, pickled Oysters, and all kinds of Potted and Collered Meat; likewise Sausages and Ham – They likewise Teach Young Ladies Pastry.[12]

A survey of the householders living on the Grosvenor Estate in Mayfair around 1790 suggests that of the 1,526

inhabitants over half earned their living through trade, with
the main trades involving food and drink. In fact some 288
tradesmen (19 per cent of the total householders) worked in
the commercial food and drink sector, the majority being
victuallers and butchers (including poulterers and tripemen).
There were twenty-eight greengrocers and fruiterers, twenty
grocers, eighteen bakers, ten cheesemongers, seven dairymen
and six fishmongers.[13]

At the opposite end of the country, in Chester, the livestock
and food markets were integral to the income for the city
corporation. The new flesh shambles built in 1827 at a cost of
over £4,000, for example, was yielding a rental of over £660
a year by 1832.[14]

The comparative table below demonstrates the growth of
food and drink trades in the city of Chester between 1781
and 1834.

Chester Retailers, 1781 and 1834

Type of business	1781	1834
Food and Drink	**218**	**494**
Provision dealers and bakers	41	143
Grocery trades	28	30
Butchers	15	33
Wine and spirit dealers	13	25
Brewers and allied trades	10	27
Inns, alehouses and eating houses	98	195
Miscellaneous	13	41[15]

The most significant increase in trading over a hundred-year
period was with the provision dealers and bakers. Provision
dealers were independent merchants trading in a variety of
goods, sometimes directly from their own homes. In fact,
according to the figures for Chester, almost every type of
food and drink retailer had doubled their trade between
1781 and 1834, apart from grocers. By the early part of the

eighteenth century, the most important product for grocers was tea and their job entailed sorting, blending, cleaning and packaging it. There remained a distinction between grocers and provision dealers, who typically sold products such as butter and cheese, alongside the new imported luxuries of smoked salmon and olives. By the middle of the 1800s this differentiation between the retailers had altered dramatically as grocers began to sell a diverse array of fresh and packaged goods. This is perhaps why the statistics for grocers trading in Chester up until 1834 do not demonstrate any significant increase, as it was before they began broadening their product range.[16]

This was the period when confectionery evolved into both a popular sweet treat and an art form of decorative fancy, thanks mainly to the French cultural influence. Sugar was, although not yet refined as we know it today, widely included in recipes for preserved fruits, jams, marzipans, jellies and sugar paste for delicately crafted items used to decorate and embellish many grand tables and dishes. Cakes and biscuits using light mixtures of whisked eggs, sugar and flour baked at low temperatures can be considered early versions of sponge cakes. Meringues were also extremely popular and recipes were converted, like gingerbread, from breadcrumb-based wholesome bakes into more luxuriant treats using molasses and different spices. Puff pastry also evolved into a product that formed the basis of both sweet and savoury elaborate dishes.[17]

The shop culture in the cities was thriving. Consumerism had arrived. We learn from the German novelist Sophie von la Roche in her journal entries of 1786, recording her visit to London, that

> everything is made more attractive to the eye than in Paris ... Behind great glass windows absolutely everything one can think of is neatly, attractively displayed, and in such abundance of choice as almost to make one greedy.[18]

Her observations of a London pastry cook shop offer an insight into just how beautifully crafted and presented these luxury new items were:

> It is surrounded, like a large spacious room, by glass cases, in which all kinds of preserved fruits and jellies are exhibited in handsome glass jars; in the middle of the shop, however, stood a big table with a white cover containing pyramids of small pastries and tartlets and some larger pastries and sweetmeats; wine-glasses of all sizes, with lids to them, and full of liqueurs of every conceivable brand, colour and taste were attractively set out in between, as might be expected, at a large and very elegant table.[19]

British ports and market towns became synonymous with endless supplies of luxury items, distributed by the growing network of internal waterways, or received directly from overseas trading links. The *St. James's Chronicle* of 1775 reports on the 'very fine Whitby and barrel cod fish' just arrived and up for sale in Salisbury's Cheese-Cross market. This was a market where you could also purchase 'fine Seville and China Oranges and Lemons, Pickled Sturgeon and Oysters in jars, Split and Boiling Pease, with Red Herrings, by the hundred or otherwise.'[20] Or at The Lamb and Gould's in Catherine Street, London, there were always on sale 'several thousand gallons of wine of various sorts, made from the grapes of Smyrna, Malaga, Calcavala, Sun, &c.' These wines were on sale from three shillings to four shillings and sixpence per gallon, 'all which are brought to such perfection, by a peculiar method in procuring the fruit from abroad, that it retains all its luscious, and essential qualities.' The Lamb and Gould's also sold 'genuine rum'. In fact they were so convinced of the level of quality of their goods, that they offered a money-back guarantee if the customer was not satisfied.[21]

Perhaps one of the most entrepreneurial of all the food

vendors in Britain at this time were the street sellers, who for a small investment could establish themselves with a barrow or a basket to sell from. House of Commons records of a loan provider to the street-trading community in London in 1746 dictate that some 24,328 pledges for this type of business were paid out in just twelve months.[22] The most valuable information to be gained about food street sellers in Georgian Britain can be gleaned from the writings of Henry Mayhew, an English journalist and social researcher who, despite being a predominantly Victorian observer, records a number of his subjects reminiscing about the Georgian age. From his writings of 1851 Mayhew talks about how pigs' trotters were sold at least fifty years before in small quantities, and had developed into quite a significant wholesale trade by the late 1880s. The trotter sellers of the Georgian period lined and prepared their pigs' or lambs' feet in tripe and cow-heel. While these types of trotters were sold primarily to manufacturers for the purposes of boiling them up for glue, by the end of the 1830s they were cooked and marketed as a cheap source of food for the poor.

Similarly, the prolific sale of bread in the street is recorded as happening very early in the era. During 1812 and 1813 bread was at its premium price and street sales were all but abandoned. Mayhew tells us that up until 1815, the Assize Acts, which had been in place since 1266, heavily regulated the bread trade, in as much as bakers were limited to bake and sell just three types of bread; 'wheaten', made of the best flour available, 'standard wheaten' involving the mix of several flours and 'household', which was the coarse, most readily available flour. By 1823 within London and its ten-mile radius a new act was passed where 'it shall be lawful for the bakers to make and sell bread made of wheat, barley, rye, oats, buck-wheat, Indian-corn, peas, beans, rice or potatoes, or any of them, along with common salt, pure-water, eggs, milk, barmleaven, potato or other yeast, and mixed in such proportions as they shall think fit'.

Mayhew speaks about one of his elder informants, who recalls his own father telling him that George III had stipulated that brown bread should be eaten in the royal household, thus earning him the nickname of 'Brown George', as brown bread was considered unfit for consumption by the poorer classes. Pea sellers were also popular street traders. In an account recorded by Mayhew of one such trader, he talks about being in business since 1825 and receiving as much as a guinea or thirty-five shillings during one day of trade – over one hundred pounds in today's money. This particular hot-pea seller was a regular at taverns and inns, working collaboratively with the owners, who encouraged him to add plenty of salt and pepper to the peas to ensure their patrons remained thirsty.[23]

Other popular street food consumed during the Georgian period included hot eels, oysters, baked potatoes and soup. Often open all day and night to cater to late drinkers, or operating seasonally with the weather, street food sellers appealed across the classes, from the stale bread sellers whose customers were the very poor, to the pie or hot potato vendors who catered to the higher-end street buyer.

Having evolved from the urban Roman infrastructures of the past, the street market has become synonymous with developments in economic trade, and the Georgian food market is no exception to this. Parliamentary papers of 1836 report that there were three principal wholesale markets in London at this time: Smithfield market, Spitalfields market and Kevin Street market. There were other smaller, specialist fish, potato, egg and fowl, butter and corn markets and around eleven general retail markets predominantly selling meat.[24] Daniel Defoe's survey of British trade during the 1720s provides a holistic economic overview of the country. *A Tour Thro' the Whole Island of Great Britain* is also classified as one of the most comprehensive travel references of the period. Within this three-volume epic, Defoe is one of the few writers of the time to focus in detail on the marketplaces of London. This may be a consequence of marketplaces being a less attractive area of commerce when the thriving ports, the business arena emerging in the City of London, the coffee-house trading and the rise of the shopkeeper were all dominating trade. Below are a number of extracts taken from Defoe's definitive volume one of *A Tour Thro' the Whole Island of Great Britain* describing some of the most dominant of London markets, many of which continue to thrive today.

Of the fourteen flesh markets, or markets for provisions, seven of them are of ancient standing, time out of mind: But the other seven are erected since the enlargement of buildings mentioned above. The old ones are, Leaden-Hall, Honey-Lane, Newgate Market, Southwark, Clare, St. James's, and Westminster; and these are so considerable, such numbers of buyers, and such an infinite quantity of provisions of all sorts, flesh, fish, and fowl, that, especially the first, no city in the world can equal them. 'Tis of the first of these markets, that a certain Spanish ambassador said, There was as much meat sold in it in one month, as would suffice all Spain for a year.

This great market, called, Leaden-Hall, though standing in the middle of the city, contains three large squares, every square having several outlets into divers streets, and all into one another. The first, and chief, is called, the Beef Market, which has two large gates, one into Leaden Hall Street, one into Grace-church Street, and two smaller, viz. ...

The second square (of Leaden-Hall) is divided into two oblongs, in the first is the fish market, and in the other, a market for country higlers, who bring small things, such as pork, butter, eggs, pigs, country dress'd, with some fouls, and such like country fare.

The north part of the fish market, the place being too large for the fishmongers use, are the stalls of the town butchers for mutton and veal, the best and largest of which, that England can produce, is to be bought there, and the east part is a flesh market for country butchers.

The third, and last square, which is also very large, is divided into three parts: Round the circumference, is the butter market, with all sorts of higglary goods, as before: The south part is the poultry market, and the bacon market, and the center is an herb market.

All the other markets follow the same method in proportion to the room they have for it.[25]

Many people drifted to the larger cities to find work in the food markets. Fruit, pea and bean picking was popular among women migrating to London from Wales and Shropshire, and the milkmaids who dominated the trade in Islington were also Welsh.[26] Rural butchers brought their carts into the city and were labelled 'foreign butchers'. They provided healthy competition for the London-based butchers, who were pressured into lowering their prices, in line with the rural traders.[27] As Defoe recorded, Covent Garden became synonymous with its fruit and vegetable markets, while Smithfield Market was a busy livestock trading centre. It was also the location for one of London's predominant annual Charter Fairs, Bartholomew Fair. The other main Georgian market places in the capital included Leadenhall and Billingsgate. In the eighteenth century there would have been a direct passage descending from Billingsgate market down to the river, enabling the boats to off-load their fresh cargoes directly into the surrounding shops and stalls.

Those who think that the coffee-shop chains that dominate the British high streets today are a modern phenomenon are very much mistaken. The same demand for coffee-shop culture was established during the seventeenth century. Just as they are present today in many cafés, newspapers and books were made available for visitors to relax with a drink while they familiarised themselves with the latest newsworthy stories. It is understood that the first coffee house opened in Oxford sometime in 1650, with a similar venture established in London about two years later. Coffee

houses were not just the preoccupation of city dwellers
either; William Bray mentions the presence of a summer
coffee house built for seasonal visitors in a remote Derbyshire
village in 1783. The owner also acted as a tour guide to assist
walkers down the steep terrain to the river.[28] They were also
built to serve as amenities within public buildings. One such
coffee house is mentioned in King's Bench Prison, originally
located in Southwark, London. An 'ordinary' (standard basic
meal) could be purchased for two shillings, an offer which
came with a pint of porter included. This particular coffee
shop also provided a bed to accommodate prisoners until
they were able to find themselves 'chummage'. Or a fee was
paid for sole occupancy of a room.[29] King's Bench Prison was
largely built to house debtors and inmates had to purchase
their own food, drink and bedding.

　　Roach's *London Pocket Pilot, or stranger's guide through
the Metropolis*, 1796, is a very early observational guide
to London written by John Roach and designed to act as
companion to a visitor's 'fortnight's ramble'. He notes that
coffee houses became venues where food was also served on
a considerable scale. As a consequence there was 'scarcely
a street in the metropolis, where the hungry passenger
of moderate fortune may not live with convenience and
elegance; and in several, not only eat and drink, but sleep
upon the most reasonable terms.' Roach provides a list of
what he considers to be the best coffee houses in London at
the time of writing:

The London Coffee House, Ludgate Hill
The York Coffee House, New Bridge Street
Anderton's Coffee House, Fleet Street
Peel's Coffee House, Fleet Street

The following coffee houses are all situated in the Temple
district of London: Joe's, Grecian, Brown's, Temple. Then
comes a list of the finest houses in the Strand, including

Nando's, George's, Holyland's, Somerset, Turk's Head, New Exchange, and Hungerford. Only three in Charing Cross are cited: Salopian, Cannon and Spring Garden. Finally Le Coq's in Parliament Street, the Prince of Wales in Conduit Street, Braund's Head in Bond Street and the Rathbone Place Coffee shop (without a location) are all recommended.[30]

The London Coffee House, Ludgate Hill, has an interesting history and urban tale attached to it. First opened in 1731, it became a place of celebrity. The first proprietor was a Mr James Ashley, who marketed the venue as a cheap alternative to other coffee houses that also served punch. This sort of punch or 'punsch' was associated with the popular liqueur of the time, arrack. The standard price for a quart of arrack was eight shillings in the early 1730s, but the London Coffee House was only charging six shillings, and only four shillings for rum and brandy. The establishment changed hands a number of times, proprietors including Messrs Leech and Dallimore and a Mr Lovegrove. The last owner was a Mr Robert Clark, who finally closed the coffee house in 1867. The building had once been a meeting place for various lodges attached to the Freemasons and was also used periodically as a central criminal court. During a night of well-oiled entertainment with a celebrity presence, a well-known opera tenor of the time, Mr Broadhurst, is believed to have sung a note so powerful that it shattered the bowl from the stem of a wine glass resting on a table.[31]

A similar 'celebrity' urban myth surrounds the Salopian coffee house in Charing Cross. The Salopian was a coffee house that was also linked to high-profile visitors. The engineer Thomas Telford was so enamoured with the premises that he was frequently cited as a permanent fixture in the lease each time the property was signed on. It is understood that he chose to leave the premises, having bought his own house, at the same time as a new landlord taking over. On hearing Telford's news it is said the new owner exclaimed 'What! Leave the house! Why, sir, I have just paid £750 for you.'

Sadly the rate books for 1823, the year that Telford bought his house, fail to corroborate this story, but it is widely documented that Telford used the Salopian coffee house as his main headquarters for no less than twenty years to both conduct his business and to live in.[32]

Nando's coffee house on the Strand, which is also listed elsewhere as being situated on the corner of Fleet Street, is believed to be the place where Lord Thurlow caught the eye of the Duchess of Queensbury. As a consequence of their meeting she recommended him into the law profession, where he succeeded as one of the most eminent legal practitioners of his generation, eventually serving as Lord Chancellor for almost fifteen years. For many years Nando's was a hairdressers and was inscribed inside with 'Formerly the palace of Henry VIII and Cardinal Wolsey'. Shortly after Henry's death the Council for the Management of the Duchy of Cornwall Estates met regularly on the same site.[33]

In 1804 the Prince of Wales coffee house was the scene of a final quarrel between 'mad Lord Camelford', so called due to his temper and slightly eccentric behaviour, and a Mr Best. Mad Lord Camelford was otherwise known as Thomas Pitt, the Second Baron Camelford and cousin to the PM William Pitt the Younger. He and his friend Mr Best argued vociferously over a lady named Simmons, a mistress to both men. This final exchange of words in the coffee house led to them fighting a duel in the grounds of Holland House, and the final fatal demise of Thomas Pitt.[34]

Curiously not included in Roach's guide under his list of top coffee houses is the Rainbow Coffee House in Fleet Street, which is often credited as the second coffee house to open in London. There are several accounts relating to the first London coffee house. The first suggests that it was established in St Michael's Alley in Cornhill by a Mr Bowman, a coachman to a turkey merchant. The second version of the story names Pasqua Rosée as the establisher, a Greek servant to a turkey merchant named Mr Edwards. Rosée prepared coffee every morning for his master, found himself to be good at it and joined forces with their coachman, namely Bowman, to open a coffee house. It is said the two men came into conflict over the business, leaving Rosée to continue running things single-handedly. The Rainbow, the second coffee house, was initiated by a Mr James Farr, originally a barber, who ventured into coffee-making as a sideline. Mr Farr was unpopular with his neighbouring traders, who took him to court in 1657, declaring that 'in making the same [coffee] he annoyeth his neighbours by evill smells; and for keeping of fire for the most part night and day, whereby his chimney and chamber hath been set on fire, to the great danger and affrightment of his neighbours'. Despite their protests Farr was allowed to continue trading and his coffee emporium grew in status across London. In 1666 he issued a special tradesmen's token engraved with the shape of a rainbow on it. One of these tokens has survived, and resides in the Beaufoy Collection, housed in the Museum of London.[35]

One of the most disreputable coffee houses of the period is undoubtedly King's Coffee House, a venue that was based in Covent Garden, London, owned and run by Tom King together with his formidable wife Moll, who inherited the shop on his death. Considered a front for prostitution, it became notorious for its fights, fraudulent selling practices and general criminal activity.[36] Moll King made a profession out of vice and was continuously being prosecuted for keeping a disorderly house and demonstrating bad public behaviour. It was said of King's Coffee House that 'here you might see Ladies of Pleasure, who apparelled like Persons of Quality, not at all inferior to them in dress, attended by Fellows habited like Footmen, who were their Bullies (Pimps), and wore their disguise, the more easily to deceive the unwary Youths who were so unhappy as to Cast their Eyes upon these deceitful Water-Wag-Tails'.

Having spent most of her life in conflict with the law,

always able to dodge imprisonment for brothel keeping on the basis that her establishment provided no beds, Moll King retired to her country house a wealthy woman and was able to send her son to Eton to receive the best education. A slim book was published about her life in 1747 by an anonymous writer, and she, along with her business, was satirised by the painter Hogarth and negatively credited in Henry Fielding's play of 1732, *Covent Garden Tragedy*. Moll King has also frequently been linked to the main character of Daniel Defoe's Moll Flanders, published in 1722.[37] The story of King's Coffee House not only emphasises the fact that many coffee houses of the Georgian period had a potential for disrepute and salacious activity, it also highlights the new role of some women who were beginning to get more involved in business activity, particularly where trade was concerned. Moll King had been a street-corner nut seller before she elevated herself to shop owner and landlady. Many of the food and drink retail businesses of the time were dominated by women, just as more of the large country and town estates were being managed by female housekeepers and domestic staff in the kitchens.

There were a number of published poems written about coffee, including 'The Coffee House: A Characteristic Poem' by Philip Smyth in 1795, 'The British Coffee House', 1764 (author unknown, reported to be a caffeine addict), and the writer and philosopher Voltaire wrote a comedic five-act play titled *The coffee-house, or fair fugitive*. The author James Miller also wrote a play that was performed at The Theatre Royal, Drury Lane, in 1743. A copy of this play published the same year reveals that a complaint was made against Miller regarding deformation of character. A local London family claimed the play was based on their own family business and coffee-house activities. The preface denounces these accusations and requests that the readers of the play appreciate that the author's inspiration was taken not from the London-based family business, but from another one-act French-language comedy written many years previously.[38]

Another of the most famed and frequented coffee houses in London was Lloyd's coffee house, which was integral to the formation of the Lloyd's of London Insurance market and its related shipping businesses. Situated above the Royal Exchange, it became the centre of British commerce, and one room was established for invited, pre-approved subscribers, who paid twenty-five old pounds to join, then a further four guineas a year in membership fees. This would have been a tidy sum in the eighteenth century. In addition to their commercial activity, as a group they established the 'Patriotic Fund', a charity to support the wounded, orphans and widows of war.[39] In 1798 this annual sum raised 32,000*l*, well in excess of £1 million in today's currency. Just as Lloyd's coffee house became concerned with insurance and commerce, many of these establishments acquired a specific association, depending on the clientèle. Since trade and shipping was so integral to the business world of the eighteenth century, many would become centres for these types of workers and investors.

There is an excellent description of one such coffee house in London, called the Jerusalem Coffee House, which appears in an 1826 copy of *The Oriental Herald and Colonial Review*. Also considered to be one of the oldest established coffee houses, the Jerusalem was said to be

the rendezvous of owners of ships engaged in the commerce of India. A stranger who enters it for the first time, is struck with astonishment at seeing a crowd of men moving around him with a kind of mercantile fury; he hears resound on all sides the words cotton, indigo, rice, insurance, bills of lading, cargo; he is every moment pushed by his neighbor ... a boy stands in the corner of the room to give the address of different captains, and to inform strangers of the hour at which they generally visit the Coffee House. The walls are

covered with hand-bills and printed placards which specify
the time at which the different vessels set sail.[40]

This description provides some indication of the energy and
pace at which these coffee houses would function. It goes
on to explain how passengers would eagerly congregate to
determine the departure times of vessels, which could often
be days or even months out. Those same passengers would
return day after day to the coffee house to find out the latest
news regarding their voyage.

One edition of the *Gentleman's Magazine*, 1785, provides
a comprehensive list of the prices of coffee at that time
on sale in the Great Turk coffee house. Coffee in the first
advertisement was from 2s 6d to 5s. In the second the same,
a better sort at 4s and the best of all at 6s per pound. The
right Turkish berry was priced at 2s 8d, the India berry,
'sweet and good', at 18d per pound. 'Chocollata' was also on
sale in pound boxes for 2s, the 'perfumed' variety between 4
and 16s and the very best chocolate would cost the customer
20s per pound. Roughly, then, the best chocolate would cost
the equivalent of around sixty or seventy pounds per pound
in today's market.[41] Even the cheapest chocolate would set
you back around twelve pounds a pound, probably the same
amount you might expect to pay in the twenty-first century
for standard chocolate. High and fluctuating costs of these
new beverages throughout the eighteenth and nineteenth
centuries saw the introduction of a cheaper alternative.
A mild stimulant, Saloop, was extracted from the roots of
orchids and was prepared in the same way as coffee and tea,
with water, milk and sugar. Sold at a fraction of the price,
Saloop was also a popular antiseptic and an aid for the relief
of certain venereal diseases, a common problem for the
Georgian population.[42]

Despite coffee houses opening throughout the country
during the seventeenth century, it wasn't until the eighteenth
century that they really established themselves as places for

men to meet and discuss business, politics, the arts and social gossip. Coffee houses are best illustrated through the works of Hogarth, who was also considered a frequent visitor. His paintings are satirical and depict the often aggressive, debauched and lewd behaviour that took place in these establishments.

It was the age of the gentlemen's club, where London's finest businessmen, politicians and nobility would meet to dine, drink, exchange discourses and more often than not gamble. Associations, informal and formal clubs and gatherings of men were established throughout London in particular, as migrants and traders formed relationships, both business and personal, across every rank of society. These clubs would often revolve around feasting and drinking. Essentially the Georgian era marked the start of modern Freemasonry.

One of the most well-known clubs of this kind, located in London and frequented by the Prince of Wales himself during the late eighteenth century, was Brooks's. From the records of the club published in 1907 we learn that

> Dinner was served at half-past four and the bill was brought in at seven. Supper began at eleven and ended at half an hour after midnight. The cost of the dinner was eight shillings a head and of the supper six; and anyone who had been present during any part of the meal hours paid his share of the wine in accordance with that old law of British conviviality which so long held good in the commercial room.

It was also reinforced that 'no gaming was allowed in the eating Room'. If caught doing so the penalty was to pay the whole bill.[43] This indicates how group dining, and making the most of your companion's company while doing so, was so highly regarded in the Georgian period.

One of the earliest clubs to open in London was White's. Originally a coffee house, White's Chocolate House was founded by one of the many Italian immigrants dominating the streets of Georgian London, a Mr Francis White. The shop itself moved premises on several occasions and it has been questioned whether chocolate was ever actually served on the premises, as it was primarily associated with London's gambling nobility and the 'fashionable gentlemen of the city'. White's final reincarnation came in 1773, when, having been destroyed by fire, it was reopened as a membership-led club. White's Club thus became the first of its kind to start a trend for other coffee houses to transform themselves into more exclusive venues to allow their clientèle to meet discreetly and away from the company of the coffee houses' less salubrious customers, such as highwaymen, rakes, con artists and petty criminals.[44]

The Beefsteak Club is the name or nickname of a number of eighteenth- and nineteenth-century male dining clubs that celebrated the beefsteak – a food item associated with liberty and prosperity, a patriotic and Whig party symbol. The actor Richard Estcourt founded the first beefsteak club in 1705, preceeded by the Sublime Society of Beef Steaks in 1735, founded by another performer and manager of the Theatre Royal in Covent Garden, John Rich, together with his colleague George Lambert. They soon acquired over twenty members, including Samuel, or Dr, Johnson. By 1785 the Prince of Wales himself became a member and weekly meetings involved eating steaks and baked potatoes, accompanied by port.[45] The Royal Society Club was another club founded in the mid-1700s; initial rules and orders included a dinner to be ordered every Thursday, at a cost of one shilling and sixpence per head. A pint of wine also had to be paid for by everyone attending.[46]

Public houses became popular venues for clubs, one such being the 'Spouting Club', where aspiring actors would drink large quantities before reciting performances in front of whoever would listen. These clubs were documented at a number of locations around London, in areas largely associated with the labouring classes. They were described as public houses 'where young people generally resort, some for amusement, and some with a view to qualifying themselves for the stage' and as 'plebians of both sexes most ridiculously misspending their time by neglecting their respective vocations'.[47] The Kit-Kat (Kit-Cat) Club was formed as early as around 1700, apparently, by a pastry cook of the name Christopher Katt, who may or may not have also been the inspiration for a renowned mutton pie of the time called the Kit Cat. It has also been argued that Christopher went by the nickname of Kit and that his shop was overshadowed by a sign bearing the image of a cat and fiddle. Initially starting as a weekly pie and pastry eating ensemble, the club expanded and attracted many prominent members over the years including Robert Walpole and Sir John Vanbrugh. There is a poem, the provenance of which is sometimes credited to Pope or Arbuthnot, about the club and its name:

> Whence deathless Kit-Kat took its name,
> few critics can unriddle:
> some say from pastry-cook it came,
> And some from Cat and Fiddle.
>
> From no trim beaux its name it boasts,
> Grey statesmen or green wits:
> But from the pell-mell pack of toasts
> Of old cats and young kits.[48]

Many dining clubs in London began to establish themselves in large private residences from about 1800, away from the coffee houses and taverns. As such the records and minutes of these meetings became obsolete and many simply could not sustain themselves without the support of all the amenities and facilities provided by their former public venues.

The word restaurant was a creation of the French and did not really enter English vocabulary with any frequency until

the late nineteenth or early twentieth centuries other than
when speaking about eating in France. Up until this time
the name given to places for purchasing and eating food in
Britain was simply 'Eating House'. However, there are some
early uses of the word 'restaurant'. An edition of the *Morning
Post* for London in 1824 carries an advertisement for a new
coffee house and restaurant owned by a Mr J. Dubourg,
declaring it to be in the 'French style',[49] and the Café De
L'Europe et Restaurant opened in Bond Street on the corner
of Park Row in Leeds in 1830.[50] Writing in 1796 John Roach
provides an interesting first-hand account of recommended
eating establishments in London during the late eighteenth
century, recounting, 'For those, whose circumstances are
barely independent there are an abundance of respectable
houses, generally known by the name of chop-houses, where
they may live altogether as comfortably as in the former,
and where they will occasionally see the best company, and
be certain of never meeting with persons of an improper
description.' This implies that chop houses in the main
were not the sort of venues where the poorer or criminal
divisions of society would frequent. He mentions that there
are other places more suited to those on a lower income,
or as Roach phrases it, of 'distressed condition'. These were
places that also sold good wholesome meals for under a
'single half-penny'. Roach then continues to list the names of
some of what he considers to be the finest taverns and eating
houses in London, including: The London Tavern, the Paul's
Head Tavern, The Globe in Fleet Street, The Saint Albans
Tavern in Saint Albans Street, The Thatched House Tavern
in Saint James's Street and The Star and Garter Tavern in Pall
Mall. These establishments provided 'all the most delicate
luxuries upon earth, and where the fortuned voluptuary may
indulge his apetite, not only with all the natural dainties of
every season, but with the delicacies produced by means of
preternatural ingenuity.'[51] For detailed information relating to
London's variety of Georgian eating houses, John Feltham's

The picture of London for 1802 offers the reader a lengthy, eloquent list and short critique of 'the most considerable Eating Houses East of Temple Bar'. These included:

The Cock, situated behind the Royal Exchange and honoured as 'one of the most celebrated houses in the metropolis for turtle, gravy and other soups, excellent dinners, and the best of wines. It is computed that 500 persons (on an average) regularly dine here every day, and from it being so contiguous to the Exchange, its truly convenient to the commercial world.' The Cock is also recommended by John Roach in his early London guide as an eating house 'where everyth1ing is of the very best quality, and where a customer, who drinks but a pint of table beer, is treated with as much deference as if he called for a bottle of burgundy'.[52]

The Crown Eating House, Bow Lane, Cheapside. 'Frequented mostly by gentlemen in mercantile situations. Well-dressed dinners every day from one to five on reasonable terms. Good wines, spirits and beds.'

The Queen's Arms Tavern and Eating House, Newgate Street. 'An established house, noted for a copious bill of fare.'

Dolly's Beef-Steak House, King's Head Court, Newgate Street. 'Well known for cooking beef-steaks in the highest perfection.'

Lamb Eating House, Bearbinder Lane, near the Mansion house. 'Dinners dressed from one to five.'

The Mitre, Fish Street Hill, 'is an eating-house, well-conducted, and on a respectable plan'.

Swan Tavern and Eating House, Fish Street Hill. 'Every suitable accommodation at a modern rate'.

The Horse-Shoe, Newgate Street. 'A very good house for beef-steaks, mutton chops etc.'

The Salutation Tavern and Eating House, Newgate Street. 'An ordinary everyday at two o'clock. And chops dressed at all hours.'

Queen's Arms Eating House, Bird-Hand Court, Cheapside. 'An excellent ordinary everyday at three and four o'clock.'

The Marlborough Head, Bishopsgate Street, near the gate of the Excise Office. 'Good rooms for the reception of company. Frequented mostly by gentlemen belonging to the Excise Office and South Sea House. No regular ordinary, but chops dressed in a few minutes.'
Guidon's French Eating House, Portland Street. 'Frequented by genteel persons; and dinners on reasonable terms.'

There were also a number of what were listed as 'Cooks Shops' – convenient and cheap eating houses, where dinners could be bought for one shilling. There were also 'Al Amode Beef Houses' (larded beef stewed with vegetables), and 'Soup Shops'. In 1802 it was estimated there were around 5000 public houses in London alone.[53]

This cynical and satirical literary descriptive piece, written in 1772, provides an illustrated idea of what a Cook's shop would have been like:

> While the keen air invites to supe-
> rior delights,
> Our appetites prone to provoke;
> How sweet is the smell, from each kitchen
> or cell!
> Of soup, how delightful the smoke!
> Still to crown the Repast, that same soup
> would you taste,
> Ye Merchants and Maidens from church
> In all its perfection, oh! Blend your direction,
> With speed towards Herton and Birch.
> There's pease, vermicelli, of Turtle a jelly,
> With delicate soup *a la Reine*;
> Capillaire, Orgeat, Lemonade, and what-not
> I'll warrant you'll go there again.
> Crouds unnumber'd may come to the little
> back room,
> Where of light there appears a faint gleam,

There you'll all sit as snug as a bug in a rug,
And enjoy both the Soup and the Steam.
There stalks Captain Bluster, of oaths with
a cluster
Zounds! Waiter, how long you're about it!
If there's no soup, you dunce, why say
so at once,
I care not, for I'll go without it.
Next, with delicate voice, and with words
of more choice,
A gentle youth makes his appearance;
he glides as he walks, he lisps as he talks
And asks for some soup with forbear-
ance.
See his cockatoo crest, how delightfully drest
With his club most prodigious behind;
With his ribbon afloat, and his long waist
ed Coat,
And his heels almost par'd of their rind.
So demure and so nice, he sits down in a
thrice,
Should some delicate damsel be near
For each spoonful of soup that his Mouth
swallows up,
His eyes fail not to give her a leer

The Nymph all the while, puts on many a
smile
Determined at heart soon to greet him
She tells him in short, that in Coventry-
court
She lives, and will be glad there to
meet him
But hark! On the block, to receive the directions shock,
A Turtle lies gaping for breath,
See with mirth brimming eyes, Common

Council man wife,
How he smiles to be in at the death.
Still with quivering life, it survives from
the knife
And vibrates with warmth left behind,
Oh! tell me ye Brokers, with fortunes ye
jokers,
Your lives, are not they of the kind
To fame long since dead, you have that in
its stead,
Which still keeps you alive, and in action,
But tho' Fortune may thrive, n'er shall
Honour survive
The just sev'ring knife of Detraction.
The truth stands most clear, then laugh not,
nor sneer,
But all that I've said lay some strets on,
There's moral enough in a Turtle as Puss,
To give to the Thoughtful! A lesson.[54]

Coventry court was a known area for prostitution in London during the eighteenth and nineteenth centuries. This short rhyme makes critical reference to the type of clientèle that would have visited the cook shops – a mix of those types of men that were forging their own elite clubs in London at the time and the prostitutes. It has a slightly sordid undercurrent and a disdainful attitude towards the food. The turtle was used widely in Georgian Britain as a French culinary import. Cook shops would have served the popular cheap soups, as well as more luxurious drinks such as Capillaire, a syrup drink often alcoholic and often mixed with orange flower water. Orgeat was also a sweet syrup drink, blended with almonds, and is still used today in some specialist cocktails.

John Perkins, writing in 1796, provides a basic recipe for Beef Alamode, a dish that was so popular in Georgian Britain that they established a number of 'houses' designed to cater just for this dish. Essentially *boeuf á la mode* is a French dish of larded beef stewed with vegetables, similar to an American pot roast or an English meat stew.

> Beef Alamode: Take a fleshy piece of beef, without fat, and beat it well with a rolling pin; then lard with pretty large pieces of fat bacon, and if you please, put it over the fire a little to fry, till the outside is brown; put it to stew in a deep stew-pan, or glazed earthen vessel, with salt, pepper, bay-leaves or Jamaica pepper; some lemon-peel, half a dozen large mushrooms, two cloves of garlick, or four or five cloves of shalot, a pint of water, and half a pint of wine; cove it close and let it stew gently till its tender; when it is enough, fry some flour in hog's lard, and add to it some lemon-juice, or a little verjuice.

Although typically eaten hot, Perkins suggests it is best served cold and cut into half-inch thick slabs.[55] A rather amusing description of an altercation that took place in an 'alamode' beef house is recounted in John Wight's *Mornings at Bow Street: A Selections of the Most Humorous and entertaining Reports which Have Appeared in the Morning Herald.* A Mr Edmund Speering, Esq., was walking past Thomas's 'alamode' beef shop in Clare Court, London, around two o'clock in the morning when he heard a 'great row and uproar' coming from inside, including the sounds of both women and men. Looking through the 'beef-besteamed windows and the sallads', Speering saw three or four men and as many women all in physical conflict. He went ahead to ask the ladies in the group if they needed help. They answered as one 'Oh! Yes, we do!' Speering ejected two of the men by their waistbands and breeches, but was then attacked by another of the men, Jemmy Green, who was also swiftly disposed of. The last man, named Snodgrass, struck Speering to the back of his head with an umbrella. He recovered to see a police officer cart away all of the offenders. The landlady, barmaid and waiter all gave evidence at the trial declaring that Green and Snodgrass, together with two other men, had come into the alamode beef shop more than a little worse for wear and had eaten large quantities of the beef and red wine, which, when mixed with gin and beer, 'produced a fume which got the better of what little sense they carried about them, and made them all agog'.[56] Perhaps the alamode was more popular with Georgian society as much for its marinade as for anything to do with French cuisine.

A slightly later account of an alamode beef house published in the *Penny Magazine* in 1843 provides us with a more civilised image of this type of establishment.

> Here a visitor takes his seat and the waiter places before him a knife, a fork and a spoon; and gives him the choice among sundry lumps of bread kept in an open basket. Meanwhile the visitor asks for a 'sixpenny plate'; and it may happen that two other customers ask at the same time, the one for sixpenny and the other for a fourpenny plate. Out goes the waiter, calling in a quick tone for 'two sixes and a four', a brevity which is perfectly well understood by those who are to lade out the soup from the cauldron wherein it is prepared. Presently he returns with a pile of pewter-plates containing the 'two sixes and a four', and places them before the diners.[57]

What this description suggests is that the types of establishment that everyday people living in the eighteenth and nineteenth centuries frequented would have been rather similar to our fast-food restaurants of today, sitting communally and ordering from a select few items designed to fill you up and keep you warm with a high calorific content – a culture of eating that was fast, cheap and practical – while the higher end of society would dine for hours at a time over many courses and with great frequency throughout the day.

There was a tragic fire in London in 1748, which famously wiped out some of the most notorious establishments in the city of the Georgian period. The fire started at a wig maker's located in Exchange Alley, Cornhill, and within twelve hours managed to burn down almost one hundred houses across three separate areas. Among these were the Fleece and Three Tuns taverns, Tom's coffee house and the Rainbow coffee house. In Exchange Alley, shops including Garraway's, the Jerusalem coffee house and the Swan tavern were also burnt down. Many others perished at a cost of around 200,000*l* just in the value of merchandise, effects and stock, exclusive of the buildings themselves.[58]

It is important to establish that the fashion for eating out and the demand for a good-quality meal was not limited to London. Many cities and towns across England, Ireland, Scotland and Wales were all benefiting. Public dining and drinking establishments listed in the 1738 Dublin Directory included taverns, eating houses, chop houses, coffee houses and a chocolate house. During the seventeenth century there were some 1,180 ale houses alone listed in in the city, and these taverns were mainly frequented by young single men, who either ate in-house or had the tavern food sent around to their lodgings.[59] Nor were these establishments only typical of Britain. Eating houses in New York are cited as 'numerous', with dinners sold 'at a very reasonable rate'. One in particular, known as Franklin House (or Plate-House), served from twelve until five from three public rooms including a bar, coffee and dining room. Plates of ham, turkey or fish with vegetables and a dessert of pie or pudding cost one shilling. Cider and beer was priced at one penny for a tumbler.[60]

Georgian Britain was a gastronomic mix of food retail, consumption and culinary commercial enterprise that would have impacted on all areas of society in one form or another. The most startling aspect of this is the very obvious comparison with today's preoccupation with food as a lifestyle mechanism. Britain has retained its pub culture and revived its obsession with coffee. Restaurants and fine dining are at the peak of popularity and society is slowly abandoning the dominant, uninspiring role of the major supermarkets in order to revisit the more artisan aspects of locally centric markets and local produce. When re-examining the gastronomic revolution of the Georgian age, it is like walking into a familiar world that is in many ways little removed from today.

5

Britain's Own French Revolution

Enchant, stay beautiful and graceful, but do this, eat well.
Bring the same consideration to the preparation of your food
as you devote to your appearance. Let your dinner be a poem,
like your dress.

Charles Pierre Monselet, French author (1825–1888)

The outlawed practice of Protestantism and enforced conversion to Catholicism during the 1680s in France left hundreds of thousands of men and women with no other choice than to be exiled to countries such as the Netherlands and America. Some 80,000 also settled in England, of which around half settled themselves in London. Doubtless, this was the first time the word refugee came into modern European use, as a word adopted to describe those of 'Le Refuge' from the country. Many French refugees arrived with skilled trades to their name, such as weaving, accounting and clock making. Despite some animosity and prejudice, French Huguenot communities settled comfortably in England. Clearly the French made an impression on the physical landscape of Britain too, as Daniel Defoe remarks in his journal *A Tour Through the Whole Island of Great Britain*, noting that in Colchester, Essex, there are a total of eight churches, of which one is a Dutch church and one a French church. He also mentions a French church in Southampton and a French hospital in the East End of London. The hospital was established to help the poor and reliant French refugees.[1] One of the earliest French Huguenot cooks to make a significant impact was Jean le Becq, who managed the Half-Moon Tavern, located in London's Half-Moon Alley; some ten years after his death, the former nearby White's coffee house, which then became White's Club, was renamed after the cook – Lebeck's Head. In her diaries of 1671 to 1714 Elizabeth Freke spoke earnestly about enrolling a French tutor, Charles Marie Du Veales, for her son's benefit as soon as he turned seventeen. This was to ensure that he learnt the French language and 'other qualifications of a gentleman'. To secure this she paid Mr Du Veales forty-four pounds annually. A considerable sum. The year was 1692, so clearly the French influence had been a dominant force from a much earlier period as a consequence of Huguenot settlers. Writing even earlier in 1663, Samuel Pepys notes that despite his misgivings he learnt two valuable lessons from the French. Firstly to have the confidence to haggle over the final cost of dinner when eating out at a tavern and secondly, to avoid recruiting new servants until references have been received from trustworthy and reputable sources. Pepys, however, is quite cynical of the French generally throughout his journal submissions. It must be remembered that Britain was in conflict with France for many years, and despite providing them with asylum and reaping the benefits of their skills and countenance, the average British opinion of the French was always a double-edged sword.

Writing in the century before, Cosmo the Third recorded in his diary, as he travelled throughout England during 1669, a theory as to why the French were so successful in England, noting that much of the everyday business transactions of the English took place in public houses over alcohol. In fact he observes that the English frequented public houses on numerous occasions throughout the day, often 'neglecting their work'. It is for this reason that he suggests the French are so successful in England as 'they are more attentive to their business, they sell their manufactures at a lower price than the English, who would fain derive the same profits as other artizans, however little they work'.[2] This is a particularly interesting theory, in light of recent contemporary debates on immigration and the argument that European migrant workers often fulfil the jobs that the English no longer want to do for considerably lower wages. The French became well known in Britain for their dentistry skills and introduced early Georgians to toothbrushes and paste. Not the type of toothpaste we are familiar with today. The French 'Dentifrice' would have been a mix of pulverised bone and sweeteners to clean and freshen the mouth. These additions to British culture came at a time when they were most needed. The significant increase of sugar in the everyday diet meant that the population's teeth were decaying at a quick rate.

Despite the ensuing influence of French style and culture that permeated many of the arts in Britain during the Georgian period, there were still a number of Anglophiles who wanted to retain the country's traditions. The newspapers were full of advertisements for 'Good, Plain, English Cooks'. By the time William IV came to the throne in 1830, the public were informed by the *London Standard* that he 'does not employ in the department of the cuisine at any of his palaces, one single French cook'.[3] This implies that the tide may have been turning for the English love affair with all things French, as Britain lurched further into the nineteenth century. The French influence on British cuisine was significant during the eighteenth century. One edition of *The Gentleman's Magazine* in 1736 makes reference to this by reiterating the recent trend for 'contempt' towards English food at the tables of 'some of our oldest English nobility'. It observes how the 'Sir Loin' is rapidly being replaced by the 'Ragoute', while 'a leg of mutton yields to a Soup Meagre'.[4]

Samuel and Sarah Adams, long-standing servants themselves in large establishments over some fifty years, informed their readers in their 1826 account *The Complete Servant* that in France all culinary business was conducted by men only, and that for every large kitchen in the country there were at least as many cooks again. The difference with English cooks was that only some 300 or 400 of the most significantly wealthy families in the country would have employed male cooks, with another forty to fifty being employed in the best hotels. Often smaller establishments would temporarily recruit a male cook to come on the premises a couple of days prior to a large event in order to help with the preparations and contribute their greater expertise. The couple also outline what they consider to be a fairly typical example of the type of staff that would be employed in a 'respectable Country Gentleman's household'. This included 'A French Man-Cook' who was paid at least four and often five times as much as the rest of the staff, including the butler. A good French cook was a truly valuable asset in a large household, as was French wine and French brandy.[5]

An excellent comparison, from American observations, of late Georgian French and English cooking and dining can be found in the *Southern Review*. The French, the reader is informed, do not eat large joints of meat, rather they use a variety of techniques to cook portions of meat that are for example stewed, fricasseed or ragoued. The meat is marinated and served with sauces, condiments and other additions. Whereas the English cook on large fires, the French utilise small brick stoves. It is emphasised that even the poorest of French men eat with silver cutlery and napkins, while the English use steel knives and forks. While the English choose to partake in entertainment and conversation after eating, the French consider the act of dining itself to be the main form of entertainment. The latter drink responsibly with their food, while the former drink to excess after their meal.[6] There were conflicting and mixed opinions about the differences between the two cultures where food was concerned in the eighteenth and nineteenth centuries. One theory as suggested in *The Nic-nac: Or Literary Cabinet* is that by eating more food in large quantities less frequently, the English had a greater mental advantage than the French. A high concentration of nutrients and meat, it is stated, encouraged a more robust and challenging attitude, which could assist positively in conflict or situations requiring bravery. Not to undermine the French entirely, it is added that smaller and more frequent portions of food, as preferred by the French, can enhance spirituality and depth of reflection.[7]

These smaller and more digestible courses of food eaten over a long period of time are documented by Joseph Woods during his travels in France in 1816. He recalls that

> the order of the dishes follows rather the mode of dressing than the substance of the meat, and you have first boiled, then fried, afterwards stewed, and at last roast. Birds in each mode follow the more solid food, and here, with the roast meat and vegetables together, each is considered as a distinct dish, and eaten separately; indeed all the mixtures are made in the kitchen, and you hardly ever see a Frenchman unite in his plate the contents of two different dishes – that is the cook's privilege ... Last came cheese, pastry and fruit. Among the last were always walnuts.[8]

There were French eating houses, as well as English establishments, that sold French fare in Georgian Britain. Macky informs his readers that in the Exchange district of London in 1722 there were 'two very good French eating Houses' called Pontack's and Kivat's. Macky defines Kivat's as an 'Ordinary'. Ordinaries became popular places to eat in a continental style, where regular meals were served up to everyone at a fixed price.[9] Pontack's in particular was a renowned establishment owned and run by Mr Pontack, a proud, confident and talkative man whose father was the President of Bordeaux. A French refugee at the end of the seventeenth century wrote of this eating house in detail, describing the 'four spits, one over another' each of which carried around five or six large chunks of butcher's meat including beef, mutton, veal, pork and lamb. He explains that 'you have what quantity you please cut off ... Those who dine at one or two guineas per head and handsomely accommodated at our famous Pontack's ...'[10]

In an article titled *English and French Cookery* published in the *Monthly Review*, 1827, French cuisine is praised as being the best form of cooking, and the former head cook to Louis XVI, Louis Eustache Ude, is cited as the leader in this field. His book, *The French Cook*, is revered as the greatest guide to cooking in the French style, with descriptive chapters on sauces, soups, fish and the dressing of game, fowl, eggs and so on. The article notes that of all the chapters, the one relating to sauces is the most critical, as sauces provide the foundation for all good cooking.[11]

Ude was an interesting, influential and poorly recognised cook, who should be remembered more in writings on the legacy of French cooking and its influence on English society. He fled to England during the French Revolution. His mother, a milliner, had married an underling working in the kitchens of Louis XVI. Rather than be apprenticed in the kitchens where he grew up, Ude attempted all manner of vocations including engraving, printing, haberdashery, gambling and even acting. He eventually returned to his original calling, and trained and elevated himself to maître d'hôtel within the house of Bonaparte within a few years. On migrating to England Ude was recruited by the Earl of Sefton, who paid him 300 guineas a year and left him a considerable sum for retirement. Ude was succeeded by Charles Elme Francatelli.[12]

In *The French Cook* Ude pays homage to his time in England, but is critical of the lack of prestige afforded to both the art of cooking and the way in which it is rewarded. He notes that there are not enough kitchen assistants provided to support head chefs in their work, which in turn diluted the quality of the dishes being prepared. He also points out the lack of recognition given to a good head chef: 'After ten years of the utmost exertion to bring his art to perfection, he has the mortification of ranking no higher than a humble domestic.'[13] Above all Ude wanted to promote the importance of cookery and establish it as a science, once announcing that the Royal Society would never be complete until it designated a 'chair of cookery'. There is a picture of Ude in the archives of the British Museum, taken from the frontispiece of *The French Cook*. Ude is drawn sitting comfortably in a chair, leaning on his walking stick and wearing a fur-trimmed jacket. The picture is engaging and Ude has a contented half-smile, the look of a man at ease with himself, confident and approachable.

One of the godfathers of French haute cuisine for the masses must be Antoine Beauvilliers, a pioneer of the restaurant in the true sense of what we consider to be a restaurant today, with a dining room, elegant waiting staff and a fully stocked wine cellar. His first significant venture was opened in the Palais Royale in 1787.[14] Beauvilliers has been described as a portly figure with a triple chin and a broad joyous face reflecting sparkling grey eyes. He was a sous chef at the palace of Versailles for Louis XV before embarking on his own business. A man that 'not only benefited mankind by his practice, but left golden maxims behind him for their future happiness',[15] Beauvilliers wrote *The Art of French Cookery*, which has become synonymous with the art of early French cuisine. In his book, Beauvilliers references the English as the most extravagant people on the face of the globe. Like so many pioneers in cooking at this time, Beauvilliers seems to have been eclipsed by Marie-Antoine Carême.

French commerce generally was at an all-time high between 1740 and 1788, with France's exports doubling and at a much greater rate than that of Britain. However, following the Revolution and the start of the nineteenth century this role was reversed, as Britain thrived and France suffered a long recovery and demise pattern over many years.[16]

An article that appears in *Blackwood's Edinburgh Magazine* focuses on the character of the French, from an English perspective, describing the French as 'Quick sensibility, superficial observation, clever thinking, and vivid passion, at once agree, and easily account for whatever we observe in the character of this people ... the French derive from their own temperamentt the most amiable, cheerfulness and gaiety, as well as love of amusement; and it is under this category that should be noticed that taste which they everywhere and so honourably shew for the elegancies of sculpture and painting'. The article continues in disdain, criticising how French men all dine at restaurants while their wives and children are left to eat at home on scraps and 'sour wine'.[17] Webster, meanwhile, writes in contrast that 'French dishes have always had a decided advantage over the English in appearance; they are made to please the eye as well as the taste. No heavy masses of viands are served at a French table; but light, elegant, and tempting forms are presented to those around it. In this respect the English cooks are beginning to reform their style, and to study, in serving, neatness and elegance in the arrangement of the contents of each dish.'[18]

Despite the rising popularity in French cuisine among the wealthy and aspirational middle classes, it is interesting to note the extent of the contradictions during this period in relation to what the French really ate and how they cooked and prepared their food. This contradiction is exemplified by Paul Cobbett, writing about his travels in France in 1824,

The French are famed for eating a great deal of vegetable, and but little of animal food. I, however, have found it quite the contrary, as far as I could judge by what I saw of their cookery at Saint Omers; for, while the people who dined at the Table d'Hote ate meat in a great variety of shapes, I never saw a any vegetables upon the table, except salad, which the French are very fond of, and some little pieces of carrot, onion and garlick, which I found mingling together in the soups, fricasees, and ragouts.

One often consistent opinion however is that, as Cobbett points out, 'the same quantity of animal food which we eat in England would feed almost double the number of persons in France.'[19]

An anonymous writer of 1827 in *Domestic Economy, and Cookery, for Rich and Poor* emphasises the importance of French ideas on cooking being imparted to English cooks or aspiring cooks, in addition to simply experimenting with French recipes, noting,

> A French cook looks upon himself as the family physician; but it is quite different with them, as they seldom leave their places. It would be a great improvement in this country to see cooks bred, as to any other business, by apprenticing them under good cooks for a certain time; this is the only way of having any number properly taught, as the best receipts will not teach much without a great deal of practice and attention, which every one cannot attain, particularly after a certain age.[20]

The popular periodical *The Monthly Review* details the travels of an English gentleman in France from 1787 to 1789, whose observations reveal, 'The common cookery of the French gives great advantage. It is true they roast everything to a chip, if they are not cautioned: but they give such a number and variety of dishes that if you do not like some, there are others to please your palate. The dessert at a French Inn has no rival at an English one.'[21] Similarly writing in the century before, the well-known diarist John Evelyn paid tribute to French cuisine, defining the sauces as the best he had ever tasted, that the meat was cooked to perfection in its own juices without the use of water (a common technique adopted by the British). Even the bones of the animals he describes eating are soft enough to spread on bread, as a result of the slow cooking process. To conclude, Evelyn describes the whole experience as one which leaves him 'exceedingly pleased'.

The French also taught the English the benefits of hygiene in the kitchen and provided them with the knowledge to improve upon safe eating, as well as alerting them to the implications of adulterating food. Friedrich Christian Accum's *Culinary Chemistry* of 1821 warns, 'If however copper utensils are to be used, they should be employed with the precautions as used in France, where the tinning of the vessels on the inside is done as regularly as the shoeing of horses in a farm-yard.'[22]

Long before germ theory and the groundbreaking discovery of how disease spread, Luis Ude's iconic book on the eighteenth century, *The French Cook*, contains some ninety-nine references to maintaining cleanliness, from the equipment that is used to cook to preparation areas, everything that comes into contact with food should be kept clean, including the cook themselves. It is ironic in many ways that in today's contemporary society there still endures an overriding derision of the French by the English. This often underlying contempt for French ways and ideals, perpetuated by the media, is contrary to the evidence that French migrants and early Huguenot refugees significantly influenced cultural and social politics in England in a way which has left a defining legacy.

The Victoria & Albert Museum have in their collection an engraving from 1757 titled *The Imports of Great Britain from France*. The painting is visually explained in *The Laudable Association of Antigallicans* as follows:

> On the front ground, a cask overset, the contents, French cheeses from Normandy, being raffinie, a blackguard boy stopping his nostrils, greatly offended at the haut-gout; a chest well crammed with tippets, muffs, ribbons, flowers

from the hair ... underneath concealed cambricks and gloves ... beauty washes, pomatums, l'eau d'Hongrie, l'eau de luce, l'eau de carme ... French wines and brandies.[23]

What this engraving implies is that a great deal of merchandise from France came into Britain via Holland and Flanders, while other items went in a slightly clandestine manner, unnoticed by customs officials. This has several implications; firstly any import figures for this period will be largely inaccurate, affecting the legitimacy of the official figures for that time, secondly it is indicative of a much wider French influence than can be assumed to have permeated England during this period. It is also useful to consider that the Anti-Gallican Society were just that – anti-French, and therefore much of their literature from the time must be viewed as controversial. The Anti-Gallican Society were established in London sometime between 1750 and 1751. They were primarily concerned with protecting and promoting domestic British industry and the discouragement of French imports. Regular quarterly meetings were held where prizes for British-made products would be awarded.[24] Little remains documented of this Georgian society, which disbanded after a brief period due to lack of substantial group objectives or interest.

A damning criticism for the British trend to recruit French chefs appears in an article in the *Ipswich Journal*, 1736, stating,

We hear a General Officer has just hir'd the famous French Cook who lately serv'd a noble duke: His wages are 125*l* per Annum, a Bottle of champagne every Day at Dinner, and clean Linen ... allow'd him daily, besides other privileges ... Immunities, altogether unknown to the Cooks of the Growth of Great Britain ... It's hop'd the Parliament will prohibit the Importation of those Fellows who 'tis thought are sent over purposely either to ruin or poison our Nobility and Gentry.[25]

Unquestionably the country was split over immigration and prejudice relating to the preservation of British identity – not unlike many of the political debates of today's contemporary society.

The charismatic English novelist and diarist Fanny Burney, having rejected many suitors in her youth, chose to marry a French exile quite late in life, and subsequently spent many years living in France. As a French sympathiser during the Revolution, she used her influence as a writer to produce literature with a French bias for the English market. One such text was *Brief reflections relative to the emigrant French clergy*. Written in 1793 it is an appeal to the women of the nation to aid charitable support for the Revolution. It is a wide-reaching political pamphlet comparing the disenfranchisement of the French clergy to the disenfranchisement of other minority groups of the time, including women. Based on this premise Burney calls for women to empathise with 'the banished men now amongst us'. The language she uses to engage with her fellow women is passionate and stirring, similar to that of the popular Gothic novels of the time, and appeals to their Christian sensibilities.

> ... behold these venerable men, collected in a body, enclosed within walls dedicated to holy offices, bewailing the flagitious actions of their country-men, yet devout, composed, earnest in prayer, and incorruptible in purity. Now, then, in mental retrospection, witness the unheard-of-massacre that ensued! Behold the ruffians that invade the sacred abode, each bearing in his hand some exterminating weapon; in his eye, a more than fiend-like ferocity. Can it be you they seek, ye men of peace? Unarmed, defenceless, and sanctuarised within the precints of your own religious functions! – Incredible! –
>
> Alas, no! – behold them reviled – chaced-assaulted. They demand their offence? They are answered by staves and pikes. They fly to the altar ... here, at least, are they not safe?

At this sanctified spot will not some reverance revive? Some
devotion rekindle? ... No! – the murderes dart after them: the
pious suppliants kneel – but they rise no more![26]

Other popular writers of the period such as William
Wordsworth wrote French propaganda with a view to
increasing support and sympathy for French migrants
arriving in England. 'The Prelude', 'Banished Negroes' and
most powerfully 'The Emigrant Mother' are all poems along
this theme. 'The Emigrant Mother' relays the story of a
woman driven out of France and forced to leave her son
behind. She befriends her English neighbour who has a
child of a similar age. She becomes deeply attached to the
child, likening it to her own son. Wordsworth describes
the woman's anguish and torment through a spectrum of
emotions that she expresses through the child. Like Burney,
Wordsworth fell in love with a French national and they had
a child together. Unlike Burney the couple were torn apart
by war and never married.[27] What these writers and many
of their contemporaries achieved was a legacy of emotion
associated with England's relationship with France at this
time, the impact of war and French immigration.

In terms of the respective attitudes of the French towards
the English, the writer Eugene Guinot's observations of an
English public dinner are contemptuous, re-enforcing the
notion of the English as staid, conventional and beholden
to traditional institutions, an attitude long associated with
the English tendency to over consume alcohol and indulge
in rich food.

Nothing is more curious than one of these repasts, which recall
to mind the feastings described by Homer. Enormous pieces
of beef, whole sheep, monstrous fishes, load an immense
table bristling with bottles. The guests, clothed in black,
calm and serious, seat themselves in silence, and with the air
which one takes at a funeral. Behind the president is placed

a functionary called the toast-master. It is he who is charged to make the speeches. The president whispers to him the mat d'ordre, and 'Gentlemen,' says he with the voice of a Stentor, 'I am about to propose to you a toast which cannot fail to be received by you with great favour – it is the health of the very honourable, very respectable, and very considerable Sir Robert Peel, &c. &c!' The guests then, shaking off their silent apathy, rise all at once, as if they were moved by springs, and respond to the invitation by thundering forth frantic cries. While the glasses are being emptied, three young girls with bare shoulders slip from behind a screen and play a tune on the piano. The toasts do not cease until the guests, having strength neither to rise nor to remain seated, roll under the table.[28]

The book *Letters describing the character and customs of the English and French* ... is a compilation of letters published in 1726 written by a Swiss national who lived in France and served for many years with the French army, called Béat Louis de Muralt. His perceptions of the English are damning, criticising the country as one riddled with corruption and considering the English people to be uneducated and generally wealthy beyond their means, making them prone to boredom and vice. While highlighting the fact that England is such a free nation, he at once attributes this again to a selfish laziness with a lack of consideration for others. He also reflects on the country's somewhat unfounded pride in itself and its citizens, but remonstrates that this is neither more nor less than any other nation. Although he does emphasise the extent to which selfishness pervades English society, making them contemptuous generally of strangers and foreigners.[29] One slightly more favourable observation of the English in terms of their cooking appears in Rosamond Bayne-Powell's eighteenth-century travel journals, quoting from the French geologist Barthelemy Faujas de Saint-Ford, who pays tribute to England's renowned cooking of beef, describing, 'Slices of beef and veal cut very thin and beaten tender, about the size of a hand, sprinkled with bread crumbs, grilled and nicely served on a silver dish, fine big potatoes with salt butter to follow, delicious beer and good Bordeau wine.'[30]

Another French traveller and social observer Pierre Jean Grosley is quoted as recognising that in most British inns of the time it was necessary to visit the kitchen to select the best steak, which was cooked to personal order. He notes, 'The sole business of the cook was to be constantly blowing the sea-coal, which was half extinguished by the fat of the steaks, and to put new steaks in the place of those which the people of the inn came, in succession, to snatch from off the gridiron.' And of British coffee he complained it resembled 'a prodigious quantity of brown water' and that 'nowhere do people drink worse coffee'.[31]

Writing a little outside of the period under discussion, around the mid-seventeenth century, François de La Rochefoucauld was, as is consistent with many French critiques, quite damning of the English custom of taking dinner, describing it as follows:

At four o'clock precisely you must present yourself in the drawing room with a great deal more ceremony than we are accustomed to in France. This sudden change of social manners is quite astonishing and I was deeply struck by it. In the morning you come down in riding-boots and a shabby coat, you sit where you like, you behave as if you were by yourself, no one takes any notice of you, and it is all extremely comfortable. But in the evening, unless you have just arrived, you must be well washed and well groomed. The standard of politeness is uncomfortably high – strangers go first into the dining room and sit near the hostess and are served in seniority in accordance with a rigid etiquette. In fact for the first few days I was tempted to think that it was done for a joke.

'Dinner', de la Rochefoucauld found, was 'one of the most wearisome of English experiences'. It lasted for four or five hours, and unlike some of his countrymen who complained that they did not get enough to eat, de la Rochefoucauld was surfeited with food. His host pressed it upon him, inquiring anxiously if he liked it, and 'out of pure politeness' he did nothing but eat from the time when he sat down to table until he got up again. The dishes consisted of various meats boiled and roasted, weighing about twenty or thirty pounds. Sauce, de la Rochefoucauld declared, was unknown and ragouts were seldom seen. 'After the sweets,' he notes, 'you are given water in small bowls of very clear glass in order to rinse out your mouth – a custom which strikes me as very unfortunate. The more fashionable folk do not rinse out their mouths; but that seems to me worse; for, if you use the water to wash your hands, it becomes dirty and quite disgusting.'[32]

In contrast are the writings of Cesar De Saussure, an early French travel writer whose book *A Foreign View of England in the Reigns of George I and George II* provides a positive account of English cooking and dining. He confirms that well-travelled noblemen regularly employed French cooks and ate in the main a combination of French and English dishes, 'adding pastries and French garnishings to the roast meats and English puddings'. He compliments the way in which the dining tables of the English nobility are usually very clean, with fresh cutlery, plates and glasses being replaced regularly throughout a meal. He notes how the English salt their beef for around seven or eight days before boiling it, which he considers a very good method for retaining the natural juices of the meat. De Saussure talks about the English fondness for puddings, the savoury as well as the sweet, observing that the main pudding served with meat is principally made of rice, flour or breadcrumbs. This pudding, he declares, is enjoyed by all 'foreigners'. However, he goes on to declare that the English are uneducated in the preparation of fish or vegetables and that vegetables are only ever eaten when accompanied by meat. De Saussure praises the quality of oysters to be found in England and notes that many of these are exported to Paris. He is critical about both the fact that supper is not customarily consumed, as well as the English custom of men and women separating after dinner. He dislikes the lack of regard or respect English men have for women compared to that of French men.[33]

Alexandre Balthazar Laurent Grimod de la Reynière is characterised as the first European food critic. A connoisseur of fine food and wines, he also established a chain of food retail shops across France. His reflections on English food and cooking were published in his periodical *Almanach des gourmands*, essentially a review of all food-related endeavours that ran from 1803 to 1812, forced into closure following a series of legal court actions involving accusations of libel.[34] Grimond de la Reynière was quite scathing of English food, declaring that the country had never been famous for its ragouts and that it was unlikely any real 'gourmets' would cross the Channel to experience an English meal, which was limited to 'boiled chickens, of extreme insipidity, and to what they call Plump Pudding, a concoction based on breadcrumbs and Corinth raisins,' making 'a bizarre and indigestible mixture rather than a healthy and skilfully-made dish'.[35]

The relationship between the French and English in terms of food and cultural influence during the Georgian era presents an interesting dichotomy. While the French clearly needed England as their refuge, and the British were keen to absorb more of the French aesthetic attitude and culinary expertise, neither appeared to genuinely respect the other. The French were in the main disdainful of British food and customs but were keen to exploit the English love and demand for French culinary expertise. In contrast there were sectors of society in England who wanted to retain British traditions and values and viewed the French migrants as a threat both within the context of food and wider social concerns. Unquestionably what the French did achieve during this period was a sustained acceptance and adoption by the English of their cuisine, together with a theoretical understanding of cooking and its numerous techniques. The very best French cooks dominated the homes of the elite across the country for hundreds of years and their publications offering advice and instruction in the kitchen adorned the bookshelves of millions of British people. This is a presence that left a tangible mark on the country's culinary history with many of Britain's best-known dishes originating from this period. *Pommes de Terre frites* (French Fries) appear in recipe books circulating in Britain as early as 1800, if not before, and the basic béchamel sauce, which has become the foundation for most British white sauces, appears in a number of recipe books throughout the early 1800s, as does mayonnaise, omelettes, consommé, soufflé, vol au vents, gateaux, croquettes potatoes and so on. In addition roquefort, brie and camembert were all being imported into Britain by 1888.

Many of Britain's most respected chefs of the twenty-first century, including more popular names such as Gordon Ramsay and James Martin, all trained in France, to learn the very best techniques in culinary aptitude. Correspondingly many French emigrants have remained in England to impart their culinary expertise in a country that they have adopted as their own, including Raymond Blanc and Michel Roux Junior.

6
Celebrity Chefs

It is almost impossible for a Cook to attend to the business
of the kitchen with any certainty of perfection if employed in
other household concerns – It is a service of such importance,
and so difficult to perform even tolerably well, that it is
sufficient to engross the entire attention of one person.

William Kitchener, *The Cook's Oracle*

Too often writers of food history give credence only to
French chefs of the Georgian period when discussing those
that achieved great status or memorability through their art.
There are many such men and women who demonstrated
their talents in the field of cooking, cookery writing and other
associated elements of culinary excellence. This chapter will
focus on some of the more traditionally well-known names
associated with cooking prowess of the eighteenth and
early nineteenth centuries, including Soyer, Carême and
Francatelli. It will also introduce some of the lesser-known
neglected purveyors of comestible trades from this age, all of
which have contributed significantly to the narrative of food
and cooking history in Britain.

The great cooks of the eighteenth and early nineteenth
centuries were innovative and knew how to self-promote.
Many were already the height of fashion by virtue of
their nationality. Cooks from Europe both enhanced and

influenced British society's perceptions and understanding of food and cooking. Despite cultural generalisations relating to the traditional role of women associated with the kitchen, rather few feature in the media as working in professional kitchens during the Georgian era. Platzer, writing in 2011, equates this to military history. From an early age it was accepted that members of the Army would cook their own meals. This in turn created a hierarchical male structure of cooks required for various tasks, a structure which eventually became the model in all professional kitchen environments.[1] The expectation that men manage the professional kitchens while women control the domestic kitchen is a tradition perpetuated by the fact that women are simply still significantly under-represented in this field, both at the training level and where recruitment and employment practices are concerned. There were a number of changes applied to guild restrictions during the eighteenth century which resulted in men inheriting many of the tasks that traditionally wives and daughters would have completed, moving women away from the production side of work.[2] Many of the women featured throughout this book are those that either wrote on the subject of cooking, worked in the food retail trade or were employed in domestic service. No women of the Georgian age received the level of notoriety that their male counterparts did, simply because they were not valued in the same way as men. These women existed, but history has neglected to record them. We know they existed because occasionally they are revealed through old, forgotten books or journals. William Hone's 1825 *Every-Day Book* is one such example. In observing the way in which Paris mobilises itself each Christmas for the traditional culinary feasts of the age, Hone mentions the vast number of English cooks working in the French capital. One of these cooks is a Ms Harriet Dunn. Working out of the Boulevard, she is labelled as a 'professor' of cooking. Not in the academic sense, but in the sense that she has become well known for this skill. In particular she produced a highly sought after plum pudding every Christmas, which she made in bulk and shipped out to all her regular English clients across the whole of France. This pudding had been thoroughly prepared, so that by the time it reached the table it simply had to be reheated.

One of the earliest celebrity chefs, who does not quite fit into the Georgian chronology but nonetheless is worthy of mention as one of the last classic cooks/writers of the Stuart period and the art of showcase cooking, is Robert May. Living at the tail end of the Stuart period, he is best known for his publication *The Accomplisht Cook* of 1660. In the tradition that many top chefs aspire to in the twenty-first century, May was an Englishman who trained to become a cook by learning and working in France. *The Accomplisht Cook* also serves as a biography of May's life. Following his training in Paris May took up an apprenticeship as cook at the Grocers' Hall and for the Star Chamber before going to work for his benefactor, Lady Dormer, who also employed his father, a well-known cook in his own right. After her death May moved around London and the rest of the south of England to work for numerous lords and countesses in large households. His book is a reflection of his passion for culinary revival and desire to return to the large-scale entertainment and theatre of cookery that existed in England before the Civil War. Consequently his ambitious recipes for pies baked within pies, decorative flowers made from all manner of ingredients and for large centrepiece statements make for enjoyable and entertaining reading.[3]

May describes one ensemble, which he advises should be made for 'Festival Times, as Twelfth-day, &c.' as follows:

Make the likeness of a Ship in Paste-board, with Flags and streamers, the Guns belonging to it of Kickses, bind them about with packthread, and cover them with close paste proportionable to the fashion of a cannon with Carriages, lay them in places convenient as you see them in Ships of war, with such holes and trains of powder that they may all take Fire; Place your Ship firm in the great Charger; then make a slat round about it, and stick therein egg-shells full of sweet water, you may by a great Pin take all the meat out of the egg by blowing, and then fill it up with rose-water, then in another. Charger have the proportion of a Stag made of course paste, with a broad. Arrow in the side of him, and his body filled up with claret-wine; in another charger at the end of the Stag have the proportion of a Castle with Battlements, Portcullices, Gates and Draw-Bridges made of Past-board, the Guns and Kickses, and covered with course paste as the former; place it at a distance from the ship to fire at each other. The Stag being placed betwixt them with egg shells full of sweet water (as before) placed in salt. At each side of the charger wherein is the Stag, place a Pye made of course paste, in one of which let there be some live Frogs, in each other some live Birds; make these Pyes of course. Paste filled with bran, and yellowed over with saffron or the yolks of eggs, guild them over in spots, as also the Stag, the Ship, and Castle; bake them, and place them with guilt bay-leaves on turrets and tunnels of the Castle and Pyes; being baked, make a hole in the bottom of your pyes, take out the bran, put in your Frogs, and Birds, and close up the holes with the same course paste, then cut the Lids neatly up ...[4]

This extraordinary complex battle scene of coloured pastry sculptures, live small animals, gold-painted bay leaves and wine and rose water is then presented to the diners, who are encouraged to engage with this culinary scene and interact with all of the intricate finer details contained within it. It is designed to titillate and conjure up 'delight and pleasure' among the men and women of the party. It is also very reminiscent of Heston Blumenthal's contemporary medieval reproductions of today.

The Accomplisht Cook is perhaps one of the last hurrahs

of the old English methods of large-scale theatrical dining, before the trend for French 'High Art' cuisine began to dominate this field, alongside the renowned cooks of the time who took great care to pitch their recipes and advice towards a broad market of readers from across the class system. This nostalgia is echoed in May's words throughout his book, including,

> Bills of fayre for every Season in the Year; also how to set forth the MEAT in order for that Service, as it was used before Hospitality left this Nation

and

> These were formerly the delight of the Nobility, before good House-keeping had left England, and the Sword really acted that which was only counterfeited in such honest and laudable Exercises as these.[5]

Another master of the pastry board, although slightly less flamboyant in his approach, was Edward Kidder. This cook and teacher/trainer was best remembered for his book of *Receipts of Pastry and Cookery*, designed specifically for scholarly purposes and to ensure his recipes were recorded for the benefit of future cooks. Kidder taught at a variety of locations around London. His main pastry school was based in Little Lincoln's Inn Fields. 'Dutch Hollow-works and butter-works' were taught here on Thursday, Friday and Saturday afternoon, while the same classes ran in the morning at another of his schools in Norris Street, in St James's Haymarket, and on Monday, Tuesday and Wednesday afternoons in yet another of his schools located in St Martin's le Grand. Each page of his printed recipes was illustrated using engraved copper plates. He died in 1739, at the age of seventy-three. His life is recorded in *A biographical history of England, from the revolution to*

the end of George I's reign, 1806. He is given great credit
and affectionately termed 'maker of puffs'. It is suggested
in this biographical account that one of his descendants
most likely took over his business, but reopened the main
premises as a slightly humbler pastry cook shop (much to
the disappointment of the writer).[6] His death is recorded in
the *Stamford Mercury* of 1739, affirming that he 'taught near
6000 Ladies'.

It wasn't just London that was producing high levels
of talented culinary expertise. Charles Gill was a pastry
cook based in Wade's Passage, Bath. Christopher Anstey,
a well-respected English writer and poet of the eighteenth
century, wrote a celebrated verse demonstrating high acclaim
for Charles Gill:

> Of all the cooks the world can boast,
> However great their skill,
> To bake or fry, to boil or roast,
> There's none like Master Gill[7]

In contrast Gill also trained under the great painter Sir
Joshua Reynolds. But perhaps the most surprising fact of all
about Gill is that as a consequence of a severe wound in his
thigh, he only had the use of one leg.[8] By the accuracy of the
description, it is also believed that in his autobiography of
1850, John Britton was writing about Gill's pastry cook shop
in Bath when he reminisces,

> I particularly remember the pastry-cooks' shops, into one
> of which we entered, and tasted some delicious tarts, the
> flavour of which seems to have dwelt on my palette to the
> present time; for I have ever regarded a raspberry tart as
> the most tempting article at the richly furnished table. The
> shop I allude to was built against the north wall of the Abbey
> church, between two buttresses, attached to one of which was
> the oven chimney.[9]

Another English Georgian culinary entrepreneur, of slightly more international notoriety, is Joseph Terry. Terry began his lifetime involvement with confectionery as a trained apothecary, manufacturing and selling medicated lozenges in Wirksworth, Derbyshire. As early as 1744 he is listed as one of the suppliers of a type of 'Chymical Drop' thought to prevent, among other ailments, wheezing and a shortness of breath.[10] It was through marriage that Joseph made the transition into the confectionery industry. One of his brothers-in-law, Robert Berry, worked in the family business, Robert Berry & Co., in St Helen's Square, York, mostly trading in candied peel. Once married, Joseph immediately joined this firm. By 1825 Robert Berry was dead and Joseph, together with Robert's son George, formed the new, rather amusingly named business Terry & Berry. According to the papers of the time, for whatever reason this partnership was dissolved in 1828, whereby Joseph then went into business with a John Coultherd, to form Joseph Terry & Co.[11] Very little seems to have been written about the early formations of Terry's dynasty. Joseph's son, Joseph junior, took over the business from 1850 and it is this period and the subsequent chocolate wars with competitors Rowntree's that receives the most attention. Rowntree became a collusive trader with John Cadbury and Joseph Fry, all of whom were Quakers. John Cadbury began trading in Birmingham as a hot drinks vendor in 1824, eventually specialising in chocolate drinks. Despite being rivals, no doubt bound by their religious beliefs and early temperance practices, the three companies operated together and maintained a cooperative among shopkeepers where pricing and display was concerned.[12]

James Gunter was an English confectioner who opened a fashionable shop in Berkeley Square in partnership with the established Italian confectioner Domenico Negri called 'The Pot and Pineapple' in 1777 (pineapples were the emblem of eighteenth-century confectioners). On Negri's death some twenty-two years later it eventually changed its name to

Gunter's Tea Shop. The British Museum have in their collection a copy of a bill receipt for the original Pot and Pineapple, dated 1760, totalling four pounds and five old pence, for two months' worth of supplies. This includes items such as dried apricots, peaches in brandy and savoy biscuits. Gunter was succeeded by his son William, who also catered for London's finest society, and was a man whose services were 'mandatory for all London's most elegant breakfasts, balls and suppers'. We are also informed that in the height of summer, ladies would assemble in their carriages opposite the shop, while waiters took trays of ices out to them. During the 1830s Gunter's tea shop was allegedly the only location respectable enough in London for ladies at the time to be seen unchaperoned with a man during the afternoon.[13] One suspects then that Gunter must have been favoured tremendously by men throughout the city, as he provided them with a rare opportunity to spend quality time alone to court.

One of Gunter's chief confectioners, William Jeanes, wrote a guide – *Gunter's Modern Confectioner* – to making and presenting confection. In the 1800s confection was a broad category that included pastries, cakes and sweetmeats. Jeanes makes a clear reference to the importance of English confectionery at the start of the book, paying homage to the early French practitioners and citing Carême as the original luminary of pastry work, but clearly stating that the recipes contained within the book are traditionally English, emphasising that as such, English confectionery 'has marked out a line of its own, and possesses peculiarities of taste widely different from those found on the Continent'.[14] Jeanes makes many references to James's son William, who wrote *Gunter's Confectioner's Oracle* in 1830, throughout his book in both an affectionate and respected way, as well as on occasion to point out slight discrepancies in his techniques.

(he) used to recommend boiling, exactly opposite to what other confectioners advise. He first boiled the loaf sugar to the 'feather' then added the gooseberries, and boiled up three times, pouring out the whole into a pan, and skimming the surface. He treated the fruit thus for six consecutive days, reducing the degree of boiling each day (instead of increasing it, as I would recommend) until at last it reached only the 'pearl'. Of course he added fresh syrup each day.[15]

There are perhaps too many cooks to mention that worked across the myriad of well-established taverns, cook shops, inns, and gentlemen's clubs of the time. One such principal cook was John Farley, who headed up the kitchen at the auspicious London Tavern. This was an establishment that boasted the largest dining facility in London, with the potential to cater for over two thousand people. Farley wrote his book, *The London Art of Cookery*, in 1783. The London Tavern was said to be so big, many people assumed it was a bank from the outside. It was also highly respectable. Unlike many other dining venues at the time it had neither a coffee shop nor a bar, defined as 'par excellence the City temple of gastronomy' by Callow in his *Old London Taverns*.[16] It was not the place to eat dinner, but rather the place to dine. It attracted royalty, the wealthy and the highly esteemed men of the age. Farley had high standards where cooking was concerned and strove for perfection in terms of cultivating, preparing and serving food. He was an advocate of progress and recognised the ongoing commitment to creativity and skill in this discipline. He notes, 'Cookery, including pickling, and the various branches of confectionery, soon became an art, and was as methodically studied as the more polite sciences. A regular apprenticeship is now served to it; and the professors of it are incorporated by charter, as forming one of the livery companies of London.'[17] Like many before and after him, Farley has often been accused of plagiarism, in particular where Hannah Glasse's work is concerned. However, he created the epitome of high-end cuisine, a unique and exclusive dining experience, cooking for some of the most important men in Europe. It is also apparent that by 1800 Farley had managed to relinquish his position of principal cook to become the proprietor of the London Tavern, as recorded in an advertisement for his book published in the *London Chronicle* for 1800. The pioneering French restaurateur Antoine Beauvilliers opened his Parisian restaurant *Grande Taverne de Londres*, and, it has been suggested by a number of academics, he chose to convey much of what Farley had achieved with the original London Tavern. This tribute to Farley's legacy is surely testament to his place in the annals of British Georgian culinary celebrity.

Another well-known cook to the paying public of the eighteenth century was William Verrall. Trained by St Clouet, the French cook to the Duke of Newcastle, Verrall, who is also cited in the chapter on recipe writing, worked at and wrote about his experiences of the White Hart Inn, Sussex. First published in 1759, his recipes are presented in a light-hearted way and have captured the imagination of modern-day culinary enthusiasts and other experts in the field. The iconic Elizabeth David quoted Verrall in her classic book of 1970, *Spices, Salt and Aromatics in the English Kitchen*, and just as Christopher Anstey proclaimed his admiration for the pastry cook Charles Gill, Thomas Gray, perhaps best known for his *Elergy Written in a Country Churchyard* (1751), kept his own copy of Verrall's book, making copious annotated recipes of his own throughout. This copy of Gray's notes was incorporated into later editions of Verrall's original book. It includes recipes for dressing eels, pike and carp, veal stewed with rice, cucumber sauce and many others. Like many other cookery books of the time, Verrall's *The Complete System of Cookery* transcends French and British culinary methods and techniques.

Marie-Antoine Carême, despite dying in his late forties, was perhaps one of the most respected of French cooks. He was also one of the most prolific writers within the Georgian celebrity chef genre. His works include:

Le Pâtissier Royal Parisien, ou Traité élémentaire et pratique de la pàrtisserie et moderne, suivi d'observations utiles au progrès de cet art, et d'une revue critique des grands bals de 1810 e 1811 (Paris, 1815)

Le Maître d'hôtel français, ou Parallèle de la cuisine ancienne et moderne, considéré sous rapport de l'ordonnace des menus selon les quarte saisons (Paris, 1822)

Le Cuisinier parisien, Deuxième édition, revue, corrigée et augmentée (Paris, 1828)

L'Art de la cuisine française au dix-neuvième siècle. Traité élémentaire et pratique. Volumes 1–5 [Work completed after author's death by A. Plumerey] (Paris, 1833–1847)

Le Pâtissier pittoresque, précédé d'un traité des cinq orders d'architecture (4ème edition, Paris, 1842)

The Royal Parisian pastrycook and confectioner [From the original of Carême, edited by John Porter] (London, 1834)

French Cookery, Comprising l'Art de la cuisine Française; Le Pâtissier royal; Le Cuisinier parisien ... [translated by William Hall] (London, 1836)

His dishes were known for their creativity and elaborate design. The ornate, many-tiered wedding cakes that we know today were made popular by his influence. Carême was keen to balance and compliment the flavours of one ingredient next to another by experimenting with combinations. While many cooks of the past had concentrated on developing sauces to mask the poor quality of food, or disguise contaminated or rotten ingredients, Carême mixed flavours to support and fuse taste sensations. These methods were often interpreted as complex and complicated, earning the label of 'Grande Cuisine'. His methods are predominantly what trainee professional chefs are instructed with today, making Carême's legacy one of the most internationally important in culinary history. Carême went to London briefly to work for the prince regent, who would later become George IV. Following a brief spell in Russia, he returned to Paris for the last years of his life to work for the banker James Rothschild.

An article composed by the renowned Irish novelist and travel writer Lady Morgan describing a dinner at the house of Baron De Rothschild in Paris, where Carême ended his service, appeared in the *Bury and Norwich Post* in 1830. The reader is informed by Lady Morgan that Carême had rejected 'la cuisine epicée et aromotisée' (the more modern-day trend for spicy food). The writer explains that she was against the French Revolution – a 'bonnet blanc' – and had read much of Carême's work. So much so, that she felt she knew Carême's style of cooking well. She declares that Carême's talents as a cook are 'unrivalled'. Rothschild introduces the writer to Carême after dinner. He is described as 'a well-bred gentleman, perfectly free from pedantry'.[18] A homage to the late Carême appeared in the 1833 edition of *The Court Journal, court circular & fashionable gazette.* It reads,

What eminently distinguished Carême was his universality. He was an elegant and exquisite 'patissier' – a correct 'Rotesseur' – a superb 'potagiste' – a superior 'Friturier'. He excelled in the oven, was great at the spit, and sublime before his stoves. Since Voltaire, no man has ever united such varied talents. He treated with the same skill, the same fucility, the hot and the cold departments; the entree, the entremet; game, fish, the hors d'ouvre and the dessert ... he wore with equal distinction, the white apron of the cook and the black coat and sword of the maître d'hotel. In short Carême was one of those privileged beings whom avaricious Nature sends into the world at 'intervals long and far between'. He was perhaps, the only man of his age capable of executing a dinner without a fault.[19]

Louis Eustache Ude has been discussed at some length already in the chapter on French influences. Defined as a popular and likeable man, with a 'numerous circle of friends',[20] like many French cooks of the time, Ude migrated to England to escape the war and persecution of France. He lived to the surprisingly mature age for the time of seventy-eight. On the death of his contemporary Alexis Soyer, *The Cheltenham Chronicle* acknowledged him as 'one of the grand gastronomic triumvirate of our day, which may be said to have comprised Louis Eustache Ude, Charles Francatelli and Alexis Soyer'.[21]

Soyer really excelled after the Georgian period, but by 1830 he was twenty years old and therefore practising his art long before Queen Victoria was crowned. Born at Meaux-en-Brie in France (that of the cheese-making), he was an apprentice cook from 1821 to 1826 near Versailles. He left France due to the Revolution in 1830, not before finding a place as second cook to Prince Polignac at the French Foreign Office. He migrated to England to work in the kitchens of the Duke of Cambridge in London. After a number of other prestigious appointments Soyer was made chef at the Reform Club in London in 1837. He was now earning a salary of 1,000 old pounds a year. He became an advocate in the press for the promotion of the famine in Ireland and was sent there by government to erect soup and economical kitchens at half the expense. This work was the inspiration for his book *Soyers charitable cookery. Or the poor man's Regenerator*. By 1849 he had turned his hand to invention and patented his 'magic stove', a portable device that enabled food to be cooked at the table. He made a series of public demonstrations of his stove. He opened his own restaurant, which made a huge loss of around 7,000 old pounds, at Gore House, Kensington. Soyer also assisted in the Crimean War by a government appointment to supervise meals served in the hospitals. His last years were spent lecturing and assisting in the design of military hospital kitchens. It is believed that Thackeray's

Above: 1. A workhouse, St James Parish.

Right: 2. Demonstrating the 'Macaroni' style, 1776.

3. Small turned wooden treen nutmeg grinder, *c.* 1830.

4. Georgian tea caddy, spoon and sugar nippers.

5. A Milinillo, or chocolate stirrer.

Below left: 6. Count Rumford, 1798.

Below right: 7. Conical decorative ice cream or pudding mould, late 1800s, and Georgian 'peg foot' earthenware jelly mould.

BENJAMIN Count of RUMFORD.

Opposite: 8. Wooden
and bone pastry cutter
and Victorian glass
juicer.

Above: 9. Georgian
pewter herb dish.

Right: 10. *Vegetable
Seller, Covent Garden,*
1726.

11. *Old Smithfield Market*, 1824.

12. *The Coffee House Politicians*, *c*. 1725.

Above: 13. *Diners in a Chop Shop*, c. 1800.

Right: 14. Engraved portrait of Moll King.

Below: 15. *A row in a city kitchen.*

Above left: 16. *French Cookery,* frontispiece illustration of cook inside restaurant, 1656.

Above right: 17. *A macaroni French Cook, c.* 1772.

Below: 18. *The Commercial Treaty: Or John Bull changing Beef and Pudding for Frogs and Soup Maigre,* 1786.

19. French iron and copper pan. Mid-1800s.

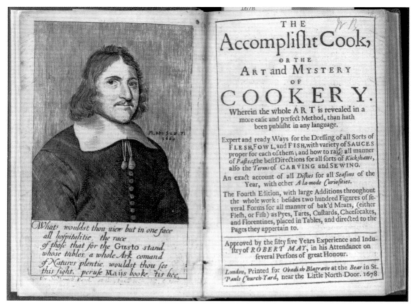

1678

THE
Accomplisht Cook,
OR THE
ART and MYSTERY
OF
COOKERY.

Wherein the whole ART is revealed in a
more easie and perfect Method, than hath
been publisht in any language.

Expert and ready Ways for the Dressing of all Sorts of
FLESH, FOWL, and FISH, with variety of SAUCES
proper for each of them; and how to raise all manner
of Pastes, the best Directions for all sorts of Kickshaws,
also the Terms of CARVING and SEWING.

An exact account of all Dishes for all Seasons of the
Year, with other A la-mode Curiosities.

The Fourth Edition, with large Additions throughout
the whole work: besides two hundred Figures of several Forms for all manner of bak'd Meats, (either
Flesh, or Fish) as Pyes, Tarts, Custards, Cheesecakes,
and Florentines, placed in Tables, and directed to the
Pages they appertain to.

Approved by the fifty five Years Experience and Industry of ROBERT MAY, in his Attendance on
several Persons of great Honour.

London, Printed for Obadiah Blagrave at the Bear in St.
Pauls Church-Yard, near the Little North-Door. 1678

What wouldst thou view but in one face
all hospitalitie, the race
of those that for the Gusto stand,
whose tables a whole Ark comand
of Natures plentie, wouldst thou see
this sight, peruse Mays booke, 'tis hee.

Above: 20. Portrait of Robert May from *The Accomplisht Cook, or the Art and Mystery of Cookery*, 1678.

Left: 21. 'Grand Buffet de la Cuisine moderne'. Taken from Carême's book *Le Maître d'hôtel français, ou Parallèle de la cuisine ancienne et moderne, considéré sous rapport de l'ordonnace des menus selon les quatre saisons*, 1822.

22. Engraved portrait of Alexis Soyer and title page of *A Shilling Cookery for the People.*

23. Title page of *La Cuisinière de ménages*, 1802.

24. From William Kitchiner's *Cooks Oracle*, 1823.

25. Victorian brass roasting jack.

26. English corkscrew with dusting brush.

27. James Ward's *Hand-rolling Machine: to Wash Potatoes*.

28. Georgian papier mâché tray, Royal Worcester blue plate, Derby factory tea cup, small 'Chinese' blue and white porcelain cup.

29. Wedgwood pattern of 1780.

Above: 30. MacFarlane, Lang and Co. biscuit barrel, 1837.

Right: 31. Richard Richardson cruet set, *c.* 1890s.

Above: 32. Multi-compartment spice tin.

Left: 33. Victorian cast-iron flat iron.

character Monsieur Mirobolant in *The History of Pendennis* is a satirical portrayal of Soyer – a likeable yet outlandish character who dresses flamboyantly, is somewhat narcissistic, prone to melodrama and subtly over-sexualised. It is left to our own judgement to decide what Soyer was really like. Soyer was also regularly belittled in *Punch* magazine, most notably, 'Affecting scene – King Soyer Resigning the Great Stewpan' (1850). He died in 1858 and wrote a number of books, including *The Gastronomic Regenerator* (1846), *The Modern Housewife or Managere* (1849), *A History of Food in all Ages* (1853) and *A shilling Cookbook for the People* (1855).[22] Just like Jamie Oliver's school meals agenda, James Martin's mission to transform hospital food, Heston Blumenthal's airline food revolution and Hugh Fearnley-Whittingstall's free-range chicken endeavours, Soyer launched a 'culinary campaign' to improve the food served in the hospitals of the British Army. The book of the title *Soyer's culinary campaign: Being historical reminiscences of the late war. With the plain wit of cookery for military and civil institutions the army, navy, public, etc. etc.* is testament to this work.

Like Soyer, Charles Elme Francatelli spanned both the Georgian and Victorian ages. His heritage was Italian, although he was born in London. Having trained under the notorious Carême, he is perhaps best known for achieving the status of chief cook to Queen Victoria when she ascended the throne. As noted above, he is often labelled alongside Soyer and Ude as being one of the most significant cooks and cookery writers of the age. Francatelli placed an emphasis on the importance of having the correct equipment available with which to cook and believed that spending large amounts of money on utensils was unnecessary. He outlines the basic essential tools in his *A Plain Cookery Book for the Working Classes.* Francatelli advocated the communal stoves in modern lodging houses of the time as perfectly adequate for all cooking needs, together with a large oval boiling pot, a one-gallon saucepan, a potato steamer, an oval frying pan, a gridiron, a mash tub and cooling tubs. It is difficult to imagine in the twenty-first century gadget-dependent kitchen that he deemed these items alone sufficient for any kitchen.

Undoubtedly a passionate man, Francatelli was frequently in trouble during his employment in the royal kitchens and he was known for his bullying, rude insults and fiery nature. In 1841 he was suspended as a consequence of his behaviour.[23] Despite his elitist background and career, Francatelli wrote extensively for the benefit of the less knowledgeable and aimed at the lower social orders of society.

Born in France in 1749, Nicolas Appert has been credited with the invention of canning, but was a trained confectioner and chef. His interesting link with Britain is with the merchant Peter Durand, who simultaneously developed containers for sealing food. Durand sold his patent, enabling the partners Donkin and Hall to open the first canning factory in England in 1811.[24]

In his patent, Durand talks about how his idea for developing the food preservation system was communicated by a 'friend abroad'.[25] Whether this was Appert is not clear. In 1807 another Englishman, Thomas Saddington, was credited by the London Society of Arts for developing a form of preservation for fruit without the need for sugar. Saddington also credited his invention on the basis of receiving inspiration from overseas.[26] Katherine Bitting's 1924 book *Un bienfaiteur de l'humanité: [a tribute to M. Nicolas Appert]*, condemns the English for defrauding Appert of both these ideas, which, she reinforces, had been evolved some years previously. While undoubtedly Durand and Saddington were inspired by the experimentations of others outside of England, there is no proof to substantiate these claims of Bitting, particularly as she mistakes Durand for Donkin when presenting her case. Nonetheless, if true, Appert must surely be credited with providing England with the means to can and preserve far quicker than it might have done, on the basis of existing research at the time.[27]

Vincent La Chapelle was another French cook working in England. Born around the turn of the eighteenth century, he was one of the earliest of the 'celebrity chefs'. While in England he remained in the employment of the Earl of Chesterfield, it was there that he wrote *The Modern Cook* around 1733, published initially in English and then later in French. Chapelle combined the old traditional styles of cooking with more modern ideas, providing new versions of dishes alongside original ones. For example, Turkey a la crème could either be tackled by roasting, pounding with veal, bacon, cow's udder and mushroom, then re-forming around a ragout of sweetbreads, cocks' combs and mushrooms, or as a simple alternative larding in bacon and ham, simmering in milk and spit roasting with a little flour to make it crusty.[28] La Chapelle was also not afraid of advocating recipes from other countries, including England and Holland. Despite his acclaimed status La Chapelle has been accused of plagiarising the recipes of Francois Massialot, a French chef often accredited with the phrase *nouveau cuisine.* There is no proof to determine whose recipes belonged to whom, although being some thirty years or so older and more experienced than La Chapelle, it would be easy to imagine that original copyright should be prescribed to Massialot. It is also not clear how talented and experienced La Chapelle was as a young cook in the service of the Earl of Chesterfield, who writes to his friend the Duke of Richmond in 1728.

Dear Duke

I believe you will easier pardon the trouble I am going to give you, than you would the excuses that I ought to make you for it. So I'll proceed directly to the business.

You must know then that I have a cook that was sent me about six months agone from Paris; who though he is not a bad one, yet is not of the first rate; and as I have in mind de faire une chere exquise [to serve exquisite fare], I should be glad to have a Maitre Cuisinier d'un genie superieur, who should be able not only to execute but to invent des morceaux friands et parfais [delectable and perfectly executed tidbits]: in short such a one as may be worthy to entertain your distinguishing palate, if you should come to the Hague. If you can find such a one, I beg of you to make the best bargain you can for me, and send him to me here.[29]

The palaces and stately homes of Britain represented the ultimate in culinary sophistication, and many European cooks of the Georgian era made their names cooking and writing about cooking within this context. Some of these names remain illustrious three to four hundred years on, while others have become almost obsolete. They all inspired and influenced aspects of British cooking and culinary literary discourse in some way, and the celebrity chef has remained a part of the culture of this art form in the country today. Well-known names in the industry in the twenty-first century continue to inspire and effect how modern cooking and dining is perceived, at both media and political levels of influence, making them comparable with their Georgian predecessors.

7
Recipes and Household Manuals

We had for Dinner a Calf's Head, boiled Fowl and tongue, a Saddle of Mutton Roasted on the Side Table, and a fine Swan roasted with Currant Jelly Sauce for the first Course. The second Course a couple of Wild Fowl called Dun Fowls, Larks, Blancmange, Tarts etc. etc. and a good Dessert of Fruit after amongst which was a Damson Cheese. I never eat a bit of Swan before, and I think it good eating with sweet sauce. The Swan was killed three weeks before it was eat and yet not the least bad taste in it.

James Woodforde, *Diary of a Country Parson*, 1780

It is difficult to determine when the first recipe or collection of recipes appeared. Many scholars consider Ibn Sayyar al-Warraq's *Kitab al-Tabikh*, which translates as 'The book of dishes', to be the earliest known documented culinary compendium, a tenth-century Islamic text. The book was translated by Nawal Nasrallah in 2007, and he describes how the chapters include information on the basic principles of kitchen utensils and ingredients. Among the 615 recipes, Warraq addresses the various stages of cooking and eating, commencing with snacks, followed by the preparation of dishes cooked on the stove, to braising and frying and outdoor cooking using grills and spits. There are chapters on preparing drinks, on social etiquette and basic hygiene as well as advice on exercise around eating and the benefits of sleeping after eating.[1]

In medieval Europe writers and cooks of the nobility such as Cristoforo di Messisbugo offered detailed descriptions of menus, as well as describing the ways in which food should be meticulously prepared and served. And Bartolomeo Scappi's renowned *Opera dell'arte del cucinare* of 1570 provides tremendous attention towards presentation and the precision with which food should be cooked.[2] Wynken de Worde, a French immigrant living in England during the 1500s, was one of the very first printers in the country to publish a cookery book. *The Boke of Kervynge* (The Book of Carving) appeared in 1508 with an introduction that states,

> Here begynneth the boke of kervynge and servyn-
> ge / and all the feestes in the yere for the servyce of a
> prynce or ony other estate as ye shall fynde eche offyce
> the servyce accordynge in this boke folowynge.[3]

Most of the early English recipe books were inspired by, or often literally copied from, overseas published works.

In 1660 William Rabisha published his surprisingly influential *The Whole Body of Cookery Dissected*. The book would go on to be published in a further five editions. In a 1900 edition of a newspaper called the *Cheltenham Looker-On*, we learn that this was a 'rather scarce little book', which is perhaps why it was so popular and easy to read. The article mentions it is one of the few books of its time offering a traditional and authentic recipe for mincemeat, within the instructions for 'Lumber Pye'. The ingredients include meat, suet, candid peels, spices, sweet herbs, marrow, breadcrumbs and rose water, among many others. Rabisha wrote instructions for another festive favourite in this book, the boil-in-a-basin Christmas pudding.[4]

By the eighteenth century recipes were appearing in

published form by numerous housekeepers and cooks, both the higher ranking cooks to nobility and royalty, and the higher- and middle-class women and men that worked in large town or country house kitchens. Many simply took an interest in cooking or taught it as a profession. Their theories, instructions and opinions can be found in the broadly published literature of the time, or simply tucked away in personal journals and diaries. According to Kate Colquhoun, incredibly by the 1740s roughly 40 per cent of all women could read. England was cited as the most literate nation in Europe. This drove the new market for an expanding media of newspapers, books and pamphlets, which would have had a wide circulation of influence.[5]

As early as the late 1500s the writer Thomas Dawson had published a number of recipe books that dealt with the subject of general cookery, preserving, animal husbandry, carving and the role of servants among other topics. His publication *The Good Huswifes Jewell* was written around 1585 in a way that readers might find more familiar today, as illustrated by his recipe 'To Make a pudding':

Take parsley and thyme and chop it small. Then take the kidney of veal, and parboil it, and when it is parboiled, take all the fat off it, and lay it that it may cool. When it is cold shred it like as you do suet for puddings. Then take marrow and mince it by itself. Then take grated bread and small raisins the quantity of your stuff, and dates minced small. Then take the eggs and roast them hard and take the yolks of them and chop them small, and then take your stuff afore-hearsed, and mingle altogether. Then take pepper, cloves and mace, saffron and salt, and put it together with the said stuff, as much as you think by casting shall suffice. Then take six eggs and break them into a vessel, whites and all. Put your dry stuff into the same eggs, and temper them all well together. So fill your haggis or gut, and seethe it well and it will be good.[6]

As England entered the seventeenth century, cookery books slowly began to become more practical. They were more specific in terms of the level of instruction, involving quantities and the processes involved in cooking, such as timings and methods. Monsieur Marnette was born in London to immigrant parents. In 1656 he wrote *The Perfect Cook*. Predominantly a book for pastry cooks, it also offered advice on dressing meat and fish and making sauces. *The Perfect Cook* is particularly important as it featured in William London's publication, *A Catalogue of the Most Vendible Books in England, between 1657 and 1660.*[7] London embarked on his task to create a definitive bibliography of the time, in an attempt to document the ever-increasing volume of printed literature circulating. His intention was to ensure that important books containing knowledge and learning were catalogued, and that this catalogue would be kept for future generations to refer to. Marnette's book was clearly regarded by London to be one that conveyed important information on the art of cooking.

Continuing the tradition of well-known cooks writing from experience, Robert May published his giant of a book *The Accomplisht Cook* in 1660. English by birth but trained in Paris from a young age at the behest of his family, May originated from a long line of distinguished cooks. His book combined English and European ideas on culinary skill, but he was also careful not to offend his English readers, by trivialising the French and other European methods of cooking in order to augment traditional English methods.

... the advantages of my Education hath raised me above the Ambitions of others, in the converse I have had with other Nations, who in this Art fall short of what I have known experimented by you my worthy Countrymen. Howsoever, the French by their Insinuations, not without enough of Ignorance, have bewitcht some of the Gallants of our Nation with Epigram Dishes, smoakt rather than drest, so strangely to captivate the Gusto, their Mushroom'd Experiences for Sauce rather than Diet, for the generality howsoever called A-la-mode, not worthy of being taken notice on. As I live in France, and had the Language and have been an eye-witness of their Cookeries as well, as a Peruser of their Manuscripts, and Printed Authors whatsoever I found good in them, I have inserted in this Volume. I do acknowledg my self not to be a little beholding to the Italian and Spanish Treatises; though without my fosterage, and bringing up under the Generosities and Bounties of my Noble Patrons and Masters, I could never have arrived to this Experience.[8]

By the end of the Georgian period there was still a tremendous emphasis on recipes and recipe writing for the benefit of curing ailments and addressing all number of problems, both mentally and physically, using various herbs and mixtures. The PR involved in selling books was extraordinary. One look at any newspaper of the Georgian era provides you with endless advertisements for new books, each promising the latest advice on cooking techniques, how to be more economical, how to achieve the new French haute cuisine, to be a better housewife, a more fashionable host and so on. Both the books and their authors were glamorised and exploited to achieve maximum impact on the reader.

The popularity of reading and acquiring cookery books, as well as adhering to the advice outlined by food writers, quelled the old notions that this activity was once solely the responsibility of paid staff. Cooks and kitchen hands had previously been the ones with the training and the knowledge, gaining basic instructions from recipe books (if they were literate) or from learning on the job. Although the cooks and other domestically employed staff prepared and cooked all of the food, as cooking was deemed inferior, it was now the householders, and in the main the mistresses of the house, who also had access to cooking information. Newspapers started promoting the trend in the cookery

literature market from the 1750s onwards. In 1782 an advert
for the latest book promising 'the least expensive receipts' and
priced at two shillings appeared in the *Leeds Intelligencer*.[9]

An article in the *Spectator* magazine of 1829 titled *Books of
Cookery* both reviews and pays homage to the recipe writers
of the eighteenth and nineteenth centuries. It distinguishes
between the fashion for economic, practical guides and the
more elaborate and highly skilled manuals such as Ude's
French Cook, designed for professional cooking on a grand
scale. Some mention is given to Hannah Glasse, but only in
the sense that her recipes are 'sometimes useful', and Mrs
Rundell's *A New System of Domestic Cookery*, published
in 1806, is cited as the forerunner of practical and simple
recipe writing, while the writer of the article appreciates that
Kitchiner has the advantage where simplicity and attention
to detail is concerned. The most critical praise is placed
upon the *Practice of Cookery* written by Mrs Dalgairns, who
the writer praises as 'economical, useful and practical', a
recipe book that can appeal to 'all families, from tradesman
to the country gentleman'. And the article reiterates that
'it is not a gourmand's book, neither does it pre-tend to
be'. The recipe book that is most damned is by the author
Dick Humelbergius Secundus and is titled *Apician Morsels*.
A book which is simply berated as 'a disgusting affair',
written with 'neither wit nor knowledge'.[10] It is important to
acknowledge that there were hundreds of recipe books and
guides for cooks published throughout the eighteenth and
nineteenth centuries, although some have received greater
recognition than others. To name a few underrated authors
and their books, John Farley's *The London Art of cookery*,
1792, *The House-keeper's Pocket-book and Compleat Family
Cook*, by Sarah Harrison and Mary Morris, Mrs Frazer's
The Practice of cookery, Pastry, Pickling, Preserving, 1791
and *The Compleat Housewife*, Eliza Smith, 1739, were all
well-respected in their time. Eliza wrote this final book on
the back of all her experience gained as a cook employed by

fashionable society and nobility. In fact many of the cook
books of the time were inspired by those working in the
capacity of cook or housekeeper. Charles Carter was the cook
to, among other nobility, the Duke of Argyle. Carter wrote
several books, the most well-known being *The London and
Country Cook* (1749) and *The Compleat City and Country
Cook* (1732).

Manuscripts and recipe, or 'receipt' writers of the Georgian
age also provided greater insight into the types and usage
of general kitchen equipment from a historical context.
One of the most notable of the eighteenth century is that
of William Verrall, the one-time publican of the White Hart
in Lewes, Sussex. He trained under the well-known French
chef St Clouet, bringing an English–French fusion of ideas
to his craft. Verrall strongly advocated the use of the correct
equipment in the kitchen, 'without which it is impossible' (to
cook). On arrival at the White Hart, he commented on the
lack of appropriate apparatus, declaring,

> A surgeon may as well attempt to make an incision with a
> pair of sheers, or open a vein with an oyster-knife, as for me
> to pretend to get this dinner without proper tools to do it;
> here's neither stew pan, soup-pot, or any one thing else that is
> useful; there's what they call a frying pan indeed, but black as
> my hat, and a handle long enough to obstruct half the passage
> of the kitchen.[11]

Another excellent and largely forgotten compendium,
written by the resident cook, Richard Dolby, of the thatched-
house tavern in London, is *The Cook's Dictionary and
House-keeper's Directory* (1830). This is an insightful and
detailed alphabetical reference manual of the time for
cooking, brewing and making confectionery among many
other domestic articles. It includes no less than thirty-five
suggestions for dressing mushrooms and a thorough
explanation of all of the terminology associated with both

French and English cooking, preparation and serving. It is a book that would still be invaluable in any kitchen today.

Rivalry between Ann Cook (who wrote *Professed Cookery*, 1755) and Hannah Glasse (*The Art of Cookery Made Plain and Easy*, 1774) was well documented at the time. In her 1755 publication, Ann Cook seeks to discredit Hannah Glasse from the outset, both personally and in relation to her lack of credentials and as a writer of cookery, dismissing her recommendations and criticising her culinary theories. In *The Analectic Magazine*, 1818, by Washington Irving there is an article on the science of cooking which exclaims that 'cookery is unquestionably the most excellent of all sciences' and cites A. Viard as the first 'homme de bouche' of cookery for his published work *Le Cuisinier Imperial*, Paris, 1806, while simultaneously damning the work of Hannah Glasse, suggesting it is high time for her to 'walk the carpet'.[12] In this same article Hannah Glasse is compared to a lesser-known writer – Susanna MacIver – who was also a teacher of cookery based in the city of Edinburgh. She penned *Cookery and Pastry* in 1789, of which there were several editions. Very little appears to have been written about Mrs MacIver. An advertisement appears in *The Edinburgh Advertiser* for 1786, stating,

Mrs McIver's Cookery,
Greatly Improved.
This day is published price 2s (sewed) and 2s 6d (bound)
Cookery and Pastry
As taught and practised by
Mrs MacIver, teacher of these Arts in Edinburgh,
A New Edition
To which are added for the first time
Figures of Dinner and Supper Coursed, from
five to fifteen dishes
Also a correct list of everything in season for every month
in the year

Nb. Those that have purchased the fourth edition of
this book lately from Mr Elliot, will have the additions
gratis.[13]

Samuel Johnson was also scathing of Hannah Glasse, pointing
out her error of referring to salt pepper and sal prunella as
two separate substances. He stresses that no truly educated
person would have written something like this.[14] In contrast
is a remark from the editor of *Notes and Queries*, published
27 November 1858, which shows Glasse's lack of pretension
is credited long after her death, and quotes the preface to her
renowned *Art of Cookery*, 'If I have not wrote in the high,
polite stile, I hope I shall be forgiven; for my intention is to
instruct the lower Sort ... For example; when I bid them lard
and Fowl, If I should bid them lard with large lardoons, they
would know what I meant: But when I say they must lard
with little pieces of bacon, they know not what I mean'. The
article commends her style; 'Would that all instructors could
be prevailed upon to drop "the high polite stile!"'[15]

Hannah Glasse would die poor and destitute, following
a series of considerable debts and bankruptcy orders as
recorded in issues of the *London Gazette* between 1754 and
1759. According to an inventory of household accounts
for a Lady Margaret Grant in 1755–6, a copy of Hannah
Glasse's renowned first book cost a total of five shillings.[16]
This totals some twenty to twenty-five pounds in today's
money. Not a cheap price for a book. Considering its vast
popularity and prior to the days of Amazon discount deals,
one wonders how Ms Glasse managed to end up so destitute.
Unlike her contemporaries, Cook and MacIver the cookery
teachers, Hannah Glasse earned her living from sewing
and 'habit-making', as credited in the *London Gazette*. What
Glasse did achieve was a more straightforward approach
to cookery, written in layman's terms for the benefit of the
mistress of the house. Recipes from the eighteenth century
were a combination of culinary know-how passed down

through the generations and a reflection of the continental trends, particularly French methods of cooking, that began to dominate the higher- and new-middle-class dining tables.

Mrs James Simpson wrote the first vegetarian cookery book as early as 1812, and by the 1880s the country had a good selection of restaurants catering specifically for non-meat eaters.[17] There was also a belief by some in society, particularly those of a god-fearing nature, that animal products were bad for the body and soul. A book published in 1830 titled *Vegetable Cookery*, by the Society of the Bible Christians, actually had claimed some one hundred members were dedicated to abstaining from meat.[18]

One author who is rather overlooked is William Kitchiner, MD (1777–1827), whose book *The Cook's Oracle and Housekeeper's Manual* was first published around 1817. Kitchiner established a *Committee of Taste* for a group of friends and colleagues 'distinguished for (their) genius and learning' by invitation only to dine at his home once a week. A trained doctor with qualifications from Glasgow, he was unable to practice medicine in England, but devoted much of his life to the science of cooking and hospitality. He was an epicure but believed vehemently that good health was integral to the proper preparation of food. He experimented with these theories in his home, together with his research partner, Henry Osborne, who was also the private cook to Sir Joseph Banks, President of the Royal Society. Osborne went on to invent a new pudding, the Boston Apple Pudding, which was said to be favoured by Queen Victoria. Osborne is credited in Kitchiner's *Cook's Oracle* together with a selection of his recipes, including the one for his Boston Apple Pudding:

> Peel one dozen and a half of good apples; take out the cores, cut them small, put into a stew-pan that will just hold them, with a little water, a little cinnamon, two cloves, and the peel of a lemon; stew over a slow fire till quite soft, then sweeten

with moist sugar, and pass it through a hair sieve; add to it
the yelks of four eggs and one white, a quarter of a pound of
good butter, half a nutmeg, the peel of a lemon grated, and
the juice of one lemon: beat all well together; line the inside
of a pie-dish with good puff paste; put in the pudding, and
bake half an hour.[19]

Kitchiner insisted that all of his dining guests arrived at
the allotted time of their invitation. On Tuesday evenings
he held conversations between the strict hours of seven to
eleven. The most notable of his regular guests were Charles
Kemble and Dr John Haslam. Kitchiner was also a prolific
collector of music manuscripts and studied and wrote at
length on the subject of optics. He died of a sudden heart
attack at his home in Fitzroy Square in London. He was
only fifty-one years old. He may have gone on to produce
other valuable writings relating to the preparation of food
and the economies of housekeeping and cooking, which
would perhaps have secured his place alongside other more
renowned cookery writers of the time, but we will never
know.[20]

Recipes were not just published in books, periodicals
and for the wider media. Many were recorded in diaries,
memoires or letters. It was typical for cooks of the Georgian
period to keep manuscripts of their recipes and techniques.
Radolphus Ayres, the cook for New College, Oxford, from
1721, left a book of instructional recipes, including one
describing in great detail how 'To hash a Calves head':

First boyle the head tendar and pull out all the bones then
Cut the meat in thin slices and put it to a stewpan or a frying
pan with half a pint of good beef grauey, a Quarter of a pint
of Clarret, a little Cattchup, some nutmeg, some salt, half
a cup of Capors, 2 anchoveys, half a lemmon Cutt in bitts,
a little vinegar, and some oysters and musheroomes if you
have them, then set it over a fire and when the anchoveys are

dissolved put in half a pound of butter and when it is melted
thicken the sauce with the yolkks of 2 Eggs beat with a little
vinegar ...[21]

Mr Ayres is also considered to be the inventor of the
popular Oxford Sausage, a distinctive mixture of pork and
veal, currently experiencing a tremendous revival in Britain
among butchers and specialist farm shops and traders. His
method involved the following:

... take of pork and veal and Equall Quantity of let it be free
from Sinues & Skin and Chopp it very small, then add to it
half as much of good beef suet as meat and Chop it together
till the suet is fine then season it with pepper, salt, nutmeg,
some sage and thyme minced small, then work it up with 2
or 3 Eggs as you see good.[22]

Other culinary writers such as John Nott and Isabella Beeton
have become known for their variations of this recipe,
including the addition of lemon. But Ayres's is no doubt the
original version, given the sausage is named after the college
he was first cook for during the early 1700s, and this is also
when the recipe first starts to appear in print.

Rebecca Price's collection of old recipes (1660–1740)
demonstrates how the fashion for copying and pasting
old recipes into new compendiums started. The diary
of Rebecca Price, who wrote up until 1740, offers varied
accounts detailing the everyday management of a large
English country house, including a number of crafty ways in
which food could be coloured in order to make it look more
attractive for the table: by adding 'clove gillyflower' for a red
hue, 'sirrup of violets' to create blue and saffron for yellow.
She suggested setting jelly in cut lemon halves, which when
cool could be cut again into quarters to create an interesting
pattern, particularly if the jelly was coloured as above to
contrast with the natural yellow of the lemons.[23]

Recipe books written by women during the Georgian period were frequently interspersed with medicinal remedies. One such journal is that of Anne Rogers from Co. Antrim, Ireland, and written in 1753. In her journals she places recipes for curing worms, dysentery and smallpox alongside instructions for pickling onions and cooking mutton.[24]

A charitable deeds book for Bradford spanning 1739 to 1777 contains a recipe book written in 1736 by a Mrs Margaret Abercromy. While nothing could be found relating to Mrs Abercromy herself, the recipe book of her notes, tips and theories offers a wonderful insight into everyday Georgian cooking practices. Un-transcripted, the book is often illegible and written in different types of handwriting on occasion. One interesting recipe exists for a type of gingerbread called 'holland pepper coken'.

> Take 3 pints of good kitchen sirop, about a pound and half of butter let the butter melt in the sirop on a soft fire and skim it often then take 6 unces of ginger, beaten and sifted and mingle it with as much flour as [the] liquor will take up to make a very hard past, and put it in 2 spoonfulls of good yest let it rise half and hour and roll it out in good cakes be sure to butter your paper, let your oven Be pretty hott and let it bake a good hour you may make your cakes as thick as a [thume].[25]

A journal which has for years baffled historians as to its validity is *The Diary of a Farmer's Wife, 1796–97.* Anne Hughes' controversial diary provides an interesting insight into eighteenth-century rural and agricultural daily life. It lacks authenticity as there has never been a sound provenance for the writing itself, which first appeared in serialised form in *The Farmer's Weekly* in the 1930s. While research continues to seek proof for the source of the diary itself, its content is considered to be a fascinating illustration of eighteenth-century domestic life by many. This is an extract describing the build up to Christmas baking on the farm and a recipe for 'meat cake'.

> Johns mother have made a verrie pretty dish wich she do call meat cake. She did mix flower and butter to a thick paste and put sum on the bottom of a bake tin, this she did cover with the chopt beef and onion and herbs, then more paste, then more meat and flavouring, and paste agen, till the tin be full. Then she do cover all with more paste and cook till done. She do say this do cut like a cake when it be cold with the meat inside.[26]

Despite the diary's lack of legitimacy, it is understood that the original transcriber, Jeanne Preston, did admit to embellishing the text with additional recipes, which she took from the period. Certainly this recipe is reminiscent of that time. For that reason, together with my own extremely dubious romantic conviction in Anne Hughes' diary, it has been included.

Another well-known diary of the 1700s is that of John Perkins, a farmer who worked and lived in the Vale of Glamorgan, Wales. This journal is in the archives of the National Library of Wales. The original copy is in bad condition and the writing is said to be almost unintelligible. However, the diary has been transcribed, studied and written about to some extent by scholars. Interestingly coffee, so fashionable at the time, is regarded as a rare commodity and referenced only once, unlike the consumption of tea, which was referenced as frequently drunk with friends and family as a regular social pastime. The diary contains recipes for 'catchups', which are more typically now known as ketchup. Of particular interest are those containing walnuts, mushrooms and cucumber. There are also recipes for apple pudding, mince pies, custard, green pease soup, potato bread, rice bread, gingerbread cakes and jelly. The diary contains instructions on how to prepare and make numerous savoury dishes including the Georgian staple, roast rump of beef, how to mash a calf's head, how to preserve eggs, make sauces and collar a round of beef. Recipes for alcoholic beverages are also listed, from ginger and elder wine to mead. The variety and range of recipes contained in Perkins' diary provides an intimate and detailed illustration of the eating habits of a typical Georgian aspiring middle-class rural family.[27] Collaring meat, most commonly beef, involved rolling it up, binding it and then preparing it for the stove. A recipe for collaring beef from around 1700 can be found in the West Yorkshire Archives:

> Take a rib piece of Beef, & do not salt it, but throw it into brine. Put into your brine some Salt petre, and when it hath laid two or three days then take it up. Lay it in well water all night. So take it up and let it drain. Then dry it well with a cloath. Season it with pepper, salt mace, cloves, nutmeg, a few sweet herbs & a little Lemon both shred small. So roul it up & bind itwell with a course Inckle (thread or yarn). So bake it in Well water, and when it comes from ye Oven take it up and tye it close in a cloath & hang it up till it is cold.[28]

Perhaps one of the most recent culinary revelations of note, left behind in a diary of personal 'receipts', is that of Baroness Elizabeth Dimsdale, the wife of a Hertfordshire doctor who copied down some 700 recipes before she died between 1800 and 1808. Discovered a few years ago by Dr Heather Falvey, this compendium of recipes includes one for fried doughnuts, or as documented by Elizabeth Dimsdale, 'dow nuts', previously attributed as an American invention. An edited version of Elizabeth's recipes for soups, fish, pies, puddings, preserves, cheesecakes, cakes, biscuits and possets among other things, along with household advice and advice on keeping the garden, has been published by the Hertfordshire Record Society. It is believed that the haphazard catalogue of transcripts was gathered from other published works and from a variety of friends and colleagues.[29]

Newspapers were prolific during the eighteenth century, with twelve circulating in London in 1712. By 1801 this had increased to a staggering fifty-two.[30] The public and notable people in Georgian society were very conscious of the need to take part in the modern debates of the time, the most important being the issue of the poor and other domestic political contentions. In the National Archive Home Office Records a letter is registered from a Dr William Augustus Howard, who writes at length about the specific combination and proportion of ingredients necessary to provide an alternative to the wheat shortage of the time. He proposes among other things a recipe for a universal bread, made of corn and starch-based vegetables, as well as for economical and nutritious puddings.[31] There are countless references to recipes sent regularly to the editors of local newspapers by philanthropic and well-meaning citizens, like this one signed simply 'A Constant Reader'. Their request to publish a soup recipe, designed to sustain 'a considerable number of persons', is granted in the 28 October 1829 edition of the *Morning Post*, and reads,

> To feed one hundred and forty persons.
> Eighteen gallons of water (but only twelve at first.)
> An ox's head, well cleaned.
> Two quarts of split peas and two quarts of Scotch barley.
> Two quarts of Scotch oatmeal, to be added an hour before it
> is finished.
> One bushel of potatoes, to be added when half boiled.
> One peck of roots, one pound of salt, one ounce of pepper.
> To boil six hours.
> This produces 140 pints, allowing one pint to each person,
> and costs altogether not more than seven shillings.

Similarly a recipe for poor farm labourers appears in the *Sheffield Independent*, 5 September 1829, this time signed 'your obedient servant'. At a cost of two pence and a halfpenny per gallon, the writer promises a wholesome beverage that is economical, with the potential to deliver thirty-six gallons.

	s	d
Hops, 8 ounces	0	9
Bran, 1 bushel	1	0
Bruised Ginger, 5 ounces	0	9
Treacle, 12 lbs, at 30s per cwt	3	3
Yeast	0	3
Fuel	1	0
Total	7	0

Home brewing was enormously popular during the Georgian period and there are many recipes circulating from that era for making a variety of fruit- and herb-based alcoholic beverages. There is a particularly jolly recipe in the form of a poem for making raisin wine, which appears in the *Derby Mercury* of 3 May, 1787:

Ye Housewifes who wish to make good Raisin Wine
Attend to these precepts; – first see your fruit's fine;
Seven Pounds to the Gallon's the Quantum 'twill take,
And measure your Water for fear of mistake:
Put into a Tub Fruit and water together,
(Take heed not to mix it in very hot Weather;)
Three weeks, at the least, to ferment, it must stand,
And stir it each Day with a resolute Hand.
Then drawing it off, put into a Cask –
If still more directions you'd willingly ask,
Don't bung it too son, but leave it quite loose,
Whilst Snake like it hisses – or more like a Goose;
Twill that hissing subsides pray let it be open,
Six Months at the least; – then the bung you may stop in.
There let it remain till 'tis perfectly fine,
Two years, I could wish – 'twill be excellent Wine.'

An interesting account relating to a recipe for a 'severe fit of the gravel', now more commonly known as gall stones, appears in *The Scots Magazine*, 3 October 1763. A supposedly secret piece of advice from a doctor specialising in this complaint is recounted, in which the patient is ordered 'to boil two pounds of the craig-end of a neck of veal in five [English] quarts ... of water, till they are reduced to three, and to send him every day three pints of broth thus made, free from all fat and other impurities'. Despite the country balancing on the verge of an industrial and cultural revolution, Britain was still naïve to the science of medicine and only just beginning to comprehend how the human body functioned.

A detailed recipe for rennet to make cheese appears in the correspondence of the Bath and West of England Society for the encouragement of agriculture, arts, manufactures and commerce in 1792. As with so many traditional methods of preparation and cooking of this period, it is a long and laborious process: 'Using the stomachs, or *abomasa* of Calves before they have eaten any vegetation, wash them in water and salt them for around two months.' Then the writer instructs to place them in a coarse bag where they should be stored in the chimney (but away from direct flames) for ten months. During the spring, collect a number of cowslips and boil them in water with salt for around fifteen minutes. This should be left to marinate for a day and then be strained. For every gallon of this liquid two of the calves stomachs should be added and soaked for a further four days before bottling with a couple of cloves. The resulting bottled rennet could then be stored for a year or more and used in measures of two large spoonfuls to 'coagulate a hogshead of milk', around fifty-four gallons in today's measures.[32]

The wealth of literature on cooking was phenomenal during the Georgian period, from the practical manuals of Hannah Glasse, to the specialised confectionery and pastry masters, through to the self-publicising works of the well-known French male cooks of the day. These works in particular often (as was fashionable) included the poor, with advice on economical cooking. Mistresses of the house were becoming more aware of the importance of a little knowledge in culinary expertise, and Britain's wealthier society voraciously consumed the latest French recipes and technical instruction. Plagiarism was common, and many keen cooks and purveyors of cooking simply copied and rewrote recipes, which they documented in their private journals or letters, or redrafted in slightly different formats to pass off and publish as their own creation. The newspapers and periodicals of the Georgian era were also replete with advice, guidance, recommendations and quotations involving recipes, methods of cooking, food preparation and serving. Almost every reader, it seemed, wanted to impart their instructions on preparing soup for the masses, and many were keen to offer opinion on modern methods as well as imparting traditional herbal remedies for medicinal purposes. Recipe books were also capitalising on the vast and varied store cupboard that transport, trade and exploration was expanding. New types of fish, vegetables, fruits, herbs and spices could be networked and sold around the country and wealthier sections of the British population had the potential to experiment with curries or pasta, given the right recipes to do so.

Recipe books represent an important resource generally for historians, as they act as a registered account of the ideas and practices, culinary, medical and scientific, recorded by people of the time. In particular the cookery books, manuals and guides of the seventeenth, eighteenth and early nineteenth centuries illustrate the extent to which material culture dominated society. The books themselves were often illustrated, either showing basic utensils, drawings of some of the dishes, or more typically containing diagrams depicting how dining tables should be laid out. These demonstrate precise dimensions detailing the correct symmetry.

Many authors of cookery books during the early part of

the eighteenth century included a substantial amount of information on homemade remedies. This trend began to shift towards the end of the century, often not featuring at all in the cookery books and manuals of professional cooks. Distinguished physicians began instead to cover this subject, which is indicative of both the advances in medicine and the focus on cookery as a consumer-driven craft in its own right.

Recipes for the Poor

Poor Man's Sauce was a simple sauce, often made by the French as an alternative to their more accustomed heavy and complicated accompaniments to meat, but was also considered the type of sauce that could be used to transform any meagre portion of food into a reasonably tasting meal. There are many variations of this recipe, but the one in B. Clermont's 1812 edition of *The Professed Cook* appears to be the basis for most of these.

> Boil half a lemon sliced in two spoonfuls of broth; add two or three chopped shallots or chibbol, pepper and salt.
> Take out the lemon before you send it up.

Chibbol is what we now more typically call a spring onion. Later recipes for Poor Man's Sauce included small pieces of ham and the addition of more herbs and spices. One of the most prolific advocates for educating the poor on the benefits of shrewd cooking practices at the time was Alexis Soyer. His *A Shilling Cookery for the People* was a bestseller and well received by the media. The book was first published outside of the Georgian period in 1855. Nonetheless it is important to include Soyer, as he was a renowned cook and social reformer whose work influenced both the Georgian and Victorian eras. He shared dialogue with people representative of all the classes, noting the ways in particular that poorer households managed to feed their families on a very low income. He would take the time to visit households in the less salubrious districts of the country, educating people about the properties of food and how to cook economically, combining ingredients to maximise both flavour and capacity. One of Soyer's simplest recipes in *A Shilling Cookery for the People* is for ox cheek. Ironically a delicacy now served in many contemporary fine dining venues, it was once one of the lowermost sweetbreads and was commonly cooked by the masses until the pan was black. Soyer's alternative below ensured people were able to get both a fine-tasting and long-lasting soup, together with a perfectly tender piece of meat.

> Rub an ox cheek (middlesize, or half a large one) with four teaspoonfuls of salt and one of pepper; put it into the iron pot, with four quarts of cold water; set it on the fire to boil; remove it then to the side, and simmer gently for three hours after it begins to boil. Skim off the fat, which will do for puddings and, at the expiration of the time, nearly three quarts of very strong gravy, in addition to the meat properly done and tender, will be found in the pot. A gillof colourinigs an improvement to the look of the broth. A head of celeryor, some leaves of it, or onions, &c, may be added in boiling. Put the head on a dish, and serve the soup separately with bread in it.

Despite the controversy that surrounds Hannah Glasse and her work, the now widely referenced manual *The Art of Cookery Made Plain and Easy* was at its time of publication one of the bestselling cookery books and remained so for the next hundred years. Her approach was practical, and while many other writers of the time were attempting to engage with cooks and other domestic staff, Glasse wrote probably in much the same way as she spoke, making the recipes more coherent and easier to replicate. The following recipe is not one that the labouring classes of Georgian Britain would have prepared for their own tables, but it is one that would have been popular to serve in affluent households. Presentation was very important to the Georgians, so it would have been important for any domestic cook and their assistant to get this exactly right before serving. It is also indicative of the opulence afforded by so many at this time.

To dress a lamb's head

Boil the head and pluck tender but don't let the liver be too much done. Take the head up, hack it cross and cross with a knife, grate some nutmeg over it, and lay it in a dish, before a good fire; then grate some crumbs of bread, some sweet-herbs rubbed; a little lemon-peel chopped fine, a very little pepper and salt, and baste it with a little butter: then throw a little flour over it, and just as it is done do the same, baste it and dredge it. Take half the liver, the lights, the heart and tongue, chop them very small, with six or seven spoonfuls of gravy or water; first shake some flour over the meat, and stir it together, then put in the gravy or water, a good piece of butter rolled in a little flour, a little pepper and salt, and what runs from the head in the dish; simmer all together a few minutes, and add half a spoonful of vinegar, pour it into your dish, lay the head in the middle of the mince-meat, have ready the other half of the liver cut thin, with some slices of bacon broiled, and lay round the head. Garnish the dish with lemon, and send it to table.

Recipes for the Tradesmen and Middle Classes

The well-known tavern cook William Verral would have served a range of clientele, serving the aspiring middle classes and also providing a quick impromptu meal for the higher class of gentleman, who may also be visiting with members of a club or social group. His 'Hors d'oeuvre',

taken from *Recipes from the White Hart Inn*, for anchovies
and parmesan cheese is also indicative of the way in which
imported dishes and ingredients were being consumed with
such conventionality as early as 1759. Verral boasts that this
was a dish that was never returned uneaten from the table.

> To make a nice whet before dinner, or a side dish for a second
> course. Fry some bits of bread about the length of an anchovy,
> with the bone upon each bit, and strew over them some
> Parmesan cheese grated fine, and colour them nicely in an
> oven, or with a salamander, squeeze the juice of an orange or
> lemon, and pile them up in your dish and send to table.

Louis Eustache Ude's once iconic manual, *The French Cook,
Or, The Art of Cookery: Developed in All its Branches*, makes
particular reference to Jus de Boeuf as being most appropriate
for the middle-class dinner in the following recipe:

> Trim with layers of bacon, the bottom of a thick stew-pan; cut
> four large onions by halves, lay the flat part over the bacon;
> take a few slices of beef, the *noix* or the *sous noix* are the parts
> that are used in preference; mark them in the same manner
> as in the *blond de veau, mouillez* with the *grand bouillon* only.
> Let this sweat in order to get all the gravy out of the beef, and
> when the broth is reduced, thrust a knife into the meat; let it
> stew gently on a slow fire, till the gravy be of a light brown,
> without burning. Next *mouillez* with some *grand bouillon,*
> throw in a large bunch of parsley and of green onions, a little
> salt and pepper corn. Let the whole boil for two hours; take
> the fat off, and drain it through a silk sieve, to use it when
> wanted.

A recipe that appears in many cookery books of the Georgian
era is for strawberry fritters. This one is taken from Jennifer
Stead's publication for English Heritage, *Food and Cooking in
Eighteenth Century Britain*, but is originally credited to William

Verral. Fritters were holiday food and particularly indulged in at Easter. This recipe has been converted for the benefit of modern-day cooks so they can try it out for themselves.

> 1 lb large dry strawberries
> 6 oz plain flour
> 2 oz caster sugar
> 2 tsps grated nutmeg
> 2 eggs well beaten
> 8 fl. oz single cream
> Lard for frying
> Sugar to finish

The strawberries must be dry. Leave the stalks on for easier handling. Sift the flour into a bowl and add the caster sugar and nutmeg. Make a well and drop in the eggs and cream. Then stir until all the flour and sugar are gradually assimilated. Let the batter stand an hour or two. Dip each strawberry in batter until it is completely coated, and fry a few at a time in hot lard. Your lard must be hot enough to puff them, but not so hot as to brown them too quickly. Drain on absorbent paper and keep hot. Pile them up in a pyramid in a hot dish and sprinkle sugar over. Decorate with leaves.

Recipes for the Higher Classes

Often credited, most notably by the food historian Ivan Day, as the first person to term the phrase 'meringue' and to invent the crème brûlée, François Massialot was a French cook to royalty. His early book, translated into English as *The Court and Country Cook*, 1702, emphasises the importance attached to mealtime etiquette at court, including the schedule of courses, number and variety of dishes and the precise layout of the table itself. Massialot's following recipe is for eggs after the Burgundian way.

Take a piece of red Beet, that has not an earthy or unsavoury tast, and pound it well with a slice of Lemmon, a few Macaroons, Sugar, and beaten Cinnamon: Then taking four or five Eggs, without the Sperm, mix all together very well, and strain them thro' the Hair-sieve, with a little Milk and Salt. Afterwards they may be dress'd in the same manner as Eggs with Milk, and brought to a fine colour.

Rather off-putting is the reference to the 'sperm' of the egg, or the membranous thread that binds the yolk to the shell. Still relatively scientifically ignorant in the 1700s, many people believed that a small man lived in the sperm of an egg and this is how babies were formed. Whether this is why Massialot instructs the reader to remove it or whether its texture may have impacted negatively on the dish itself is not known. Attempts to find Massialot's Eggs Burgundy recipe in use have so far been unsuccessful. The predominant traditional recipe using eggs in the Burgundy region of France is today Eggs in Red Wine.

Many cookery writers of the Georgian age plagiarised or simply 'cut and pasted' their recipes. One exception was Charles Carter, whose *Complete Practical Cook*, published in 1730, makes clear in its preface that all the recipes included have been tried and tested personally and Carter credits none of the dishes to himself. While the title of his book is misleading in the sense that the recipes are designed to suit 'the more Grand and Sumptuous Manner of Entertainments', Carter's objective was to persuade anyone with little knowledge of cooking that if given the right instruction they would be capable of cooking dishes of the highest standard. The following recipe is taken from a section in *Complete Practical Cook* devoted entirely to 'Torts' – a sort of pie meets pancake type of dish that could be sweet or savoury. Sack refers to a type of imported fortified wine and Naples biskets were what we might define as sponge fingers today.

Asparagus or Artichoke Tort

Take of Asparagus one hundred pretty large, boil them, and take the heads and Green, all of it that is tender, and beat in a mortar, with a quarter of a Pound of Naples Bisket, some beaten cinnamon and Ginger, some sack, Orange flower and Rose-water, and sugar, mingle it with the yolks of ten Eggs and a little cream, and boil up a Quart of good ceam, and thicken it with this, drawing it up thick, and bake it in puff-paste, with citron at the bottom.

Artichoke Tort – is, To take the Bottoms of three good Artichokes boil'd, and cut and pare out the strings, and beat them in a mortar, with a quarter of a Pound of bisket or white bread, mince the Marrow of two large bones, of small three, season with Sack, Sugar, Salt, Cinnamon, Ginger and Nutmeg, work it up with the Yolks of ten Eggs and a little cream, boil up a Quart of cream, and draw it up thick with this, and sheet your Dish with puff-paste, bake it, and serve it away to the Table, stick it over with candy'd Citron.

8

Innovation and Invention

Genius is shown only by invention.

Samuel Johnson, 1759

Many people continue to consider the Victorians as the pioneers of invention and industrialisation, but it was undoubtedly during the Georgian era that the foundations for innovation and change, visible by the latter part of the 1800s, were instigated. The transformation of the metal-working industries occurred during the eighteenth century with pig iron being converted to stronger bar iron, the smelting of ores and the invention of cast steel. Hammers, blowing machines and metal lathes were just some of the new mechanical equipment that emerged which would greatly enhance the iron industry. Large ironworks opened, such as The Darbys at Coalbrookdale, and Wilkinson based at three locations in Bersham, Bradley and Broseley. The great Scottish Carron ironworks founded by John Roebuck and the Samuel Walker steelworks at Rotherham all emerged in the 1700s. Similarly the textile industry was transformed, in part by the entrepreneurial spirit of Richard Arkwright, with his inventions that enabled the mass production of yarn and his model of the first factory systems of working.[1] The northern and midland towns became the focus of industrialisation and began to transform England's geographical and subsequent social diversification and population distribution.

The invention and application of the steam engine was used to create an operational network for the new metalworks, mills and factories. New manufacturing of a higher artistic value seen in the growth of the potteries, instigated and popularised by Josiah Wedgwood, would also dramatically change the way certain sectors of society chose to enhance their drinking and dining ware. From the wider impact on the public overall to the small inventions for the domestic, all these new developments began to significantly impact on the way in which people started to think about convenience, practicality and technology in the process of preparing, cooking and serving food.

When comparing the methods adopted by the respected cookery writers Hannah Glasse in 1747 and Mrs Beeton in 1861 for roasting mutton, their approaches are identical, but on closer analysis the differences in equipment generally referred to by both culinary campaigners are worthy of mention. The French influences are also more prevalent in Mrs Beeton's recipes and tips published between 1859 and 1861, with references given to béchamel sauce and meringues.

Hannah Glasse mentions the use of stone jars for preserving, storing and cooking over twenty times in *The Art of Cookery Made Plain and Easy*. Compared to the single reference Mrs Beeton makes in her *Book of Household Management*, this illustrates the extent to which glass pots or bottles were being slowly substituted for the same purposes. Similarly while Hannah Glasse demands that her readers use copper pots and pans to cook with, her hundred-year contemporary Mrs Beeton cautions against the use of all copper utensils, warning 'food may become dangerously contaminated'.[2] However, the cooks of the Georgian era were clearly becoming aware of the dangers of contamination to food, as this narrative demonstrates. An account of a dinner on 29 March at the Castle Inn at Salthill, attended by the commissioners of Colnbroke Turnpike, including a captain, a chemist, a brewer and Eton bookseller among others, had tragic fatal consequences for its diners. The dinner consisted of soup, jack, perch and eel spitchockt, fowls, bacon and greens, veal cutlets, ragout of pig's ears, chine of mutton and salad [*sic*]; course of lamb and cucumbers; crawfish, pastry and jellies. Typical to Georgian dining, Madeira wine and port of the best quality was provided. The company ate and drank moderately. Before dinner, several paupers were examined, and among them 'one miserable object' that they found to be quite remarkable in terms of his illness.

It transpires from reading the rest of this diary entry that the 'one miserable object' was carrying a particularly deadly and infectious disease and was deemed most likely responsible for killing the entire dining party, with the exception of the one member who remained. However, it later emerged that one item was omitted from the menu as listed above, and that this may well have been the cause of the mass disaster. The innkeeper also died, the inn was closed immediately and his widow and children moved away. It was not until her death that the innkeeper's widow admitted that her husband had been a cook of some merit, renowned for his signature dish – a special dressing for turtle. The turtle was supposed to be stewed overnight, but the chef had fallen asleep and let the fire go out. The next day he simply reheated the turtle soup without removing it from the original pan, and the acids from the pan reacted with the copper, turning it to verdigris and poisoning everyone who ate it. It is not made clear what became of the accused pauper ... the one remaining survivor had clearly managed to avoid eating any of the poisoned food.[3]

Georgian society was beginning to recognise the dangers of poisoning as a consequence of contamination. Many were beginning to equate hygiene with health. The revelations of germ theory were some years away, but communities were not ignorant to the correlation between sickness, dirt and decay. A number of cookery books of the age emphasised the importance of cleanliness when preparing, cooking and serving food. As Kitchiner wrote in his *Cook's Oracle* of 1822, 'Cleanliness, and a proper ventilation to carry off smoke and steam, should be particularly attended to in the construction of a kitchen,' and, 'Let the young cook never forget, that cleanliness is the chief Cardinal Virtue of the Kitchen.'[4]

Scientific journals highlighted the dangers of cooking with copper and the newspapers regularly reported deaths caused by corrosive copper poisoning. By the start of the nineteenth century improvements in iron and steel production and manufacture provided safer alternative cooking utensils. Tin was also a metal increasingly in use by the mid-nineteenth century. The tin can was patented in 1809 by the French inventor Nicolas Appert, about whom more has been written in the chapter on celebrity chefs. The patent was then later sold to two Englishmen, Bryan Donkin and John Hall. By 1813 they had established a canning factory, selling tins of food to the British Army and Navy.[5] Mrs Beeton makes continuous reference in her *Book of Household Management* to storing food in tin cannisters.[6] By 1850 meat prices began to significantly fall across Britain and canned meat also provided a much cheaper alternative.[7]

Long before James Osborn Spong invented his ice cream maker, the ice box was a household item that was becoming more relied upon in the modernised kitchens of the 1700s. The Scottish scientist William Cullen is accredited with the ability to develop a machine for evaporating water in a vacuum as early as 1755. The early founding father of the United States, Benjamin Franklin, makes reference to this in his personal diaries, noting that 'Dr Cullen, of Edinburgh has given some experiments of cooling by evaporation'.[8] This process would later be modified by George Bevan Sloper, who patented a machine for refrigeration in 1858. The water to be frozen was stored in canvas bags, so the surface of the water would be more exposed and evaporation would be more effective.[9]

One of the most difficult tasks in any Georgian kitchen was storing the meat. Methods ranged from preserving it in salt and spices to drying it by hanging it in the air, burying it in boxes or even immersing it in skimmed milk.[10] A Mr Peschier invented a method for preserving eggs, which was submitted in the British Annual Register of Useful Inventions for 1829. He suggested immersing them in lime-water, a process which, according to Peschier's tests, enabled the eggs to remain fresh for up to six years. This method was adopted by a confectioner in Geneva, who preserved whole casks of eggs in this way. The recommended ratio of water to lime was twenty or thirty pints mixed with five or six pounds of quicklime, placed in a covered vessel. One can only imagine that this technique did not become popular due to the typical poisonous effects that quicklime can have on the human system over time, including vomiting, abdominal pain and diarrhoea.[11]

There were countless theories during this period about how to preserve and store various types of food. Many in particular related to potatoes, as they were the most valued and consumed vegetable of the age. Methods ranged from exposing them to frost before storage, maintaining them in an airtight area surrounded by soil or straw, to parboiling them, or even searing them on a fire to seal them first before storing them. It is frequently recorded during this period that bread was eaten black. Often bread was kept in damp places or wrapped in wet cloths, which as we know today would probably have escalated the process of generating mould. Individual storage units for bread began to appear around the 1820s. These would have been earthenware pots or tin plate 'bins'.

People were aware of the detrimental effects of poor-quality water and there were a number of patents to filter water in domestic kitchens. These filters worked on the principal that water could be purified by being filtered through either sand or porous stone. The most popular of these domestic filters were Bennet's Patent Filtering Machine and Robin's Royal Filter.[12] These two names often appear in advertisements of the time for house clearance auctions, where items such as this were considered marketable. In fact any items with the word 'patent' placed in front of them seem to be immediately elevated in terms of denoting status and value.

A total of 199 patents were lodged between 1750 and 1851 for general items relating to cooking.[13] These included a 'Machine for roasting, boiling, and baking, consisting of a portable fire-stove, an air-jack, and a metal-screen, to be used in the field in ships and houses, where they may be separately used.' This was the invention of the brothers Joseph and Jedediah Strutt in 1770. A Jedediah Strutt is cited just three years earlier in the *Newcastle Courant*, 1767, as the licence holder for a machine for making ribbed stockings. Whether this is the same man or not is not known, but if it was, he must have been both productive and diverse in terms of his innovative engineering abilities. Similarly, the rather uncommonly named Bartholomew Dominicetti appears to have been attributed with inventing a unique type of Turkish bath system for the British market in 1764, in addition to being listed in 1770 as receiving a patent for 'dressing from one to twenty-one different dishes at once, with one fire'.[14] Peter Clare patented a horizontal smoke-jack in 1770, which is labelled as 'curious', while William Hanscomb's machine for 'roasting many joints of meat, turkey's, geese, fowls, ducks &c, both horizontally and vertically, at the same time or separately, and to the weight of one hundred pounds or more, in such a manner that several joints may be ready at one time, or progressively one after another as wanted' sounds both complicated and ambitious. George Stratton was an ironmonger by trade and is mentioned as living and trading in Surrey in an 1801 edition of the *Lancaster Gazette*, found in an article listing new patents granted. The Patent Office lists his patent simply as 'Machines for cooking'.[15]

William Davis's machine for chopping meat to make

sausages received a patent in 1811. A set of knives were fixed by shanks and screws to enable the knives to rise and fall. The chopping board attached is moved from one end to another by way of rollers and there are references to complicated ratchets, frames and troughs.[16] As to whether this device became popular or not is difficult to determine, but it does not appear to have received much publicity in the media of the time. The newly prized corkscrew, patented as early as 1795 by the Revd Samuel Henshall, had evolved in response to the increasing popularity for importing wines and the development of the wine stopper.[17] Wine and beer were utilised in the same way as we might use water today for daily consumption and in cooking. These new corkscrews would have become useful household items, as well as a travel aid for opening bottles, which were more commonly beginning to be sealed in this way.

As early as 1790 a new 'Travelling Kitchen' was being sold at G. Gregory's Tin Shop in Edinburgh. It is advertised in the *Caledonian Mercury*, 24 July 1790, as being of particular benefit to gentlemen of the muirs (moors), or military officers. Capable of preparing a variety of dishes economically, it was so small it could be carried as a piece of luggage. Readers are invited to visit the shop, where the item is on display and can be better explained in detail. Much like the kitchen shops such as Lakeland in high streets today, shops specialising in kitchenalia were emerging across towns and cities across the country as early as the late 1700s. Thomas Harker advertises his shop in the *Newcastle Courant*, 22 April 1797, as one that specialises in Double Block Tin kitchen furniture, sold either in complete sets or as separate articles. He also sold dish covers, jelly moulds, roasting jacks, tea and coffee urns, plate warmers and candle sticks, among many other items specific to the kitchen.

Another useful object that appears to have received considerable mention in the British media throughout the 1800s is the American-designed 'apple parer'. Invented by

Moses Coates in 1802, the apple was placed on a rotating fork which comes into contact with a stationery knife, which succeeds in peeling the apple for use in a variety of desserts and confections. The British equivalent didn't materialise until 1856, with advertisements for Parnell's 'Apple, Turnip and Potato Parer[18] This exemplifies the race for invention in the field of kitchenalia between Britain and America that is apparent when researching the origins of kitchen equipment.

Advertisements in the local and regional British press of the time indicate that washing machines were available as early as 1801, for those fortunate enough to have the funds to purchase one. The British Museum have on file an early draft advertisement for Edward Beetham's Royal Patent Washing Mill, which is dated around 1790. Beetham was a part-time actor and an inventor, and his washing mill claimed to 'wash more in one hour than ten women, or any other two machines can in the same time'.[19] Beetham's contraption seems to have generated a lot of interest at the time, with some commentators thinking his machines were too commercial. It was believed that the washing mill might encourage people to become lazy, when hard labour meant healthy exercise for both the mind and body. Others, like the writer of this letter written by a follower of Beetham in 1790, celebrated the potential of the machine itself for domestic households and commercial enterprises:

> ... The advantage of cleaning by pressure frequently occurred to me – your method to that effect is so complete, *that it will not injure a cobweb*; it struck me, that washing and wringing by hand, the common way, wore and tore the linen, &c. very much, and required the power of strong men to make them clean. You have eased the lower class of females from a scene of drudgery they have too long experienced; and at the same time, you have effected an immense saving to the publick at large.[20]

In fact the trend for washing many items in bulk was popular in the eighteenth and early part of the nineteenth centuries. Around 1829 John Lawson of Elgin designed a machine for washing potatoes, using an open cylinder which was hand turned in a cistern of water. A wooden or iron trough with a moveable bottom was secured and the potatoes were shifted back and forth by a wooden hoe. Clean water was dispersed at one end, while the dirty water was removed at the other.[21] An illustration of a similar type of machine was sketched by the artist James Ward and can be found in the image section in this book. By 1836 there were a number of washing machines and new ways to mangle and wring clothes. Examples that appeared in the press a great deal include Thomas Bradford and Co.'s 'Vowel' range of patented washing machines and mangles, built in a variety of sizes to suit both domestic and commercial needs. Bradford's also invented a 'Drying Closet'. This appears to be a portable contraption, including a stove for heating flat irons and for drying clothes. The 'Drying Closet' claimed to have everything free of moisture in around twenty minutes.[22]

Other innovative inventors of the time include the Birmingham iron founder Archibald Kenrick, who patented a specific type of coffee grinder in 1815. He improved the technology in the milling process itself for grinding coffee and malt in its design.[23] Papier-mâché became a low-cost alternative product during the Georgian era and featured heavily in the production of tea trays. Advertising in 1775, Brasbridge and Slade of London were stocking 'a fresh Collection of those much-esteemed Patent Trays, which, for their Lightness and Elegance, are so peculiarly adapted to the most curious Setts of China, that many of the principal Nobility and Gentry have discarde the Use of the Silver Tray, as destructive to that delicate Ware, the Machee-Tray having besides the further Advantage of being no Temptation to House-Breakers.'[24] To accompany this fashionable beverage, tea caddies, cups and pots were all very popular and the

patent tea kitchen, or tea urn, was invented during the mid-
to late 1700s. In particular, Wedgwood became well known
for making decorative tea kitchens. John Sibbald, advertising
in the *Caledonian Mercury*, 8 May 1784, mentions selling
'Brown Patent Tea Kitchens' alongside spits, jacks, sugar
nippers and many other metal-worked items. Sugar nippers
are frequently quoted as being invented from around 1800,
although the media cites them from at least as early as 1773.

Spit roasting meat was the favoured method of the
Georgians, with boiling or stewing being the main alternatives.
Smoking (or roasting) jacks, which were positioned inside
the chimney, were replacing the traditional basket spit that
sat on the hearth by the middle of the 1700s.

Wealthier households were also installing brick stoves
heated by charcoal in their kitchens during this period. It is
understood that the iron, or 'perpetual', oven first appeared
in the mid-1700s. One is believed to have been installed at
Shibden Hall, Halifax, at a total cost to the owner of four
guineas.[25] However there seem to be a number of patented
variations of the perpetual oven catalogued much later
throughout the 1800s, and it is difficult to determine who
established what first. Sir Isaac Coffin has frequently been
linked to the invention of the perpetual oven, and his
product was not patented until 1811. His patent, however,
does stipulate being a perpetual oven for the 'baking of
bread', which may be where the confusion exists.[26] It was
also common in the eighteenth century for new patents
to be issued against existing ideas and products. Until the
nineteenth century, when new laws were implemented,
patents were less about inventive activity and more about
the royalties charged by the patentee to the consumer.

By the mid-1800s it is clear that the popularity of the closed
kitchen range, labelled 'the most useful and economical
invention, so admirably adapted for supplying hot baths, or
cooking the largest quantity at the least cost',[27] had made a
tremendous impact on the way in which domestic kitchen

cooking was able to progress. Sir Benjamin Thompson, also known as Count Rumford, is the person most associated with the progressive invention of the early fireplace for the benefit of cooking and heating. Essentially he altered the amount of air that circulated up a chimney, streamlining the flow, which enabled kitchen staff to eventually work in a smoke-free environment. Thompson's aim was to enhance the productivity of fireplaces, utensils, laundry appliances and stoves to improve conditions for the poor.[28]

Portable stoves that could be used for domestic purposes, on holiday or during military conflict, were a hugely popular concept in the Georgian age. In fact, due to the extent England was at war during this period, inventors were no doubt marketing many of their portable cooking utensils to the armed services and government. Mr James Tate did this in 1796, with his portable cooking machine 'for the use of officers in the army or navy, which is provided with lamps'.[29] Similarly, in the same year, a patent was granted to Mr William Whittington of Sheffield for his invention of a portable baking stove. Whittington advises that it could be heated with 'coals, coke, wood, charcoal or any other kind of fuel' and was suitable to be used in 'houses, gardens, fields, camps, on board vessels of every description, at sea or upon rivers ... being portable, and immediately moveable to any situation, and made ready to operate in a few minutes'.[30] It could even be cast in the metal of the consumer's choice, including wrought iron, copper, tin or cast iron among others.

The Georgian age was the age of steam, and numerous steam-powered ovens were being manufactured and marketed as a healthier and lighter alternative to the stove. One of the earliest patents, dated 1793, for a steam-powered cooking contraption was the 'Pneumatic Kitchen' invented by Stanley Howard. It simply consisted of a boiler supplied with water from a small reservoir, creating steam from a number of different cocks and pipes.[31] It is a simple object, yet indicative of a time when almost every conceivable alternative to cooking was being tried and tested for the market. A much later and yet very similar patent is granted to William Erskine Cochrane, whose portable oven and portable steamer of 1828, heated by a lamp, is described thus:

> ... the burner ... is inserted into an opening in the bottom of the boiler and the heat of the flame acting against the under surface of the central compartment of the water chamber, distributes itself through the flues, and causes the water to boil throughout the whole vessel. The steam thus generated rises in the upper part of the boiler and passes off by the pipe for any heating purpose to which it may be desirable to apply it ... [the] portable oven, consisting of a dish or pan, into which the burner of a lamp is inserted for to generate the heat. The cover has a damper to regulate the heat, and also an aperture by which access may be had to the interior.[32]

By the time Cochrane's invention was patented, the new laws involving patents would have ensured that his product was unique, unlike Howard's 'Pneumatic Kitchen', which would, and did, have many copies created, based on its original concept. Somewhat harshly, Cochrane's invention is criticised with tremendous sarcasm in *The Repertory of Patent Inventions* for 1828:

> ... As to the heating it by a lamp, we own our inability to conceive its utility, in any place, where charcoal, peat, or tan-cake can be had; and think that the employment of it for cooking, as described could only be advantageous to the Esquimaux (Eskimo Inuit), who are unhappily bereft of any means of producing heat, but through the scanty and inadequate assistance of a lamp; and we are inclined to imagine that it can only be used in that way here as an ingenious toy, which will, after a few exhibitions, be consigned to the lumber-room ...[33]

A pioneer of domestic gas cooking, James Sharp patented the gas stove as early as 1826. An example of one of the first of these manufactured designs resides in the collections of the Science Museum. An Anglo-American, Abel Stowell, developed the 'economical oven' in 1830. Stowell proposed a cast-iron 'chest' with an oven door to be suspended over ignited fuel. The original design drawing looks a lot like our ovens of today, with the exception that it was suspended over heat, rather than being fitted with heating elements.[34]

Other chapters in this book have explored the influence of overseas trade and migration in relation to what people living during the eighteenth and nineteenth centuries were consuming. There were also a number of new dishes in circulation that originated from Britain itself. There is a tendency to associate roast beef, puddings and pies with the Georgian age, although these were introduced much earlier in Britain's culinary history. In fact it is difficult to determine dishes that are specifically unique to this period, as so many recipes have changed, and been altered, adulterated and renamed throughout history. However, there are some that appear to be consistent with this time. By the middle of the eighteenth century ketchup was the predominant condiment served with many fish and meat dishes in England. It was not like the tomato ketchup that we are most familiar with today. The ketchups, or 'catsups', of the Georgian period were predominantly made of mushrooms, fish or walnuts. One of the earliest recipes appears in Richard Bradley's *The Country Gentleman and Farmer's Monthly Director.*

Take the Gills of large mushrooms, such as are spread quite open, put them into a skellet of Bell-Metal, or a vessel of Earthen Ware glazed, and set them over a gentle Fire till they begin to change into Water; and then frequently stirring them till there is as much Liquor, and put to every Quart of it about eighty Gloves, if they are fresh and good, or half as many more, if they are dry ... add to this about a Pint of strong

red Port Wine that has not been adulterated, and boil them
all together till you judge that every Quart has lost about a
fourth Part or half a Pint; then pas it thro' a sieve, and let it
stand to cool ...[35]

Probably the most famous culinary creation of the 1700s
is the sandwich. Credit is attributed to John Montagu, the
fourth Earl of Sandwich, although it is his cook who should
be honoured. Addicted to gambling, while immersed in a
long game one night in 1762 he requested a meal that would
be quick to digest and not interfere with his concentration.
What his cook prepared was some sliced meat resting between
two pieces of toast. This enabled the Earl to continue playing
and eat simultaneously. From that moment the unique snack
has continued in its popularity and inherited the name of its
honorary inventor.[36] Printed recipes for sandwiches began to
appear in the 1820s, the most popular of which were ham,
tongue, roast beef and potted shrimp.[37]

Having experimented at length with adding gasses to
liquid, the English chemist Joseph Priestly produced the
first artificial carbonated water in 1767. This discovery was
further developed by the Swedish scientist Torbern Bergman,
who introduced the concept of sparkling fortified waters
throughout Europe, an idea which was quickly picked up by
the German entrepreneur Jacob Schweppe, who established
the famous Schweppe & Co. soft drink manufacturers in
London during the 1790s.[38] An advertisement for the new
Schweppe artificial mineral water appears in a 1799 edition
of the *Caledonian Mercury*, boasting its abilities to alleviate
bilious complaints, calm the nervous system and generally
invigorate the whole body. Another carbonated beverage also
conceived at the beginning of the 1800s and hugely popular
across Britain was ginger ale.

The first references to Eccles cakes appear in the Georgian
period. The commercial directory for Manchester 1828–1829
records several Eccles cake makers in the city, and a number

of street sellers trading this product are also referenced in the media at the time. A recipe for Mrs Raffald's 'sweet patties', published in her cookery book of 1769, *The Experienced English Housekeeper*, has been accredited as the first recipe for Eccles cakes to appear in print. Another British classic dish that emerged in the eighteenth century, the name and recipe of which has been slightly adulterated, is Toad in a Hole. One of the earliest recipes is published in *The English Art of Cookery, According to the Present Practice*, 1788, by Richard Briggs. Traditionally this dish was prepared with any meat that was readily available, and Briggs suggests a piece of beef sprinkled with salt. Unlike today's typical version, the batter recipe includes ginger and grated nutmeg.

References to Scotch eggs start to make an appearance around the beginning of the 1800s, one of the earliest recipes of which appears to be published in 1808, in Lady Maria Rundell's *A New System of Domestic Cookery*. This early recipe does not include breadcrumbs, and suggests serving the eggs in a hot gravy. 'Boil hard five pullet's eggs and without removing the white, cover completely with a fine relishing forcemeat in which let scraped ham bear a due proportion. Fry of a beautiful yellow brown and serve with a good gravy in the dish.[39] It seems it was even possible to take out patents on cooked dishes, such as this one for 'Simolina Rice Pudding' cited in Richard Briggs's *The English Art of Cookery, According to the Present Practice*. It is assumed that since this was published in a book that reproduction rights were not linked to the patent itself. Consequently, if the recipe could be freely reproduced and published for public consumption, it raises the question of why someone would choose to patent it at all? It is noted that the patented version is to be made without eggs under the following instruction:

put a quarter of a pound (of the rice) into a sauce-pan with a quart of new milk, boil it gently till it is thick, and keep it stirring all the while, to prvenet its being in lumps and burning; then stir in a quarter of a pound of fresh butter, a little grated nutmeg and ginger, a little lemon-peel shred fine, sweeten it to your palate, and put it in a pan to cool; lay a puff paste round the edge of the dish and when the pudding is cold pour it in, put some candied sweetmeats over it, bake it in a gentle oven three quarters of an hour, and send it to table hot.[40]

Similarly it was recorded in 1832 that a wagonload of patented bread arrived in a Leicestershire town from Bilston. It was patented on the basis that the recipe itself extracted a 'spirit, from the dough' while it was being proved, obviously something no other baker was doing. Any savings that the baker made by carrying out this process enabled him to pay for the distribution of the bread. This was then sold at 8*d* per stone in weight below the typical baker's price. It is reported that the wagon was 'besieged by crowds'. Having been emptied of its contents, the town was informed that the wagon would replenish and return. As a consequence, that evening a sign was erected in the nearby baker's shop advertising all of its bread at the same discount price as the patented variety.[41] This is a nice example capturing many aspects of social historical reference. Firstly it is an early illustration of retail price warring, secondly it shows that if something comes attached with a status label, in this case a patent, at a reduced price, people will always be keen to buy the product. The power of retail competition would have been at its peak during the mid-1800s, as innovation and manufacturing was excelling. Competition in almost every marketplace was becoming integral to the way in which tradesman operated.

Some of the most well-known traders of the Georgian era continue today. Huntley and Palmer biscuit manufacturers were founded in 1822 by Thomas Huntley and George Palmer. They established the business in Reading, with the marketing strapline 'The Most Famous Biscuit Company in the World'. At one point in their career Huntley and Palmer accounted for 75 per cent of the total British export market in cakes and biscuits.[42] Following a history which includes several takeovers and mergers, the company re-established itself in 2006 as a growing independent trader. W. H. Brakspear and Sons have been trading in the brewing industry since 1711. The company owns a chain of pubs and has franchised out its brewery houses, which according to their company website still incorporate some of the original brewing equipment from 1779. Another of Britain's most respected and largest brewery businesses is Greene King. Although it did not acquire this name until the later 1800s, the Greene family started the venture in Suffolk in 1799 and it remains today a thriving enterprise, having recently acquired the renowned chain of Loch Fyne fish restaurants. Similarly, Guinness began brewing in County Kildare around the 1750s and has become perhaps one of the most iconic and globally recognised beers of today.

Although no longer a British-owned company, Cadbury continues to operate from its head office in London as a multinational subsidiary of Mondelez International. Cadbury's was founded by John Cadbury in 1824. He started the empire operating out of a tea and coffee warehouse in Birmingham, and is described in the *Birmingham Gazette*, 1824, as being regularly furnished 'with coffess of the finest quality, and a supply will be kept fresh roasted, which alone can insure a fine and delicate flavour'. It is also here in this advertisement that the first inklings of John Cadbury's future are revealed, as it states 'J.C. is desirous of introducing to particular notice Cocoa Nibs, prepared by himself, an article affording a most nutritious beverage for breakfast'.

Like Cadbury, J. S. Fry and Sons began trading as early as 1761. On the death of her husband, Anna Fry took responsibility of the company, which was then named Anna

Fry & Son. In 1790 the company was selling 'Churchman's Patent Chocolate' and patented cocoa in Bristol. Other items included cocoa nuts and shell, ground cocoa-sago, China cinnamon sticks and refined liquorice.[43] Some years later her son, together with his own children, formed J. S. Fry and Sons, a business that would become the largest commercial chocolate manufacturer in Britain. Now known simply as Fry's, the company became consumed by Cadbury during the early part of the twentieth century.

Now part of the American 'Smucker's' group, Edmund Crosse and Thomas Blackwell were just young London-based entrepreneurs back in the 1830s, when they became well-known for their sauces, in particular the Soho Sauce with a 'very delicious piquant flavour it imparts to game, bashed venison, made dishes &c'.[44] Crosse & Blackwell went on to build an empire which gave us the famous Branston Pickle, before finally being sold in the 1960s.

Matthais Robinson and Co., later to become Robinson and Bellville, were manufacturing barley waters for 'children, Invalids and others' as early as 1823, and managed to patent these drinks a few years later in Pigot and Co.'s national commercial directory for 1828–9. Robinsons took their patent seriously, submitting an article in the *Norfolk Chronicle* on 28 June 1823 stating,

> The Prepared Barley and Prepared Groats are particularly Patronized by the first Medical Practitioners in the Metropolis, and in every part of the Kingdom where they have been introduced, and as they are generally used in cases of illness, or as a peculiar fine food for Infants, too much care cannot be taken to prevent an improper commodity being substituted. M.R. begs to state his preparations are made from the finest Pearl barley, and best Embden Groats, under his own immediate inspection, and will keep in any Climate.

Perhaps their most famous product of all, Robinson's Barley Water, was created specifically for Wimbledon and other major tennis tournaments under Colman's.[45] The company was eventually acquired by Britvic in the 1990s, but has retained its brand under them. Other notable trademarks of this period include James Keiller and Son, trading since 1797, of the Keiller marmalade dynasty, now owned by Centura Foods. Thomas Sarson began marketing his specially brewed malt barley in 1794. Sarsons was recently acquired by the Japanese company Mizkan, along with Branston Pickle.

Although not trading under their original name, MacFarlane Lang were very early biscuit manufacturers, established in Glasgow initially as a bakery in 1817, and then later as a biscuit factory. During the early twentieth century the company commissioned an inventor to develop a biscuit sandwiching machine called the 'streamline', which they patented. Following the Second World War, MacFarlane Lang and Co. Ltd became absorbed into United Biscuits.[46]

The following general overview provides some examples of kitchenware to be found during the Georgian period, which are both typical to the era and still utilised in the twenty-first century. In terms of cutting and chopping, items such as mincers, bean slicers and shredders would not be marketed until the late nineteenth century and curiously no patents, either in Britain or America, were issued for bread or cake knives between the years 1790 and 1873. Thereafter they appear to be in abundance. One theory is that this may have had something to do with restrictions coming from cutlers guilds, considering their autocratic reputation; otherwise it is quite a mystery. Cucumber slicers were being manufactured at least as early as 1790. Not all Georgians favoured this vegetable; as Samuel Johnson noted, 'A cucumber should be well-sliced, dressed with pepper and vinegar, and then thrown out.' Iron chopping knives with wooden handles that could chop by way of a rocking movement were produced by blacksmiths until around the beginning of the nineteenth century. These types of chopping tools are favoured among many chefs today, particularly for chopping herbs. Pestles and mortars and also remain the same fundamental shape and are used for the same purpose today. Once used by apothecaries and as tools for domestic remedies, they soon transferred to the kitchen in the Middle Ages, became decorative by the Renaissance and then became a culinary accessory once again by the Georgian era, mainly because the guilds that controlled their manufacture became less powerful. Typically cast in bronze, brass, cast iron or marble, by the mid-1800s pestles and mortars were being made in the latest fashionable earthenware material and being sold by the big potteries like Wedgwood. In the early 1800s families would still celebrate Hallowe'en on what was also sometimes called 'Nutcrack night' in the North of England. This trend for cracking and then eating the nuts would become somewhat easier by the early to mid-1800s, when mechanical and decorative iron nutcrackers were readily available to consumers. Nutcrackers have existed since at least the fifteenth century, but only as basic wooden levers. Figural nutcrackers were particularly fashionable in later Georgian Britain, carved into anything from full character human figures to a variety of animals.

Despite whisks and beaters not being introduced until the middle of the nineteenth century, Georgians were already experimenting with the process of mixing ingredients for greater ease. One method involved taking a number of pieces of cane, often six, each slightly longer than an average ruler. These were then tied together at one end, with some rods left deliberately shorter to provide a variant of volume to mix with. This makeshift tool was simply called a mixing rod.

The fashion for confectionery during the eighteenth and nineteenth centuries fuelled a new industry of related sugar-craft tools, forcing bags for icing, and jelly bags and strainers which were constructed out of fine woollen weaves. Nothing inspired the baking and consumption of luxury confectionery like religious festivals and specialist commemorative days in the eighteenth and early nineteenth centuries. The following extract is taken from William Hone's *Every-Day Book* of 1825. It describes the activities of a confectioner's shop on Twelfth Day (now known as Twelfth Night) celebrations in London.

> From the taking down of the shutters in the morning, he, and his men, with additional assistants, male and female, are fully occupied by attending to the dressing out of the window, executing orders of the day before, receiving fresh ones, or supplying the wants of chance customers. Before dusk the important arrangement of the window is completed. Then the gas is turned on, with supernumerary argand-lamps and manifold wax-lights, to illuminate countless cakes of all prices and dimensions, that stand in rows and piles on the counters and sideboards, and in the windows. The richest in flavour and heaviest in weight and price are placed on large and massy salvers; one enormously superior to the rest in size, is the chief object of curiosity; and all are decorated with all imaginable images of things animate and inanimate. Stars, castles, kings, cottages, dragons, trees, fish, palaces, cats, dogs, churches, lions, milk-maids, knights, serpents and innumerable other forms in snow-white confectionery, painted with variegated colours, glitter by 'excess of light' from mirrors against the walls festooned with artificial 'wonders of Flora'. This 'paradise of dainty devices', is crowded by successive and successful desirers of the seasonable delicacies ...[47]

One can only wonder at how sumptuous the displays of the high-end retailers of the Georgian streets were in relation to today's high-street offerings, comparable only to the larger city stores such as Selfridges, Harrods or Fortnum and Mason. In fact many of those same stores originate from this same period.

The trend for ice cream and sorbet fitted within the context of confectionery in the early nineteenth century. At the very end of the Georgian period an illustration of the types of utensils required to make this increasingly popular sweet treat are recorded in the correspondence between a reader and the editor of *The Magazine of Domestic Economy*.

> Mr Editor – Can you give me any practical directions for the making Ice creams? I have this year an opportunity of procuring ice in a rough state, but being unacquainted with the management of it for cream &c., I shall be obliged by your giving the necessary directions through your valuable magazine ...
>
> Editor – Sorbetieres or moulds for cream or fruit-ices, are made of two sorts of materials, block-tin and petwter; of these the latter is the best, the substance to be iced congealing more gradually in it than in the former; an object much to be desred, as when the ice is formed too quickly, it is very apt to be rough, and full of lumps like hail, especially if it be not worked well with the spatula; the other utensils necessary for this operation are a deep pail, with a cork at the bottom, and a wooden spatula about nine inches long; being so far provided, fill the pail with pounded ice, over which spread four handfuls of salt; then having filled the sorbetiere, or mould, with cream, &c. put on the cover, and immerse it in the centre of the ice-pail.[48]

There is then a long explanation about removing the mould every fifteen minutes or so to stir or shake the setting ice cream until it is completely 'congealed' and ready to be turned out on to a plate. The process is not that different to today for those households that do not own an ice-cream maker, the exception being that we no longer require a bucket of ice; most of us simply walk to the freezer.

There are many more objects that could be included as part of this list, too many. The intention is to emphasise the extent to which the Georgian period had, and continued to develop and enhance, practical items for the kitchen. The advancements and enlightenment of the eighteenth and early nineteenth centuries were germinating the seeds of the great Victorian chain reaction.

9

From Georgian Seeds to Victorian Acorns: The Dawn of the Kitchenalia Revolution

As to the Art of Cookery, it is rapidly retrograding, and will retrograde more swiftly still, as well-to-do middle class people grow more and more 'stuck up', and have their 'set dinners' sent in from the pastry cook's instead of having them cooked at home.

The Illustrated London News, 1882

Industrial, labour and employment practices were altering significantly in Britain as early as the end of the eighteenth century, and by the end of the first half of the nineteenth century an increasing number of the working classes were being employed by the expanding factories and workshops. Farm labourers no longer lived on site with their employers, and were hired on a more casual and flexible contract. A growing surge in union recognition, workers' rights and opportunities also gave way to the abolition of the old Law of Master and Servant, to be replaced by the Employer and Workman Act in 1875.[1]

The slum kitchens of the previous century, although still prevalent, were beginning to witness improvements as a consequence of the philanthropic activities of the Victorian elite. In particular, George Peabody's extensive housing projects for the poor were constructed as larger, better-equipped buildings. These were designed for rental and included separate kitchens that moved away from the one-room open fire design, where families had traditionally cooked, eaten and slept. He also provided cupboards for storage, a boiler, an oven, drained ventilation and adequate water supplies.[2] A study of 300 random women aged between twenty and thirty-five born in London, but living throughout the UK and Ireland, from the census returns of 1901 is enlightening in its demonstration of the shift in social demographics in this period. Many of the 300 remain as 'occupation unknown' and twenty-one claim to be living by their own means. However, the highest number of women listed as employed are those working as teachers in schools – a total of sixteen – followed by domestic governesses and dressmakers, both totalling nine. Six women are employed as clerks and six employed as hospital nurses. One woman is cited as studying at university, another as a scientist and one a hotel manager. Only four of the women are employed in general domestic service and three separately as cooks and a kitchen maid. This reveals a stark transition already for many women as early as just one year after the death of Queen Victoria, in addition to a shift in occupational patterns away from domestic service and the need to employ cooks and kitchen staff. In contrast, the percentage of female labour employed in domestic service in 1851 can be approximated at somewhere between 18 and 40 per cent.[3]

Taking the sample above as an example of the 1901 census occupations for women, this equates to just 7.2 per cent of the female population being employed in domestic service, a significantly lower number than the estimated figure for fifty years previously. This continued decline is echoed in the census returns for Ireland that recall 193,620 men and women employed in domestic service in 1901 compared to the 151,534 in 1911,[4] a loss of over forty thousand in this field of work. Henrietta Thornhill was a nineteenth-century middle-class diarist. She makes frequent reference to cooking and keeping her own house, stepping in when the cook and laundry maid were ill or on leave. She provides the housemaid with cooking lessons and on one occasion makes her own potato pudding.[5] This illustrates the extent to which the women of the nineteenth century were engaging more with household domestic chores.

In line with the beginning of the sharp rise in popularity in the trade noted earlier, there are a total of 6,976 pastry cook and confectioners listed in the 1841 census for Great Britain. But by the time the 1881 census was conducted, the figure for both men and women employed in this same capacity had risen to a staggering 25,534. This is unquestionably indicative of the popularity for new cooking techniques and cooking specialisms.[6] It is unlikely the majority of these confectioners would have been employed on a domestic basis, rather they were self-employed with small businesses. From the numerous citations that appear in newspapers and archives of the time, there were a vast number of confectioners operating wholesale and retail outlets across the UK and Ireland from the mid-nineteenth century. As the fashion for decorative food products was becoming more popular, these practitioners were sometimes found guilty of using substances that were dangerous to consumers in their pursuit for achieving the most ornate delicacies. *The Penny Illustrated Paper* reports on one such case in 1871, when a description of a sugary masterpiece produced by a Dublin confectioner included a cradle made of plaster of Paris, containing the body of a baby moulded out of sugar and rice starch, its rosy cheeks fashioned in cochineal beetle and its clothes coloured using chromate of lead.[7] In this same year a young boy is recorded as dying from eating poisonous chocolate creams purchased from a confectioner's shop in Brighton.[8] This highlights the extent to which cakes, pastries and confection epitomising extravagance and indulgence had expanded beyond the confines of the kitchens of the rich, and were now fully available to consumers on almost every high street. It also indicates the lengths to which these skilled craftsmen would go to produce the most aesthetically pleasing items, often at the expense of human health.

During the mid-1800s many references to public lectures on hygiene in cooking began to emerge. And articles such as one published in the *Leicester Chronicle* in 1852 discuss links between diseases such as consumption and food adulteration, citing legitimate published studies by the pioneering medical journal the *Lancet*, founded in 1823.[9] We know from an article in the *Tamworth Herald* of 1875 that the *Lancet* had recently published research on the importance of improvements in cooking for the benefit of the poor.[10] Methods as well as ingredients were being challenged nationally, even to the extent of a great debate as to whether potatoes should be peeled or left in the skins prior to cooking.[11] By the time the country rolled into the early twentieth century the government had instigated whole new departments to manage the issue of educating society at large about food preparation and the manufacture of food, by establishing special schools and creating new jobs that maintained sanitary standards. One such training centre was the Clapham Tennyson Street Cookery Centre, and a photograph of young girls participating in this type of training at the turn of the twentieth century, learning to wash and dry dishes after a meal, can be found in the archives of the Women's Library.[12]

By the turn of the twentieth century Britain and Ireland were dominated by widespread local and regional demonstrations highlighting the benefits of both gas and electric cooking. For example, the *Dundee Courier* of 1902 advertises a series of 'Art of Cooking Demonstrations' in the city, stressing the advantages of cooking with gas during the summer months,[13] while members of Southport Electricity Committee held an electricity exhibition[14] and Bristol extolled the merits of gas cooking and its 'ever increasing popularity' during their 1900 'Gas Cooking Exhibition at Fishponds'.[15] These types of events grew in size, culminating in the first Ideal Home Exhibition hosted in London's Olympia in 1908, the brainchild of the then owner of the *Daily Mail* newspaper, Lord Northcliffe. The Ideal Home Exhibition was to become a regular platform for showcasing the latest developments in domestic architecture, design and gadgetry.[16] In 1898 one in four households with a gas supply possessed a gas cooker; by 1901 this had increased to one in three households, although this was less common in rural areas. Electricity as a cooking fuel was introduced in 1890; it was used less than gas due to its expense. But, as electric cooker designs improved and prices slowly decreased by the beginning of the twentieth century, electricity slowly began to replace gas.[17]

It has been accepted that cookery schools had long been established a century before, but it is the Victorians who took this concept for the benefit of educating the masses. While much of the documentation relating to the day-to-day running of early cookery classes was not archived, a great deal of the Victorian literature is accessible, including that pertaining to the National Training School. It is described here by Charles Dickens in 1879. He writes,

The National School of Cookery, Exhibition-road, South Kensington, commenced its work in the year 1873 under the title of the Popular School of Cookery, and was located in the building of the International Exhibition of that year. At the close of the International Exhibition the commissioners granted to the executive committee of the National School of Cookery the temporary use, free of rent, of that portion of the building already occupied by it, together with some more space for an additional kitchen and offices. Up to the present time it has not been found possible for the school to provide its own premises, and therefore the use of the exhibition building is continued to it. Lectures and demonstrations are now given daily in this school by students going through a course of training as teachers. Cooks and others are instructed in all branches of cookery, and lessons can be had singly or in a course. The public are admitted to see the school at work every afternoon, except Saturday, between three and four o'clock. The Crystal Palace classes for cookery and domestic economy were commenced in the Ladies' Division of the School of Art, Science, and Literature in the year 1875. On the removal of the school to its present position in the tropical department of the palace, Miss Mary Hooper was entrusted with the formation of a new series of classes for instruction in cookery and every branch of domestic economy. These classes have been continued to the present time. The instruction is given by practical illustrations, and is designed for ladies, from a lady's point of view, and not for the training of servants. It includes all that is necessary to make home comfortable and attractive, and a lady accomplished ruler of her own house. At each cookery lesson, two or more dishes are prepared which are tasted by the students. At this school single lessons are not given, and the number of students received for each course is limited.[18]

One early training manual for the school reveals the lessons were thorough and classified into subject areas, including stews, tripe, the cooking of meat, the cooking of poultry, stock and soups, vegetables, sauces, pastries, puddings, pickles, cakes and even how to work with canned meats. Instructions for each area of cooking or cleaning were numbered. For example, lesson four in the section on 'Cleaning Ranges, Stoves and Kitchen Utensils' deals with how to clean copper stewpans:

1. Mix some sand and salt together on a plate – half the quantity of salt to that of sand.
2. Wash the stewpan well in hot water and soda.

3. Soap the hand, or a brush, dip it in the salt and sand, and rub the inside of the pan until all stains are removed and it has become clean and bright.
4. Rinse it out well in the water, dry the inside quickly, and then rub over the pan and clean the copper outside.
5. Rub it in the same way with a soaped hand, or a brush dipped in sand and salt.[19]

One of the most eminent educationalists of domestic economy and hygiene of the late 1800s and early 1900s was Margaret Eleanor Pillow, *née* Scott. Margaret was a Cambridge University graduate and a teacher, as well as being the only female sanitary inspector in the United Kingdom. She co-authored the manual *Domestic Economy: Comprising the Laws of Health in their Application to Home Life and Work* in 1897 and lectured prolifically on this subject and the theory of cooking.[20] Sadly her legacy has not remained as iconic as some of her contemporaries. This newly available and accessible education provision began to raise awareness of the importance of cooking independently and cooking to healthy standards in hygienic environments.

The public cooking depots created to provide cheap, hot food for the poor and working classes at a low fixed rate were very popular in Glasgow throughout the nineteenth century. By 1863 it appears that London had adopted this trend and built a similar model in Lambeth, which it later rolled out across the city, where young girls were trained in kitchens to 'roast and boil plain food, so that when they become heads of families they may not be so helpless in the kitchen as so many poor women now are'.[21]

The street sellers of the last century were also expanding and evolving into more sophisticated enterprises. By 1840 ham sandwiches were being sold on the streets as the latest snack. It is understood that an unsuccessful coffee shop owner in Westminster, London, came up with the idea when he hit bad times and started to sell ham sandwiches outside the theatre doors. His success was so great that he soon had competition in the form of errand boys, pot boys and foot boys, all profiting from this lucrative business. It is estimated that by the mid-1800s around thirty-three traders were operating along the Strand side of London's theatreland, with approximately seventy in all working across the theatres in the East End of London. An estimated 436,800 sandwiches were believed to have been sold annually in this way during the early part of the Victorian era.[22] Slowly the bustling, energetic coffee shops of the Georgian age were beginning to be replaced by mobile hot tea and coffee vendors, who steadily appeared just after 1830. By 1842 it is believed that some 300 of these stalls were active throughout London.[23]

Similarly the 'Bazaars' of the later Georgian era were transformed into the types of shops that we are more familiar with today, with elaborate glass display windows and eye-catching awnings. What were once tradesmen's houses became extended buildings with showrooms, work rooms and living quarters for the staff. Consumers in late Victorian and Edwardian Britain were also beginning to be much more conscious of what they ate. Advertisements for vegetarian restaurants became more visible in this period, as the British Library poster for the 'Wheatsheaf' vegetarian restaurant in Oxford Street, London, 1884, denotes.[24] It was inspired perhaps by Mrs James Simpson's theories outlined in the first vegetarian cookery book of 1812. Other cookery writers of note include Eliza Acton and her 1845 *Modern Cookery, in all its branches*, together with Isabella Mary Beeton and her now iconic *Book of Household Management*, written in 1861. Both these publications and their popularity are synonymous with the kitchenalia revolution. Eliza Acton provides an exactness of proportions and measurements when delivering recipe instructions that had previously not existed. She talks about the increasing popularity in people steaming their food, from fish, butcher's meat, poultry, vegetables, puddings and macaroni, and notes the advantages in being able to cook in this way 'at a distance from the fire'.[25]

By the mid-1800s it is clear that the popularity of the closed kitchen range, labelled 'the most useful and economical invention, so admirably adapted for supplying hot baths, or cooking the largest quantity at the least cost',[26] had made a tremendous impact on the way in which domestic cooking was able to progress. It is important to rationalise the difference class would have had within the context of the development of the kitchen and kitchenalia. The wealthy kitchens of the nineteenth century would have stood in stark contrast to the less modernised domestic kitchens of the labouring working classes. This is exemplified in an issue of *The Builder* published in 1852, describing a new construction of labourers' cottages in London consisting of two cottages converted into seven apartments, denoting that 'one single brick oven should be built in the outhouse for the joint use of the cottages'. It was stipulated that 'one of very moderate size will be sufficient for six or even twelve families'.[27]

Fredrich Engels' *Study of the Working Classes* of 1844 records the ten plus pawnbrokers to be found operating in just one street alone in most working-class areas of Manchester. Residents would regularly pawn their furniture, clothing and kitchen utensils every Wednesday, returning to reclaim them on the Saturday night.[28] Due to the growing desire to improve the conditions of the working classes, many fountains were constructed throughout London during the nineteenth century to assist the poor in their daily lives, and an article featured in the *Penny Illustrated Paper* of 1861 announces the opening of one such fountain in Tower Hill that 'conferred upon the poor, both by reason of the purity of the water and the extent to which it is used for cooking purposes'.[29]

Despite the advent of the closed range, most average households were still fitted with open ranges, one of the best of which is highlighted by Eliza Acton in 1845 as 'Arnott's

Stove', which provided 'the perfect regulation of the heat ... better than most others we apprehend'.[30] Arnott was credited with the invention of the smokeless grate around 1854. Arnott's fame must have been a little short lived, considering the announcement of his death exactly twenty years later.[31] Eliza also recommends investing in the newly imported Forneau Économique, or French furnace. At a cost of 'not more than seven shillings', this portable smokeless stove could rest comfortably on the kitchen table, and was ideal for making jams and preserves.[32]

It is important to consider the extent to which the kitchen also served as the laundry area and as such, items related to washing, drying and preparing laundry must also feature within this narrative. Larger appliances, such as the wash tub and wash board, were slowly being replaced. Following on from Edward Beetham's first patented washing machine of almost a century earlier, by 1888 the London firm Harper Twelve Trees had established themselves as one of the predominant manufacturers of the new popular rotary washing machine.[33] As more items of kitchen paraphernalia entered the market, the old tools were becoming less acceptable. By 1854 one of the most well-known publishers of domestic cooking, Alexis Soyer, refers to the gridiron as a 'primitive utensil',[34] while advocating the multi-purpose benefits of the new frying pan.[35] In his popular Victorian women's manual *The Modern Housewife*, Soyer provides a definitive list of essential kitchen utensils, which includes stew pans, a fish kettle, a braising pan, a bain-marie, sauce pans, frying pans, pie-moulds, jelly moulds, baking sheets, a salamander, vegetable cutters, pastry cutters, tartlet pans, scissors, pastry brushes, pudding cloths, larding needles (a thin shaft of steel, tapering into a sharp point used for inserting fat into joints of meat), a meat saw and meat chopper, rolling pin and tammies (fabric kitchen cloths used to strain sauces and stocks).[36]

Other small appliance inventions included George

Kent's Rotary Knife Cleaning Machine business, which was established in 1838. A substantial wooden rotating barrel with slots to insert the knives into sharpeners and buffers would have been an extremely valuable asset to any large home prior to the discovery of stainless steel. Advertisements for this new contraption began appearing in the popular press from around 1848.[37] Similarly the British inventor James Osborn Spong had established himself as a manufacturer of economic household utilities, which he had labelled 'domestic machinery', by 1856. Among these items was the steel Spong Meat Mincing Machine and the Spong Ice Cream Freeze, all British inventions that were patented in the United States in 1893.[38] At the same time Ebenezer Stevens is mentioned in the *London Gazette* for his invention of 'an improved cooking utensil'. Stevens' patent was an early form of a bread maker, suitable for preparing dough for biscuits, pastries and cakes, as well as bread products, as early as 1859.[39] This trend for enhancing bread making in the home to make it an easier and faster process continued, as Lucy H. Yates stipulates in her guide to essential equipment for kitchen flats in 1905, *The Model Kitchen*. Her list of essential items includes a bread mixer and a 'Spong' chopper,[40] suggesting that Spong's inventions also sustained their longevity and popularity well into the twentieth century. One of the most insightful and detailed compendiums of Victorian kitchen utensils can be found in *Cassell's Dictionary of Cooking*, published as several editions towards the end of the nineteenth century. It advises the reader on the types of metals that kitchen items are manufactured in and what precautions to take when cooking with these metals. Iron is declared the safest, copper and brass are heavily scrutinised and lead is considered inadvisable for use with milk or cream, which it taints. Lead is also deemed unsafe for storing meat. *Cassell's* recommends every kitchen should keep a variety of frying pans; one simply for frying, one to sauté, one for omelettes and one for fish. Many items from the Georgian era remain integral to the kitchen, such as the nutmeg grater, the pestle and mortar, the spit, the salamander, the tea kettle and saucepan, among others. There are also various new items, such as a mincing machine, freezing machine and egg slicer.

A somewhat lesser-known female writer of the time who was inspired by cooking and its methods is Mary Holland, whose compilation *The Complete Economical Cook and Frugal Housewife* mentions beating eggs with a hand-held whisk as early as 1837. Similarly the American-born Eliza Leslie, who was a prolific mid-1800s culinary writer, makes reference to the new metal egg beaters of the time as being counter-productive, in that the metal 'retards the lightness of the eggs'. Instead Leslie recommends beating eggs with wooden rods, as many were utilising in Britain the century before, preferably with an unflinching elbow close to your side and placing the egg beater 'always down to the bottom of the pan'.[41] It is evident that British kitchens were also becoming stocked with these labour-saving small appliances, as the first British egg beater was patented in 1857, invented by E. P. Griffiths, whose 'compound action egg whisk and batter mixer' was retailing in 1861 for thirty shillings,[42] around sixty pounds in today's money.

The ascendance of the French celebrity chef continued into the late nineteenth and early twentieth centuries, with names such as Urbain Dubois, Jules Gouffé and Auguste Escoffier working in some of the most prestigious foreign courts. Dubois was a celebrated chef who cooked for the Rothschild family and for Prince Orloff of Russia, among others. Many of his eight published works were translated into English and he has been credited with the invention of 'service a la russe', a concept that enabled diners to just eat one dish for each course, the modern menu as it's known today.[43] Gouffé became Carême's protégé at an early age and is most known for his comprehensive writings, including *Le Livre de Cuisine* and *Le Livre de Pâtisserie*, known for their systematic approach to cooking methods and techniques, and written with the assumption that all his readers had some basic professional training. It was Escoffier that made the greatest impact on Britain and its newly emerging restaurant culture. Taking inspiration from the famous chefs of the Regency period, Escoffier lightened French cuisine, created delicate mousses, miniaturised delicacies, steamed vegetables and thinned soups and sauces while inventing classics like Peach Melba and Melba toast. He wrote what would become one of the most important culinary manuals of his generation, and one which is still used today, *Le Guide Culinaire*. Escoffier famously partnered with César Ritz. As Ritz built up the Carlton and Ritz hotels in London, Escoffier was charged with designing and supervising the kitchens in both.[44]

Arguably the most prolific female culinary entrepreneur of the Victorian era was not Mrs Beeton or Eliza Acton, but rather the largely forgotten Agnes Bertha Marshall. Agnes wrote four manuals, the best-known being *The Book of Ices*, published in 1885. Agnes had a wide repertoire, from running a cookery school, Marshall's School of Cookery, to inventing kitchen appliances and running an agency for domestic staff. It is understood she was a trained and experienced cook and toured the country delivering lectures about her branded products, including freezers and the first edible ice cream cone.[45] The emergence of females as inventors was seen during the Victorian period. More women were coming through the education system and this meant that they were entering areas of work previously unknown to them. Elizabeth Saunders invented the quaintly named Aunt Iza's Princess Tray Rack in 1880, boldly advertised as the 'handiest domestic article ever offered to the public'.[46] Similarly, Sarah Anne Blundell invented a 'new or improved coal economiser for kitchen and other grates' in 1893.[47]

Labour-saving products were to dominate the late nineteenth and early twentieth centuries, with many products that are still familiar in today's society, such as Bovril,

Bird's custard and Quaker oats. Edmund Crosse and Thomas Blackwell had also mastered the process of canning, drying and bottling to preserve food by the middle of the nineteenth century.[48] The emphasis was on manufacturing less-work-intensive items for the kitchen in addition to ensuring that food preparation and cooking methods maintained new standards of hygiene. There was also a growing awareness that vitamins and certain dietary necessities were essential to good health. In particular, breastfeeding and babies' milk became more important. Samuel Clarke had invented the food warmer, fuelled by a tea light, which could be used to heat a pint of milk, keep food warm or, more commonly, in the preparation of pap – a mixture of flour or bread and diluted milk used to wean infants. The food warmer remained in circulation until around 1920.[49]

The British Empire was at its strongest during the nineteenth century. Large numbers of officials and families of officials were travelling to the colonies and territories ruled and administered by the British crown. This involved transporting domestic goods, including kitchen equipment, across considerable distances. Special metal carrying containers were specifically designed and developed to hold kitchen equipment, such as those to be found in the collections of the Museum of London that were used by a British family between 1881 and 1920.[50]

While the Georgians had mastered steam and gas, the Victorians are credited with electricity. Founded in 1886, The General Electric Apparatus Company began selling over-the-counter electrical products, and by 1901 there were some 50,000 electrical apparatus makers, 42 per cent of which were based in London.[51] Wenham and Waters were an engineering company based in Croydon. In December 1894 they were just one of seven companies at that time who responded to an invitation by Croydon's town clerk to submit a tender to run the proposed electric lighting in the town.[52] Works carried out, particularly in large country houses, included installation of electric lighting, sanitary fittings, central heating, cooking apparatus, water mains and fire mains. Britain had a public supply of electricity by 1881. The company Siemens began a small hydroelectric plant in Surrey that was successful until 1894, when it moved to Brighton; electricity was nationalised in the 1940s.[53]

Just as the smart bazaars of the Georgian age had evolved into large commercial enterprises, these had once again transformed by the 1860s and 1870s into the elegant department stores that we are most familiar with today. Names such as Whiteley's of Bayswater, Dickins and Jones, Swan and Edgar, Marshall & Snelgrove, Broadbent's of Southport and Lewis's of Liverpool all became synonymous with the same business model, to buy in bulk and sell at a lower price, with cash-only sales to undercut competitors. Many of these stores featured large-scale food halls and tea rooms, which attracted female visitors from all over the country, as venues where they could conduct most of their domestic shopping under one roof, in addition to enjoying lunch or afternoon tea. Independent grocers also expanded, like the family business Sainsbury's. Once a humble family dairy store in Drury Lane selling butter and eggs in 1869, just fifteen years later it had expanded into a small chain of three branches across London.[54] The coffee shops and cook shops of the previous era either became obsolete or continued to reinvent themselves as either clubs, restaurants or genteel tea rooms. *Bentley's Miscellany, Volume 5* of 1839 notes that the renowned London-based old eating house, the Cock, and the Rainbow coffee shop of the century before were still popular venues, both known for their brown stout, European-inspired lunches and straight-talking clientèle.

In addition to its established traditional dining and gentrified tearooms, the Victorian era was known for the rise of the foreign restaurant. Curry had already become reinforced as a staple diet of Empire and the French cuisine of old had inspired the evolution of sophisticated restaurants modelled on Parisian convention. There was another influence, in the form of an increasing migrant German community, which was establishing itself in Britain's major cities including Liverpool, Manchester, Bradford, Glasgow and London. These communities introduced their own food businesses, particularly in the London area. By the 1860s there were a number of specialist German restaurants; a German baker, John Wittich, trading in the Docklands; a 'Konditorei', or Germanic patisserie, selling 'German tarts, cakes and pastries' operating in Whitechapel and another baker in Leman Street, East London, who sold Konigsberg marzipan, Nuremberg and Basle pepper cakes and fresh German black bread.[55] There was an increasing demand for dining out and procuring specialist, fashionable artisan food. Considered one of the first legitimate food guides to London, *London at Dinner; or Where to Dine* was published in 1858. It shared useful advice on suggested places to dine depending on your circumstances. If in a small group, the Blue Posts in Cork Street offered a 'snug place during the winter for a dinner for four', or before going to the theatre The Bedford Hotel or Clun's Hotel would both serve you in a hurry, while providing an excellent claret. For a guaranteed good night of dining in a venue that wasn't going to leave you bankrupt, the Wellington was said to have provided a mix of comfort, luxury, elegance and economy.[56]

Public dining and food retail boomed; the scope for kitchen gadgetry across a rapidly increasing and economically mobilised population and a competitive international market for developing new inventions makes the Victorian age synonymous with culinary elevation and technology. The real desire for these products and labour-saving devices existed well before this period, with many of the items that were developed in the eighteenth and early nineteenth centuries maturing into a holistic commodity by the end of the 1800s. The early transport networks established in the 1700s became more sophisticated by the end of the nineteenth century and fresh, diverse food products became readily available across the country as a whole. Factory production also became more sophisticated and convenience foods were increasing in popularity. Methods of bottling and canning practices were enhanced and tradesmen delivered to domestic kitchens on a daily basis. The potential to cook more diversely and more regularly would continue to change the way Britain ate. Larger numbers of staff were required to create and serve the elaborate courses presented at breakfast and dinner, and lunchtime eating had also been revived. The rise in commerce generated an emphasis on dining and networking from home. Much like the Georgians, the Victorians entertained, but with more frequency. Cooking and eating remained integral to society, just as the Georgians had established it.

Notes

Introduction

1. P. Deane & W. A. Cole, *British Economic Growth, 1688–1959, Second Edition* (Cambridge, University of Cambridge, 1962), p.62.
2. K. Colquhoun, *Taste: The Story of Britain Through its Cooking* (London, Bloomsbury, 2007), p. 233.
3. Royal Commission on the Ancient and Historical Monuments of Scotland, ScotlandsPlaces, *Female Servant Tax Rolls, 1785–1792* (Scotland, 2009).
4. Royal Commission on the Ancient and Historical Monuments of Scotland, ScotlandsPlaces, *Male Servant Tax Rolls, Volume 06, 1785–1786* (Scotland, 2009).
5. DEFRA, *United Kingdom Slaughter Statistics, 2014* (London, DEFRA, 2014).
6. M. Levy (ed.), *Medicine and Healers Through History* (The Rosen Publishing Group, 2011), pp. 42–4.
7. Marshall Cavendish, *Exploring Life Science: Lymphatic Systems – Organisms* (Marshall Cavendish, 2000), p. 495.
8. Nottinghamshire Archives, DD/E/120/11, 26 March, 1756.
9. York City Archives, Acc. 54:1, *Household inventory of the furnishings of Rev. John Forth and Mrs Elizabeth Forth at Slingsby and Ganthorpe, 1791–1806.*
10. Lincolnshire Archives, 1ANC2/B/19/II/6, Manuscripts of the Earl of Ancaster.
11. Colquhoun, *Taste: The Story of Britain through its Cooking*, p. 90.

12. P. Earle, *The Making of the English Middle Class: Business, Society and Family Life* (California, University of California Press, 1989), pp. 297–8.

13. T. Scully, *The Opera of Bartolomeo Scappi (1570): L'arte et prudenza d'un maestro Cuoco (The Art and Craft of a Master Cook)* (Toronto, University of Toronto Press, 2008), pp. 765–74.

14. A. E. Richardson, *Georgian England* (Yorkshire, Jeremy Mills Publishing, 2008), p. 33.

15. P. Giuseppe, *Semi-serious observations of an Italian exile during his residence in England* (Philadelphia, Key and Biddle, 1833), pp. 140–41.

16. R. Bayne Powell, *Travellers in Eighteenth-Century England* (London, J. Murray, 1951), p. 48.

17. S. Mennell, *All Manners of Food* (Illinois, University of Illinois Press, 1996), p.126.

18. D. Dean, A. Hann, M. Overton & J. Whittle, *Production and Consumption in English Households 1600–1750* (Routledge, 2004).

19. C. Dukes, *Work and overwork in relation to health in schools; an address delivered before the Teachers Guild of Great Britain and Ireland at its fifth general conference held in Oxford, April, 1803* (London, Percival & Co, London), p. 55.

20. F. Eden, *The state of the Poor: An History of the labouring classes in England, from the conquest to the present period* (London, J. Davis, 1797), p. 822.

21. D. Wilmeth & L. T. Miller (eds), *Cambridge Guide to American Theatre* (Cambridge, Cambridge Uni Press, 1996), p. 24.

22. Eden, *The state of the Poor: An History of the labouring classes in England, from the conquest to the present period*, p. 822.

23. *Cobbett's Weekly Political Register* (London, Clement, Saturday 14 July 1821), p. 23.

24. The Sussex Advertiser, various editions: 11 July 1785, p. 3; 30 April 1792, p. 4; 26 August, 1799, p. 4; 7 October 1811, p. 2; 20 March 1815.

25. Eden, *The state of the Poor: An History of the labouring classes in England, from the conquest to the present period*, pp. cccxxxix – cccl.

26. Mennell, *All Manners of Food*, p. 136.

27. Eden, *The state of the Poor: An History of the labouring classes in England, from the conquest to the present period*, p. iv.

1 Trade and Early Empire: Overseas Influence and New Ingredients

1. P. Langford, *Eighteenth-Century Britain: A Very Short Introduction* (Oxford, Oxford University Press, 2000), pp. 38–41.

2. CIA Factbook <www.cia.gov/library/publications/the-world-factbook>.

3. R. Davis, 'English Foreign Trade, 1700–1774' (*The Economic History Review*, New Series, Volume 15, No. 2, 1962), pp. 285–303.

4. L. Mason, *Food Culture in Great Britain* (Wetsport, USA, Greenwood Publishing, 2004), p. xviii–xix.

5. F. Martin, *The History of Lloyd's and of Marine Insurance in Great Britain* (The Lawbrook Exchange Ltd, 1876), p.55.

6. J. Stobart, S*ugar and Spice: Grocers and Groceries in Provincial England, 1650–1830* (Oxford, Oxford University Press, 2013), pp. 53–4.

7. Stobart, S*ugar and Spice: Grocers and Groceries in Provincial England, 1650–1830*, p. 56.

8. J. S. Brewer (ed.), *Letters and Papers, Foreign and Domestic, Henry VIII, Volume 1: 1509–1514* (London, IHR, 1920).

9. W. Andrews, *Historic Byways and Highways of Old England* (London, Andrews, 1900), pp. 175–6.

10. *Salisbury and Winchester Journal* (London, Mon. 1 Oct 1810), p. 4.

11. E. J. Burford, *Wits, Wenchers and Wantons* (London, Robert Hale Ltd, 1990), p. 57.

12. I. Day, *Cooking in Europe 1650–1850* (Westport, USA Greenwood Press, 2008), p. 4.

13. E. Smith, *The Household Companion* (Hertfordshire, Wordsworth Editions Limited, 2006), p. 31.

14. *Londonderry Corporation Minute Book, Volume 4 (1720–1736)* (1915), pp. 114–202.

15. E. J. T. Collins, 'Dietary Change and Cereal Consumption in Britain in the Nineteenth Century', *The Agricultural History Review, Volume xxm (2)* (1975), p. 97.

16. A. D. Salaman, M. Ghadiri & M. Houslow (eds), *Particle Breakage* (Amsterdam, Elsevier, 2007), p. 390.

17. A. Wild, *The East India Company Book of Spices* (London, Harper Collins, 1995), p. 39.

18. L. Collingham, *Curry: A Tale of Cooks and Conquerors* (New York, Oxford University Press, 2006), p. 129.

19. Collingham, *Curry: A Tale of Cooks and Conquerors*, p. 113.

20. W. Kitchiner, *The Cook's Oracle: Wherein Especially the Art of Composing Soups, Sauces, and Flavouring Essences is Made So Clear and Easy ... Being Six Hundred Receipts, the Result of Actual Experiments Instituted in the Kitchen of a Physician, for the Purpose of Composing a Culinary Code for the Rational Epicure* (London, 1817), p. 4.

21. Wild, *The East India Company Book of Spices*, pp. 48–9.

22. Mrs Dalgairns, *The Practice of cookery: Adapted to the business of every day life* (Edinburgh, 1830), p. 364.

23. *The True Briton, Volume III* (London, 1752), p. 576.

24. A. Dodd, A. Smith, *The Gentlemen's Magazine, Volume 86, Part 1* (London, Nichols, Son and Bentley, 1816), p. 230.

25. J. F. Curwen (ed.), *Supplementary Records: Troutbeck, Records relating to the Barony of Kendale: Volume 3* (IHR, 1926), pp. 192–9.

26. J. A. Vallejo and J. A. González, J. Ramón, J. Antonio, 'The use of head louse as a remedy for Jaundice in Spanish folk medicine: an overview', *Journal of Ethnobiology and Ethnomedicine, Volume 9* (2013), p. 52.

27. J. Hill, *A History of the Materia Medica* (London, T. Longman, C. Hitch and L. Hawes, 1751), p. 476.

28. J. Mitchell, *A Dictionary of Chemistry, Mineralogy, and Geology* (London, Sir Richard Phillips and Co., 1823), p. 560.

29. Wild, *The East India Company Book of Spices*, pp. 24–7.

30. R. Hewitt, *Coffee: Its History, Cultivation, and Uses* (New York, D. Appleton and Company, 1872), pp. 96–7.

31. The British Library, *Ipswich Journal* (Saturday 24 July, 1736), pp. 2–3.

32. A. F. Smith, *The Oxford Companion to American Food and Drink* (New York, Oxford University Press, 2007), p. 138.

33. National Archives, Cornwall Record Office (25 August 1712), AR/10/408.

34. British Library, *The Preston Chronicle*, Saturday 11 February, 1832, 2.

35. *Western and Midland Directory; or Merchant's and Tradesman's Useful Companion, for the year, 1783, Pigot's Directory of Hampshire, 1828, Pigot's Directory of Kent, 1824, Universal British Directory of Trade, Commerce & Manufacture, 1792–98. Hampshire extracts.*

36. National Archives, D5459/1/28/6, 1785.

37. Patent no. GB189819164 (A) – 1899-03-18, *Percolator Packages or Infusers for Tea, Coffee, and other Substances.*

38. National Archives, Hackney Archives, D/F/BRA 6/9, *c.* 1880.

39. British Library, *Birmingham Daily Post* (February, 5 July 1878), p. 6.

40. G. A. Sala, *Paris Herself Again in 1878–9* (London: Remington and Co. 1879), pp. 37–8.

41. C. E. Pascoe, *London of To-day: an illustrated handbook for the Season* (London, Roberts, 1890), p. 281.

42. J. Stead, *Food & Cooking in 18th Century Britain: History and Recipes* (London, English Heritage, 1985) p. 22.

43. E. Young, *Poetical Works of the Rev. Dr. Edward Young* (London, printed for Benjamin Johnson, Jacob Johnson & Robert Johnson, 1805), pp. 88–9.

44. D. Campbell, *The Tea Book* (Louisianna, USA, Pelican Publishing, 1995), p. 27.

45. B. A. Weinberg, B. K. Bealer, *The World of Caffeine: The Science and Culture of the World's most Popular Drug* (London, Routledge, 2004), p. 105.

46. *Kelly's Directory of North & East Ridings of Yorkshire, [Part 1: Places]* (1893), p. 14.

47. R. O. Mennell, *Tea. An Historical Sketch* (London, E. Wilson, 1926), p. 29.

48. J. Murray, *The Quarterly Review, Volume 42* (London, John Murray, 1830) pp. 354–60.

49. S. Wise, *Inconvenient People: Lunacy, Liberty and the Mad-Doctors in Victorian England* (London, Vintage, 2012).

50. Murray, *The Quarterly Review, Volume 42*, p. 368.

51. D. McKinley, 'The Tea Caddy', Article 128, *The Early History of the English Tea Caddy* (Association of Small Collectors of Antique Silver, 2010).

52. Nottinghamshire Archives, Executorship Papers, Reference DD/BK16/36, 1843–1847.

53. Oxfordshire Record Office, Reference GIL/XIV/vii/2, 30.

54. H. Broadbent, *The Domestick coffee-man. Shewing the true way of preparing and making of chocolate, coffee and tea* (1722), p. 74.

55. J. Radcliffe, *Pharmacopoeia Radcliffeana* (London, Charles Rivington, 1716), p. 425.

56. J. Bradley, *Cadbury's Purple Reign: The Story Behind Chocolate's Best-Loved Brand* (Chichester, John Wiley & Sons, 2011), p. 32.

57. Broadbent, *The Domestick coffee-man. Shewing the true way of preparing and making of chocolate, coffee and tea*, pp.4–5.

58. L. Grivetti, H. Y. Shapiro (eds), *Chocolate: History, Culture and Heritage* (New Jersey, USA, Wiley-Blackwell, 2009), pp. 129–30.

59. J. S. Ubrey-Rees, *The Grocery Trade: Its History and Romance* (London, Duckworth & Co., 1910), p. 47.

60. L. Inglis, *Georgian London: Into the Streets* (London, Viking, 2013), pp. 224–5.

2 From the Streets to Fashionable Society

1. A. J. S. Gibson & T. C. Smout, *Prices, Food and Wages in Scotland, 1550–1780* (Cambridge, Cambridge University Press, 1995) p. 228.

2. J. Mackintosh, *An Essay on ways and means of enclosing* (Edinburgh, 1729) p. 131.

3. Gibson, *Prices, Food and Wages in Scotland, 1550–1780*, p. 234.

4. Public Record Office for Northern Ireland, *A collection of moft of the publications*, 1806.

5. Public Record Office for Northern Ireland, *Letter from Shannon to Boyle, circa. 1791*, Ref:D2707/A/3/3/13.

6. B. A. Weinberg & B. K. Bealer, *The World of Caffeine: The Science and Culture of the World's Most Popular Drug* (London, Routledge, 2002) p. 106.

7. J. Stead, Food and Cooking, History and Recipes in 18th-century Britain (London, English Heritage, 1985.) p. 15.

8. E. Chadwick, *Report on the Sanitary Conditions of the Labouring Population of Great Britain* (W. Clowes and Sons, 1843), p. 33.

9. A. S. Wohl, *Endangered Lives: Public Health in Victorian Britain* (Taylor and Francis, 1884), p. 48.

10. London Metropolitan Archives, 1886, ref: B/EGLC/031/004.

11. Londonderry Corporation Minutes, Volume 9 (1788–1793), pp. 31–63.

12. W. R. Louis, A. M. Low, N. P. Canny, P. J. Marshall (eds), *The Oxford History of the British Empire: The Eighteenth Century, Volume 2* (Oxford, OUP Oxford, 1998), p. 47.

13. Public Record Office for Northern Ireland, *Diary of John Galt, 1796–1837*, ref: D561.

14. Public Record Office for Northern Ireland, *Ward Papers, 1691–1745*, ref: D2092.

15. Public Record Office for Northern Ireland, *Letter from Sir John James Burgoyne from Strabane to the the Marquess of Abercorn, 30 July 1817*, ref: D623/A/130/38.

16. T. Bernard, *The Reports of the Society for bettering the condition and increasing the comforts of the poor* (S. Bulmer & Co., 1798), pp. 148–9.

17. Bernard, *The Reports of the Society for bettering the condition and increasing the comforts of the poor*, p. 104.

18. J. Dennie, *The Port Folio* (Philadelphia, USA, 1812), p. 342.

19. R. Griffiths, *The Monthly Review, Volume 31* (1800), p. 326.

20. G. B. Hindle, *Provision for the Relief of the Poor in Manchester, 1754–1826* (Manchester, Manchester University Press, 1975), p. 49.

21. Anonymous, *Domestic Economy and Cookery for rich and poor* (London, Longman Rees, Orme, Brown and Green, 1827), p. 21.

22. M. A. Espriella, *Letters from England Volume One* (Edinburgh, James Ballantyne and Co, 1814), p. 158.

23. S. C. Brown, *The Collected Works of Count Rumford, Volume V: Public Institutions* (Harvard University Press, 1970), p.180–2.

24. *Kentish Gazette* (Tues 24 Nov., 1812), p. 2.

25. Brown, *The Collected Works of Count Rumford, Volume V: Public Institutions*, p. 215.

26. *Society For Bettering The Condition And Increasing The Comforts Of The Poor, fourth edition, Volume 1* (London, 1805), p. 108–12.

27. R. Owen, *Report to the County of Lanark: Of a Plan for Relieving Public Distress, and Removing Discontent, by Giving Permanent Productive Employment, to the Poor and Working Classes* (University Press for Wardlaw & Cunninghame, 1821), pp. 26–35.

28. M. Witzel, *Management History: Text and Cases* (London, Routledge, 2009), p. 46.

29. Q. R. Skrabec, *William McKinley, Apostle of Protectionism* (USA, Algora Publishing, 2008), p. 43.

30. T. C. Smith, *The Naval and Military Magazine, Volume three* (1828), p. 520.

31. T. Gisborne, *An enquiry into the duties of men in the higher and middle classes of society in Great Britain, resulting from their respective stations, professions and employments* (London B&J White, 1797), pp. 507–8.

32. L. E. Ude, *The French Cook* (J. Ebers, 1822), p. 7.

33. S. Smiles, *Thrift* (Chicago, Donohue Henneberry, 1800), p. 370.

34. J. Strype, *A Survey of The Cities of London and Westminster, Ancient Housekeeping* (London, HRI, 2007).

35. *The Court and City Register* (London, 1801), p.107–8.

36. Public Record Office for Northern Ireland, 'Minutes of meetings of the Governors of the County Down Infirmary, with accounts, 1767–1848', HOS/14/2/1/A/1.

37. J. Strype, *Survey of the Cities of London and Westminster, Book 1, Chapter 26: Colleges and Hospitals, Christ's Church Hospital. Their Diet; And good Orders* (1720), p. 182.

38. E. Gambier-Parry, *Annals of an Eton House: with some notes on the Evans family* (London, John Murray, 1907), p. 28.

39. G. Pecchio, *Semi-serious observations of an Italian exile, during his residence in England* (London, Effingham Wilson, 1833), p. 305.

40. J. Strype, *Survey of the Cities of London and Westminster, Book 1*, Chapter 26, 'Colleges and Hospitals', p. 196.

41. K. Olsen, *Daily Life in 18th Century England* (Westport, USA, Greenwood Publishing Group, 1999), p. 237.

42. M. DeLacy, *Prison Reform in Lancashire, 1700–1850: A Study in Local Administration* (Manchester, Manchester Uni Press, 1986), p. 110.

43. *Morning Post* (Tuesday 25 Aug., 1818), p. 2.

44. M. DeLacy, *Prison Reform in Lancashire, 1700–1850: A Study in Local Administration*, p. 109.

45. P. H. Wilson, *A Companion to Eighteenth-Century Europe* (USA and Oxford, Blackwell Publishing Ltd, 2009), p. 161.

46. R. Hickox, *All you wanted to know about 18th Century Royal Navy* (USA, Rex Publishing, 2007), p. 20.

3 Price, Profit, Pilfering and Probate: The Value of Kitchenalia

1. J. H. Parker, J. Parker, *Our English Home* (London & Oxford, J. H & Jas. Parker, 1861), p. 77.

2. R. Griffiths, G. E. Grifiths, *The Monthly Review, Or, Literary Journal, Volume 76* (1787), p. 431.

3. Royal Institution of Great Britain, *Royal Institution of Great Britain Journals Volume 1*, Issues 1–8 (London, The Royal Institution of Great Britain, 1802), p. 11.

4. M. Dods, *The Cook and Housewife's manual: A Practical system of Modern Domestic Cookery and Family Management* (Edinburgh, Oliver and Boyd, 1829), p. 34.

5. The Old Bailey, Ref: t17860222-91, 'Richard Smith, Theft, grand larceny', 22 February 1786.

6. The Old Bailey, Ref: t17611209-16, 'Ann Ford, Theft, theft from a specified place', 9 December 1761.

7. The Old Bailey, Ref: t17740518-74, 'William Healey, Theft, pocketpicking', 18 May 1774.

8. The Old Bailey, Ref: t17761204-13, 'John Kelly, Thomas Latham, Theft, theft from a specified place', 4 December 1776.

9. The Old Bailey, Ref: s17141209-01, 'Old Bailey Proceedings punishment summary', 9 December 1714.

10. E. Burke, *Annual Register, or, a view of the history and politics of the year* (London, J.Dodsley, 1762–1838), pp. 202–3.

11. *The Morning Post* (Sat 24 January 1818) p. 3.

12. *London Standard* (Thursday 20 March 1828), p. 4.

13. *The Spectator* (4 October 1828), p. 6.

14. The Old Bailey, Ref: s17141209-1, 'Proceedings punishment summary', 9 December 1714.

15. The Old Bailey, Ref: s17160906-1, 'Old Bailey Proceedings punishment summary', 6 September 1716.

16. The Old Bailey, Ref: t17210712-43, 'Ann Richardson, theft, grand larceny', 12 July 1721.

17. The Old Bailey, Ref: OA17280626, 'Ordinary's Account', 26 June 1728.

18. The Old Bailey, Ref: OA17330129, 'Ordinary's Account', 29 January 1733.

19. *London Gazette* (28 November, 1734), pp. 1–2.

20. *London Gazette* (1716), p. 2.

21. Gwynedd Archives, Meirionnydd Record Office, Trinity Quarter Sessions, Reference ZQS/T1778, 1778.

22. Shropshire Archives, Wills, Probate, Administrations and Inventories, Reference 741/67, 6 December 1774.

23. *Staffordshire Advertiser* (Saturday 22 August 1807), p. 1.

24. *Sussex Advertiser* (Monday 25 September 1815), p. 1.

25. Science Museum Group, Art Collection, object number: 2002–98, *c.* 1830.

26. Science Museum Group, Art Collection, object number: 1983–516.

27. I. W. Archer, *Transactions of the Royal Historical Society: Volume 19: Sixth Series* (Cambridge, Cambridge University Press, 2009) p. 193.

28. *Bury and Norwich Post* (Wednesday 4 July 1804), p. 3.

29. *Derby Mercury* (Friday 17 October, 1755), p. 4.

30. *Caledonian Mercury* (Saturday 25 November 1780), p. 1.

31. *The Ipswich Journal* (Saturday 8 August 1789), p. 3.

32. S. Richards, *Eighteenth-century Ceramics: Products for a Civilised Society* (Manchester, Manchester University Press, 1999), p. 153.

33. S. Richards, *Eighteenth-century Ceramics: Products for a Civilised Society*, p. 111.

34. H. Mayhew, *London Labour and the London Poor; A Cyclopaedia of the condition and earnings of those that will work, those that cannot work and those that will not work, Volume 1* (London, G. Woodfall & Son, 1851), p. 338.

35. P. Mantoux, *The Industrial Revolution in the Eighteenth Century* (Oxford, Routledge, 2013), p. 278.

36. R. Eadon, *History of the Company of cutlers in Hallamshire, in the*

county of York, by Leader (Sheffield, Pawson & Brailsford, 1905–6),
p. 35.

37. P. Mantoux, *The Industrial Revolution in the Eighteenth Century*, p. 363.

38. R. Eadon, *History of the Company of cutlers in Hallamshire, in the county of York, by Leader*, pp. 22–4.

39. R. Eadon, *History of the Company of cutlers in Hallamshire, in the county of York, by Leader*, p. 23.

40. *Edinburgh Gazzette* (21 October, 1828), p. 253.

41. *Edinburgh Gazette* (20 January, 1829) p. 15.

42. *Edinburgh Gazette* (16 July, 1830), p. 201.

43. R. J. Cheeswright, *An historical essay on the livery companies of London, with a short history of the Worshipful company of cutlers of London, and combining an account of its charters, fundamental laws, bye-laws, estates, and charities* (Croydon, J. W. Ward, 1881), pp. 38–9.

44. S. Shackleford, *Blades Guides to Knives and their values* (Iola, USA, Krause Publications, 2009), p. 125.

45. S. Shackleford, *Blades Guides to Knives and their values*, p. 125.

4 The New Gastronomic Culture

1. J. Brillt-Savarin, *The Phisiology of Taste* (Createspace, 2011), p. 18.

2. T. Bradshaw Belfast, *General and Commercial Directory for 1819* (Belfast, Francis Finlay, 1819).

3. National Archives of Scotland, *Scottish Shops in the Eighteenth Century*, Ref: CC8/8/126.

4. University of Portsmouth, *A Vision of Britain, Census Reports* (2009).

5. University of Portsmouth, *A Vision of Britain, Census Reports* (2009).

6. *Directory, General and Commercial, of the Town & Borough of Leeds, for 1817, containing an alphabetical list of the merchants, manufacturers, tradesmen, and inhabitants in general... to which is prefixed, a brief but comprehensive history of the borough ...* (Edward Baines,Yorkshire, 1817), pp. 189–94.

7. *Pigot's Directory of Cornwall* (Pigot & Co., 1830).

8. J. Chamberlayne, *Of Vices and Punishments. The Present State of Great Britain, Part One, Book 3* (London, 1736), p. 190.

9. W. Bailey, *T**d no tansey, or The disappointed pastry-cook* (London, William Bailey, 1790).

10. C. Matthews, *J. Duncombe's second, and only correct, edition. Mr. Mathews 'At Home', etc.* (Duncombe, London, 1826), p. 10.

11. *Leeds Intelligencer* (11 March 1777), p. 1.

12. *Kentish Gazette (*14 September 1768), p. 2.

13. F. H. W. Sheppard, *The Social Character of the Estate: A Survey of Householders in c. 1790, Survey of London: Volume 39: The Grosvenor Estate in Mayfair, Part 1, General History* (London, Athlone Press, 1977), pp. 86–9.

14. T. W. Scragg, *Chester City Council, Old and New* (Liverpool University thesis, 1971), p. 14.

15. S. I. Mitchell, *Urban Markets and Retail Distribution, 1730–1815, with Particular Reference to Macclesfield, Stockport, and Chester* (Oxford, Oxford University thesis, 1974).

16. G. M. Koot, *Shops and Shopping in Britain: from market stalls to chain stores* (History Department, University of Massachusetts Dartmouth, 2011), p. 23.

17. L. Mason, *Food Culture in Great Britain*, p. 32.

18. S. La Roche (trans. C. Williams), *Sophie von. Sophie in London – 1786, Being the Diary of Sophie v. la Roche* (London, Jonathan Cape, 1933), p. 87.

19. S. La Roche, *Sophie von. Sophie in London – 1786, Being the Diary of Sophie v. la Roche*, p. 112.

20. *St. James's Chronicle* (30 March to April 1775).

21. *St. James's Chronicle* (April, 1775).

22. J. White, *A Great and Monstrous Thing: London in the Eighteenth Century* (USA, Harvard University Press, 2013), p. 198.

23. H. Mayhew, *London Labour and the London Poor; A Cyclopaedia of the condition and earnings of those that will work, those that cannot work and those that will not work, Volume 1*, p. 171–80.

24. *Parliamentary Papers, House of Commons and Command, Volume 24* (London, HM Stationery Office, 1836), p. 218.

25. G. E. H. Cole, *A Tour Through the Whole Island of Great Britain, Volume 1* (New York, Everyman's Library, 1962), pp. 343–6.

26. J. White, *A Great and Monstrous Thing: London in the Eighteenth Century*, pp. 93–4.

27. T. Allen, *The History and Antiquities of London, Westminster, Southwark, and Parts Adjacent* (London, Cowie and Strange, 1829), p. 345.

28. W. Bray, *Sketch of a Tour Into Derbyshire and Yorkshire* (London, B. White, 1783), p. 240.

29. J. Neild, *State of the prisons in England, Scotland and Wales* (London, John Nichols & Son, 1812), p. 307.

30. J. Roach, *Roach's London Pocket Pilot, or stranger's guide through the Metropolis* (J. Roach, London, 1796), pp. 44–5.

31. W. Thornbury, *Old and New London, Volume 1* (London, 1878), pp. 220–33.

32. G. H. Gater, E. P. Wheeler (eds), *Survey of London: Volume 16, St Martin-in-the-Fields, Charing Cross* (London, 1935), pp. 75–81.

33. J. Timbs, *Club Life of London, Volume II (of 2) With Anecdotes of the Clubs, Coffee-Houses and Taverns of the Metropolis During the 17th, 18th, and 19th Centuries* (London, Richard Bentley, 1866), pp. 18–19.

34. E. Walford, *Old and New London: Volume 4* (London, 1878), pp. 314–26.

35. J. Timbs, *Club Life of London, Volume II (of 2) With Anecdotes of the Clubs, Coffee-Houses and Taverns of the Metropolis During the 17th, 18th, and 19th Centuries*, pp. 15–17.

36. J. D. Pelzer, 'The Coffee Houses of Augustan London', *History Today, Volume 32, Issue 10*, 1982, pp. 40–7.

37. E. Eger, *Women, Writing and the Public Sphere, 1700–1830* (Cambridge, Cambridge University Press, 2001), p. 35–6.

38. J. Miller, *The Coffee-House, a dramatick piece, etc. By James Miller. With musical notes* (J. Miller, 1743 Miller), p. 2–3.

39. J. Robertson, *London or Interesting Memorials of its Rise, Progress and Present State.* (London, T. Boys, 1824), p. 78.

40. J. S. Buckingham (ed.), *The Oriental Herald and Colonial Review* (London, Sandford Arnot, 1825), p. 284.

41. F. Jeffries, *Gentleman's Magazine, Volume 57* (London, John Nichols, 1785), p. 28.

42. A. I. Coffin, *A Botanic Guide to Health, and the Natural*

Pathology of Disease (London, British Medio-Botanic Press, 1850) p. 154.

43. Brooke's Club, *Memorials of Brooks's from the Foundation of the Club 1764 to the close of the Nineteenth Century* (London, Ballanntyne & Co. Ltd, 1907), p. x.

44. J. D. Pelzer, 'The Coffee Houses of Augustan London', *History Today, Volume 32, Issue 10,* 1982, pp. 40–7.

45. J. Timbs, *Club Life of London, Volume II (of 2) With Anecdotes of the Clubs, Coffee-Houses and Taverns of the Metropolis During the 17th, 18th, and 19th Centuries,* pp. 123–50.

46. J. Timbs, *Club Life of London, Volume II (of 2) With Anecdotes of the Clubs, Coffee-Houses and Taverns of the Metropolis During the 17th, 18th, and 19th Centuries,* p. 67.

47. J.White, *A Great and Monstrous Thing: London in the Eighteenth Century,* p. 334.

48. *Sketches of club-life, hunting and sports* (New York, Hurd and Houghton, 1868), p. 45.

49. *Morning Post* (Thursday 11 March, 1824), pp. 1–4.

50. *Leeds Intelligencer* (Thursday 18 February, 1830), p. 1.

51. J. Roach, *Roach's London Pocket Pilot, or stranger's guide through the Metropolis,* p.43.

52. J. Roach, *Roach's London Pocket Pilot, or stranger's guide through the Metropolis,* p. 54.

53. J. Feltham, *The Original Picture of London. A Correct Guide for the Stranger, as well as for the Inhabitant to the Metropolis of the British Empire* (London, Longman, Rees, Orme, Brown and Green, 1802), pp. 340–57.

54. *Stamford Mercury* (Thursday 19 November, 1772), p. 4.

55. J. Perkins, *Every Woman Her Own House-keeper; Or, The Ladies' Library: Containing the Cheapest and Most Extensive System of Cookery Ever Offered to the Public. ... Also, The Family Physician; Or, A Complete Body of Domestic Medicine* (London, James Ridgway, 1796), p. 66.

56. J. Wright, *Mornings at Bow Street: A Selections of the Most Humorous and entertaining Reports which Have Appeared in the Morning Herald ...* (London, 1824), p. 237.

57. *The Penny Magazine* (11 February, 1843), p. 56.

58. J. Timbs, *Club Life of London, Volume II (of 2) With Anecdotes of the Clubs, Coffee-Houses and Taverns of the Metropolis During the 17th, 18th, and 19th Centuries*, p. 290.

59. M. Mac Conlomaire, 'Public Dining in Dublin: the history and evolution of gastronomy and commercial dining, 1700–1900', *International Journal of Contemporary Hospitality Management, Volume 25, Issue 2*, 1989, pp. 11–12.

60. J. Stuart, *Three Years in North America, Volume 1* (Edinburgh, Cadell.Robert,1833), p. 447.

5 Britain's Own French Revolution

1. G. E. H. Cole, *A Tour Through the Whole Island of Great Britain, Volume 1*, pp. 141–376.

 2. *Travels of Cosmo the Third, grand duke of Tuscany, through England during the reign of King Charles the Second (1669) tr. from the Italian manuscript in the Laurentian Library at Florence* (London, Mawman, 1821) p. 398.

 3. *London Standard* (Saturday 20 November 1830), p. 4.

 4. Bodleian Library, *The Gentleman's Magazine, Volume 6* (August 1736), p. 455.

 5. S. Adams & S. Adams, *The Complete Servant* (1826: London. Knight & Lacey), p. 369, p. 7.

 6. A. E. Miller, *The Southern Review, Volume 5* (USA, Charleston, A. E. Miller, 1830), pp. 406–7.

 7. T. Wallis, *The Nic-nac: Or Literary Cabinet, Volume 2* (London, T. Wallis, 1824), p. 287.

 8. J. Woods, *Letters of an Architect, from France, Italy, and Greece: In Two Volumes, Volume 1* (London, John and Arthur Arch, 1828), p. 61.

 9. J. Macky, *A Journey through England: In familiar letters from a Gentleman here, to his friend Abroad, Volume 1* (London, J. Hooke, 1722), p. 175.

10. H. B. Wheatley, P. Cunningham, *London Past and Present: Its History, Associations, and Traditions* (Cambridge, Cambridge University Press, 2011), p. 102.

11. H. Robinson, *The Monthly Review, Volume 5* (London, Thomas Hurst, Edward Chance & Co., 1827), p. 42.

12. A. Hayward, *The Art of Dining, Gastronomy and Gastronomer's* (London, John Murray, 1852), p. 75.

13. L. E. Ude, *The French Cook* (London, John Ebers, 1822), p. 6.

14. R. Spang, *The Invention of the Restaurant* (USA, Harvard Uni Press, 2001), p. 140.

15. W. Harrison (ed), *New Monthly Magazine* (London, Chapman and Hall, 1847), p. 57.

16. W. Brownlie, D. Brownlie, *A System of Geography; Or, A Descriptive, Historical, and Philosophical View of the Several Quarters of the World, and of the Various Empires, Kingdoms, and Republics which They Contain: Particularly, Detailing Those Alterations which Have Been Introduced by the Recent Revolutions* (Glasgow, Niven, Napier and Khull, 1807), p. 427.

17. 'Character of the French', *Blackwood's Edinburgh Magazine, Volume 26, Issue 156*, 1829, pp. 309–19.

18. T. Webster, Mrs Parkes, *An encyclopœaedia of domestic economy: comprising such subjects as are most immediately connected with housekeeping as, the construction of domestic edifices, with the modes of warming, ventilating, and lighting them ...* (New York, Harper and Brothers, 1815), p. 900.

19. P. Cobbett, *A ride of eight hundred miles in France* (London, Charles Clement, 1824).

20. Anon., *Domestic Economy, and Cookery, for Rich and Poor* (London, Longman, Reese, Orme, Brown and Green, 1827), pp. 117–18.

21. R. Griffiths, G. E. Griffiths, *The Monthly Review* (London, R. Griffiths, 1793), p. 5.

22. F. C. Accum, *Culinary Chemistry* (London, R. Ackermann, 1821), p. 333.

23. D. G. C. Allanrsa, 'The Laudable Association of Anti-Gallicans', *Royal Society for the Encouragement of Arts, Manufactures and Commerce, Journal Volume. 137, Issue Number 5398*, 1989, p. 623–8.

24. H. T. Wood, *A History of the Royal Society of Arts* (London, John Murray, 1838), p. 4.

25. *Ipswich Journal* (Friday 12 November, 1736), p. 1.

26. F. Burney, *Brief reflections relative to the Emigrant French Clergy: earnestly submitted to the humane Consideration of the Ladies of Great Britain* (London, Thomas Cadell, 1793), pp. 22–4.

27. M. Wiley, *Romantic Migrations: Local, National, and Transnational Dispositions* (New York, Palgrave Macmillan, 2008), p. 51.

28. National Archives of Scotland, *Early Gaelic Book Collections, Chambers's Edinburgh Journal, no.305* (1849), p. 40.

29. B. L. De Muralt, *Letters Concerning the English and French, Describing the Character and Customs of the English and French* (London, Edlin, 1726), p. 1.

30. R. Bayne-Powell, *Travellers in Eighteenth Century England* (J. Murray, 1951), p. 46.

31. R. Bayne-Powell, *Travellers in Eighteenth Century England*, p. 45.

32. R. Bayne-Powell, *Travellers in Eighteenth Century England*, p. 137.

33. C. de Saussure, *A Foreign View of England in the Reigns of George I and George II* (Plymouth, Van Muyden), pp. 221–3.

34. C. Coff, 'The Taste for Ethics: An Ethic of Food Consumption', *The International Library of Environmental, Agricultural and Food Ethics, Volume 7*, 2006, p. 75.

35. S. Mennell, *All Manners of Food*, p. 3.

6 Celebrity Chefs

1. R. Platzer, *Women Not in the Kitchen: A Look at Gender Equality in the Restaurant Industry* (California Polytechnic State University, 2011), p. 3.

2. D. E. Hussey, M. Ponsonby, *Buying for the Home: Shopping for the Domestic from the Seventeenth Century to the Present* (Hampshire, Ashgate Publishing, Ltd, 2008), p. 28.

3. S. R. Charsley, *Wedding Cakes and Cultural History* (London, Taylor and Francis, 1992), p. 47.

4. R. May, *The Accomplisht Cook or The Art & Mystery of cookery* (London, Obadiah Blagrave at the Bear and Star, 1685).

5. R. May, *The Accomplisht Cook or The Art & Mystery of cookery*.

6. M. Noble, J. Granger, *A biographical history of England, from the Revolution to the end of George I's reign* (London, W. Richardson, 1806), pp. 436–7.

7. C. Anstey, *The New Bath Guide: Or, Memoirs of the B-n-r-d Family* (Bath, J. Dodsley, 1779), pp. 80–5.

8. J. Northcote, *Memoirs of Sir Joshua Reynolds ...: Comprising Original Anecdotes of Many Distinguished persons* (M. Carey & Son, 1817), p. 98.

9. J. Britton, *Autobiography* (London, 1850), p. 58.

10. *Derby Mercury* (Friday 23 March, 1744), p. 4.

11. *Yorkshire Gazette* (Saturday 25 October, 1828), p. 1.

12. R. Fitzgerald, *Rowntree and the Marketing Revolution, 1862–1969* (Cambridge, Cambridge University Press, 2007), p. 51.

13. A. Adburgham, *Silver Fork Society: Fashionable Life and Literature from 1814 to 1840* (U.S.A., Constable, 1983), p. 216–21.

14. W. Jeanes, *Gunter's Modern Confectioner* (London, Dean & Son, 1870), p. iv.

15. W. Gunter, *Gunter's Confectioner's Oracle* (London, Alfred Miller, 1830, p. 34.

16. E. Callow, *Old London Taverns* (London, Downey and Co.,1899), p. 79.

17. J. Farley, *The London Art of Cookery and Domestic Housekeeper's Complete Assistant* (London, Scatcherd and Letterman, 1811), p. ii.

18. *The Bury & Norwich Post* (Weds. 13 October 1830), p. 4.

19. *The Court Journal, Court Circular & Fashionable Gazette, Volume.* 5 (London, Alabaster, Pasemore & Sons ltd, 1833), p. 174.

20. *Cork Examiner* (Wednesday 15 April, 1846), p. 4.

21. *Cheltenham Chronicle* (10 August, 1858), p. 5.

22. S. Lee, *Dictionary of National Biography, Volume 18* (London, Macmillan, 1889), p. 22.

23. *Dublin Evening Mail* (1841), p. 4.

24. L. Day, I. McNeil (eds), *Biographical Dictionary of the History of Technology* (London, Routledge, 2013), pp. 30–31.

25. J. Wyatt, *The Repertory of Arts, Manufactures, and Agriculture* (London, John Nichols and Son, 1811), p. 193.

26. E. Bronson (ed.), *Select Reviews of Literature, and Spirit of Foreign Magazines, Volume 2* (Philadelphia, Hopkins and Earle 1809), pp. 141–2.

27. K. Bitting, *Un bienfaiteur de l'humanité* (USA, 1924), p. 8.

28. A. Wilan, *The Cookbook Library: Four Centuries of the Cooks, Writers, and Recipes That Made the Modern Cookbook* (University of California Press, 2012), p. 216.

29. B. K.Wheaton, *Savoring the Past: The French Kitchen and Table from 1300 to 1789* (USA, Simon and Schuster, 2011), pp. 167–8.

7 Recipes and Household Manuals

1. N. Nasrallah, *Annals of the Caliphs' Kitchens* (The Netherlands, BRILL, 2007), p. 13.

2. K. Albala, *Food in Early Modern Europe* (Westport, USA, Greenwood Publishing Group, 2003), pp. 125–31.

3. A. Oxford, *English Cookery Books* (Germany, Unikum, 2012) p. 1–2.

4. *Cheltenham Looker-On* (Saturday 29 December, 1900), p. 9.

5. K. Colquhoun, *Taste: The Story of Britain Through its Cooking*, p. 207.

6. K. Albala, *Food in Early Modern Europe*, p. 170.

7. A. Oxford, *English Cookery Books*, p. 29.

8. R. May, *The Accomplisht Cook or The Art & Mystery of cookery*, p. 4.

9. British Library, *The Leeds Intelligencer*, Tuesday 15 October (1782), 1–4.

10. Spectator, *Books of Cookery* (13 June, 1829), p. 12.

11. W. Verrall, *Recipes from the White Hart Inn* (Originally published 1759) (London, Penguin Books, 2011), pp. 7–8.

12. W. Irving, *The Analectic Magazine, Volume 11* (Philadelphia, Moses Thomas, 1818), p. 388.

13. *The Edinburgh Advertiser* (31 October 1786), p. 286.

14. J. Boswell, C. Hibbert, *The Life of Samuel Johnson* (Penguin, 1979), p. 246.

15. *Notes and Queries, Series 2, Volume 6* (Bell & Daldy, London, 1858), p. 444.

16. National Records of Scotland, *Papers of the Ogilvy Family, Earls of Seafield (Seafield Papers)*, c. *1205–1971, Miscellaneous household accounts mainly due by Sir Ludovick and Lady Margaret Grant*, Ref: GD248/208/12.

17. The British Library, *Advert for the Wheatsheaf Vegetarian Restaurant, 1887*, Ref: 6812.

18. W. Alcott, *Vegetable Diet* (New York, Fowlers and Wells, 1838), p. 214.

19. W. Kitchener, *The Cook's Oracle*, Fifth edition (New York, Evert Duyckinck, George Long, E. Bliss and E. White, 1825), p. 312.

20. *Dictionary of National Biography, Volumes 1–20, 22.* (London, Oxford University Press), p. 231.

21. G. Midgley, *University Life in Eighteenth-Century Oxford* (New Haven & London, Yale University Press, 1996), p. 45.

22. G. Midgley, *University Life in Eighteenth-Century Oxford*, p. 38.

23. M. Masson, *The Compleat Cook: or the secrets of a seventeenth-century Housewife* (London, Routledge & Kegan Paul, 1974), p. 171.

24. A. Bourke (ed.), *The Field Day Anthology of Irish Writing: Irish women's writing and traditions. Vols. 4-5* (USA & Canada, NYU Press, 2002), p.708.

25. West Yorkshire Archives, *Bradford election leaflets and cartoons for parliamentary and municipal elections*, Ref: DB39/C29/1.

26. *The Diary of a Farmer's Wife 1796–1797* (London, Penguin, 1981), p. 89.

27. W. Linnard, *John Perkins of Llantrithyd: The Diary of a Gentleman Farmer in the Vale of Glamorgan, 1788–1801* (The National Library of Wales, 1987), p. 23.

28. West Yorkshire Archives, *Ramsden Family of Ovenden and Norfolk and Estate Papers*, Ref: RMP: 1117.

29. H. Falvey (ed.), *The Receipt Book of Baroness Elizabeth Dimsdale, c. 1800* (Hertfordshire Record Society, 2013).

30. I. Tieken-Boon van Ostade, *An Introduction to Late Modern English* (Edinburgh, Edinburgh University Press, 2009), p. 142.

31. National Archives, Folio(s) 157–158. Letter from Dr William Augustus Howard, Gray's Inn Square, 1795, Ref: HO 42/35/68.

32. Bath and West & Southern Counties Society, *Letters and Papers on Agriculture, Planting, &c. Selected from the Correspondence of the Bath and West of England Society for the Encouragement of Agriculture, Arts, Manufactures and Commerce, Volume 4* (Bath, R. Crutwell, 1792), p. 291–2.

8 Innovation and Invention

1. P. Mantoux, *The Industrial Revolution in the Eighteenth Century* (Oxford, Routledge, 2005), pp. 11–12.

2. I. M. Beeton, *The book of Household Management* (London, Jonathan Cape Limited, 1861), p. 31.

3. T. Stephen, *The Diaries of Dummer: Reminiscences of an Old Sportsman* (London, Unicorn Press, 1934), pp. 64–6.

4. W. Kitchener, *The Cook's Oracle*, p. 19.

5. J. W. Klooster, *Icons of Invention: The Makers of the Modern World from Gutenberg to Gates* (USA, ABC-CLIO, 2009), p. 103.

6. I. M. Beeton, *The Book of Household Management*, p. 30–100.

7. A. Broomfield, *Food and Cooking in Victorian England* (USA, Greenwood Publishing Group, 2007), p. 8.

8. B. Franklin, *The Writings of Benjamin Franklin, Volume IV* (New York, Haskell House Publishers, 1907), p. 132.

9. N. Selfe, *Refrigeration and Refrigerating Machinery* (Chicago, H. S. Rich & Co, 1900), p. 18.

10. A. F. M. Willich, *The Domestic Encyclopaedia*, Volume II (London, Murray and Highle, 1802), p. 404.

11. J. Limbard, *Arcana of Science and Art; Or, an Annual Register of Useful Inventions and Improvements, Discoveries and New Facts, in Mechanics, Chemistry, Natural History, and Social Economy* (London, J. Limbard, 1829), p. 252.

12. J. A. Paris, *A Treatise on Diet* (London, Sherwood, Gilbert, & Piper, 1837), p. 259.

13. H. I. Dutton, *The Patent System and Inventive Activity During the Industrial Revolution 1750–1852* (Manchester, Manchester University Press, 1984), p. 206.

14. *Morning Post* (Wednesday 25 December 1833).

15. Patent Office, *Subject-matter Index of Specifications of Patents By Great Britain.* (London, HM Stationery Office, 1857), p. 211.

16. *The Repertory of Arts, Manufactures, and Agriculture* (London, Nichols & Son printers, 1820), pp. 199–200.

17. S. J. Gendzier, 'The Corkscrew', *The Journal of Food and Culture, Volume 1, Issue number 3*, 2001, pp. 67–71.

18. *Tauton Courier and Western Advertiser* (Wednesday 12 March, 1856), p. 4.

19. British Museum, Reg Number: D, 2.4139.

20. *Observations on the Utility of Patents* (London, Ridgway, 1791), p. 37.

21. J. Limbard, *Arcana of Science and Art; Or, an Annual Register of*

Useful Inventions and Improvements, Discoveries and New Facts, in Mechanics, Chemistry, Natural History, and Social Economy, p. 236.

22. W. Blackwood, *The Quarterly Journal of Agriculture Volume. VI, June 1835 – March 1836* (London, John Murray,1881), p. 3.

23. *The Repertory of Patent Inventions: And Other Discoveries and Improvements in Arts, Manufactures and Agriculture; Being a Continuation, on an Enlarged Plan, of the Repertory of Arts & Manufactures* (London, T & G.Underwood, 1830), p. 382.

24. Some Selected Reports from the *St James's Chronicle,* 'New Invented Patent Papier-Machee Tea-Trays and Caddys' (London, Thursday 30 March to Saturday 1 April 1775. Thursday, 30 March to Saturday 1 April 1775).

25. P. Brears, *Traditional Food in Yorkshire* (Edinburgh, John Donald Publishers, 1987), p. 50.

26. *The Monthly Magazine: Or, British Register, Volume 32* (London, J. Adland, 1811), p. 50.

27. British Library, *The Staffordshire Sentinel and Commercial and General Advertiser* (Saturday 8 December 1855), p. 8.

28. British Library, *The Graphic,* Issue 1541 (1899).

29. A. Wilich & J. Mease, *The Domestic Encyclopaedia: Or, A Dictionary of Facts and Useful Knowledge, Comprehending a Concise View of the Latest Discoveries, Inventions, and Improvements, Chiefly Applicable to Rural and Domestic Economy* (Philadelphia, W. Y. Birch and A. Small, 1803), p. 204.

30. *The Repertory of Patent Inventions, and other Discoveries and improvements in Arts, Manufactures and Agriculture Volume 12* (T and G Underwood Publishers, 1800), p. 78–80.

31. *The Repertory of Patent Inventions, and other Discoveries and improvements in Arts, Manufactures and Agriculture Volume 10* (London, G. and T. Wilkie, 1799), p. 148.

32. W. Newton, *The London Journal of Arts and Sciences,* Sherwood, Neely and Jones (London, Sherwood, Gilbert and Piper, 1831), pp. 283–4.

33. *The Repertory of Patent Inventions And Other Discoveries and Improvements in Arts, Manufactures, and Agriculture* (T. and G. Underwood, 1828), pp. 225–6.

34. *Mechanics' Magazine and Journal of Public Improvement, Volume 1* (Boston, Samuel N. Dickinson, 1830), pp. 371–2.

35. R. Bradley, *The Country Gentleman and Farmer's Monthly Director* (D. Browne, 1736), pp. 142–3.

36. J. La Boone, *Around the World of Food: Adventures in Culinary History* (Lincoln USA, iUniverse, 2006), p. 113.

37. K. Colquhoun, *Taste: The Story of Britain Through its Cooking*, p. 264.

38. J. Blocker, D. Fahey, I. Tyrell, *Alcohol and Temperance in Modern History* (California, ABC-CLIO, 2003), p. 569.

39. M. Rundell, *A new system of domestic cookery* (London, John Murray, 1808), p. 207.

40. R. Briggs, *The English Art of Cookery, According to the Present Practice* (G. G. J. and J. Robinson, 1788), p. 373.

41. *Leicester Chronicle* (24 March 1832), p. 1.

42. T. Griffiths, *Slicing the Silence: Voyaging to Antarctica* (USA, Harvard University Press, 2007), p. 347.

43. *Caledonian Mercury* (Monday 26 April 1790), p. 1.

44. *The Examiner* (Sunday 10 November 1833), p. 13.

45. H. Frenk & R. Dar, 'A Critique of Nicotine Addiction', *Neurobiological Foundation of Aberrant Behaviours, Volume 2,* 2000, p. 41.

46. D. Manley (ed.) *Technology of Biscuits, Crackers and Cookies* (Cambridge, Woodhead Publishing, 2011), p. 5.

47. W. Hone, *The Every-Day Book* (London, 1825), pp. 47–8.

48. *Magazine of Domestic Economy and Family Review* (London, W. S. Orr & Co., 1838), p. 30.

9 From Georgian Seeds to Victorian Acorns: The Dawn of the Kitchenalia Revolution

1. L. Davidoff, 'Mastered for Life: Servant and Wife in Victorian and Edwardian England', *Journal of Social History*, Volume 7, Issue Number 4, 1974, p. 406.

2. The British Library, 'The Late Mr.Peabody', *Penny Illustrated Paper* (13 November, 1869, Issue 424, 312).

3. J. Burnette, *Gender, Work and Wages in Industrial Revolution Britain* (Cambridge, Cambridge University Press, 2008), p. 58.

4. M. Mac Con Iomaire, 'Searching for Chefs, Waiters and Restauranteurs in Edwardian Dublin: A Culinary Historian's Experience of the 1911 Dublin Census online', *School of Culinary Arts and Food Technology*, Volume 86, 2008, p. 95.

5. National Archives, *The Diaries of Henrietta Thornhill*, Reference IV/81.

6. University of Portsmouth, *A Vision of Britain, Census Reports* (2009).

7. The British Library, *Penny Illustrated Press* (Saturday 11 March 1871, Issue 493), p. 155.

8. The British Library, *Penny Illustrated Press* (Saturday 25 August 1871, Issue 517), p. 126.

9. The British Newspaper Archive, *Leicester Chronicle* (Saturday 3 April 1852), p. 4.

10. The British Newspaper Archive, *Tamworth Herald* (Saturday 30 October, 1875), p. 3.

11. The British Newspaper Archive, *Huddersfield Chronicle* (Monday 27 October 1879), p. 4.

12. The Women's Library, Ref No. 10/08/1/08.

13. The British Newspaper Archive, *Dundee Courier* (Wednesday 30 April, 1902), p. 3.

14. The British Newspaper Archive, *Manchester Courier and Lancashire General Advertiser* (Wednesday 15 November, 1905), p. 11.

15. The British Newspaper Archive, *Bristol Mercury* (Wednesday 18 April, 1900), p. 2.

16. T. Chapman and J. Hockey, *Social Change and the Experience of the Home* (London, Routledge, 1999), p. 1.

17. L. Mason, *Food Culture in Great Britain*, p. 125.

18. C. Dickens, *Dickens's Dictionary of London* (London, H. Baker Press, 1879).

19. E. Youmans, *Hand-Book of The National Training School For Cookery, South Kensington, London* (New York, D. Appleton & Company, 1879), p. 4.

20. The Women's Library, 'Notes of lectures given by Margaret Pillow', Ref No. 7MEP/1/3.

21. The British Library, *Penny Illustrated Paper* (7 February 1863, Issue 70), p. 87.

22. H. Mayhew, *London Labour and the London Poor; A Cyclopaedia of the condition and earnings of those that will work, those that cannot work and those that will not work, Volume 1*, p. 177.

23. H. Mayhew, *London Labour and the London Poor; A Cyclopaedia of the condition and earnings of those that will work, those that cannot work and those that will not work, Volume 1*, p. 183.

24. The British Library, 'Advertisement for the Wheatsheaf Vegetarian Restaurant', Ref. 6812.

25. E. Acton, *Modern Cookery in all its Branches* (London, Longman, Brown, Green & Longmans, 1845), p. 157.

26. British Library, *The Staffordshire Sentinel and Commercial and General Advertiser* (Saturday 8 December, 1855), p. 8.

27. Bodleian Library, *The Builder, Volume 10, Number cccclxvi* (Saturday 10 January, 1852), p. 24.

28. F. Engels, *The condition of the working class in England in 1844* (New York, Cosimo Inc., 2009), p. 127.

29. British Library, *The Penny Illustrated Paper* (Saturday 2 November 1861), p. 50.

30. E. Acton, *Modern Cookery in all its Branches*, p. 320.

31. British Library, *The Graphic* (7 March 1874), p. 223.

32. E. Acton, *Modern Cookery in all its Branches*, p. 463.

33. British Library, *The Engineer* (3 February, 1888), p. 98.

34. A. B. Soyer, *A Shilling cookery for the people* (London, Geo Routledge and Co., 1854), p. 17.

35. A. B. Soyer, *A Shilling cookery for the people*, p. 55.

36. A. B. Soyer, *The Modern Housewife* (London, Simpkin, Marshall and Company, 1851), p. 413.

37. British Library, *Manchester Times*, Issue 199 (29 August, 1848).

38. United States Patent Office, *Patent no: 505731* (1893), p. 100.

39. *The London Gazette* (24 May, 1859), p. 2075.

40. L. H. Yates, *The Model Kitchen* (New York, Longmans Green and Co., 1905), p. 13–15.

41. E. Leslie, *The Lady's receipt-book, A useful Companion for large or small families* (Philadelphia, Carey and Hunt, 1847), p. 193.

42. *The Farmer's Magazine*, Volume 20 (London, Rogerson and Tuxford, 1861), p. 348.

43. R. Sokolov, *Why We Eat What We Eat* (New York, Simon and Schuster, 1993), p. 232.

44. K. Colquhoun, *Taste: The Story of Britain Through its Cooking*, p. 304.

45. H. Walker, *Cooks and Other People* (Totnes, Prospect Books, 1996), p. 109–10.

46. The British Library, *Advert For Aunt Iza's Princess Tray Rack*, 1880.

47. European Patent Office, Patent no. GB189319852.

48. A. F. Smith, *Pure Ketchup: A History of America's National Condiment, with recipes* (USA, University of South Carolina Press, 1996), pp. 44–82.

49. Science Museum Archives, 'Pyramid' Food Warmer, invented by Samuel Clarke, England, Ref. A639882.

50. Museum of London Collections, *'Moving Here' catalogue*, Ref. 86.228/2.

51. J. White, *London in The Nineteenth Century* (London, Bodley Head, 2011), p. 178.

52. Croydon Corporation, *General Purposes Committee Minute Book, January 1891 – January 1898. Electric Lighting Sub Committee, 10 December 1894.*

53. J. Surrey, *The British Electricity Experiment: Privatization: the Record, the Issues, the Lessons* (London, Earthscan, 1996), p. 14.

54. G. Randall, A. Seth, *The Grocers: The Rise and Rise of Supermarket Chains* (London, Kogan Page, 2011).

55. P. Panayi., 'Sausages, Waiters and Bakers' in S. Manz (ed.) et al., *Migration and Transfer from Germany to Britain, 1660–1914* (Germany, Walter de Gruyter, 2007), pp. 147–8.

56. Anon., *London at Dinner, or Where to Dine* (London, Robert Hardwicke, 1858).

Bibliography

Accum, F. C., *Culinary Chemistry* (London, R. Ackermann, 1821).

Acton, E., *Modern Cookery in all its Branches* (London, Longman, Brown, Green & Longmans, 1845).

Adams, S. & S. Adams, *The complete servant* (1826: London, Knight & Lacey).

Adburgham, A., *Silver Fork Society: Fashionable Life and Literature from 1814 to 1840* (USA, Constable, 1983).

Albala, K., *Food in Early Modern Europe* (Westport, USA, Greenwood Publishing Group, 2003).

Alcott, W., *Vegetable Diet* (New York, Fowlers and Wells, 1838).

Allanrsa, D. G. C., 'The Laudable Association of Anti-Gallicans', *Royal Society for the Encouragement of Arts, Manufactures and Commerce* (1989).

Allen, T., *The History and Antiquities of London, Westminster, Southwark, and Parts Adjacent* (London, Cowie and Strange, 1829).

Andrews, W., *Historic Byways and Highways of Old England* (London, Andrews, 1900).

Anon., *Cassell's Dictionary of Cookery* (London, Paris & New York. Cassell Petter & Galpin, 1892).

Anon., *Domestic Economy, and Cookery, for Rich and Poor* (London, Longman, Reese, Orme, Brown and Green, 1827).

Anon., *London at Dinner, or Where to Dine* (London, Robert Hardwicke, 1858).

Anon., *Sketches of club-life, hunting and sports* (New York, Hurd and Houghton, 1868).

Anon., *Domestic Economy and Cookery for rich and poor* (London, Longman Rees, Orme, Brown and Green, 1827).

Anselment, R. A. (ed.) *The Remembrances of Elizabeth Freke 1671–1714* (Cambridge, Cambridge University Press).

Anstey, C., *The New Bath Guide: Or, Memoirs of the B-n-r-d Family* (Bath, J. Dodsley, 1779).

Bailey, W., *T**d no tansey, or The disappointed pastry-cook* (London, William Bailey, 1790).

Bath and West & Southern Counties Society, *Letters and Papers on Agriculture, Planting, & c. Selected from the Correspondence of the Bath and West of England Society for the Encouragement of Agriculture, Arts, Manufactures and Commerce, Volume 4* (Bath, R. Crutwell, 1792).

Bayne-Powell, R., *Travellers in Eighteenth-Century England* (London, J. Murray, 1951).

Bedoyere, G. (ed.), *The Diary of John Evelyn* (Suffolk, Boydell Press, 1995).

Beeton, I. O., *Englishwoman's Domestic Magazine, Volume 4* (Leamington, C. F. Blackburn, 1855).

Bentley, R., *Bentley's Miscellany, Volume 5* (London, Samuel Bentley, 1839).

Beresford. J. (ed.), *James Woodeforde. The Diary of a Country Parson, 1758–1802* (Norwich, Canterbury Press, 1999).

Bernard, T., *The Reports of the Society for bettering the condition and increasing the comforts of the poor* (S. Bulmer & Co, 1798).

Bitting, K., *Un bienfaiteur de l'humanité* (USA, 1924).

Blackwood, W., *The Quarterly Journal of Agriculture Volume. VI, June 1835 – March 1836* (London, John Murray, 1881).

Blocker, J., D. Fahey & I. Tyrell, *Alcohol and Temperance in Modern History* (ABC CLIO, 2003).

Boswell, J., C. Hibbert, *The Life of Samuel Johnson* (Penguin, 1979).

Bourke, A. (ed.), *The Field Day Anthology of Irish Writing: Irish Women's Writing and Traditions. Vols. 4–5* (USA & Canada, NYU Press, 2002).

Bradley, J., *Cadbury's Purple Reign: The Story Behind Chocolate's Best-Loved Brand* (Chichester, John Wiley & Sons, 2011).

Bradley, R., *The Country Gentleman and Farmer's Monthly Director* (D.Browne, 1736).

Bradshaw, T., *Belfast General and Commercial Directory for 1819* (Belfast, Francis Finlay, 1819).

Bray, W., *Sketch of a Tour Into Derbyshire and Yorkshire* (London, B. White, 1783).

Brears, P., *Traditional Food in Yorkshire* (Edinburgh, John Donald Publishers, 1987).

Brewer, J. S. (ed.), *Letters and Papers, Foreign and Domestic, Henry VIII, Volume 1: 1509–1514* (London, IHR,1920).

Briggs, R., *The English Art of Cookery, According to the Present Practice, 1788* (G. G. J. and J. Robinson).

Brillt-Savarin, J., *The Phisiology of Taste* (Createspace, 2011).

Britton, J., *Autobiography* (London, 1850).

Broadbent, H., *The Domestick coffee-man. Shewing the true way of preparing and making of chocolate, coffee and tea* (1722).

Bronson, E. (ed.), *Select Reviews of Literature, and Spirit of Foreign Magazines, Volume 2 (*Philadelphia, Hopkins and Earle 1809).

Brooke's Club, *Memorials of Brooks's from the Foundation of the Club 1764 to the close of the Nineteenth Century* (London, Ballanntyne & Co. Ltd, 1907).

Broomfield, A., *Food and Cooking in Victorian England* (USA, Greenwood Publishing Group, 2007).

Brown, S. C., *The Collected Works of Count Rumford, Volume V: Public Institutions* (Harvard University Press, 1970).

Brownlie, W., D. Brownlie, *A System of Geography; Or, A Descriptive, Historical, and Philosophical View of the Several Quarters of the World, and of the Various Empires, Kingdoms, and Republics which They Contain: Particularly, Detailing Those Alterations which Have Been Introduced by the Recent Revolutions* (Glasgow, Niven, Napier and Khull, 1807).

Buckingham, J. S. (ed.), *The Oriental Herald and Colonial Review* (London, Sandford Arnot, 1825).

Burford, E. J., *Wits, Wenchers and Wantons* (London, Robert Hale Ltd, 1990).

Burke, E., *Annual Register, or, a view of the history and politics of the year* (London, J. Dodsley, 1762–1838).

Burnette, J., *Gender, Work and Wages in Industrial Revolution Britain* (Cambridge, Cambridge University Press, 2008).

Burney, F., *Brief reflections relative to the Emigrant French Clergy: earnestly submitted to the humane Consdieration of the Ladies of Great Britain* (London, Thomas Cadell, 1793).

Callow, E., *Old London Taverns* (London, Downey and Co., 1899).

Campbell, D., *The Tea Book* (Louisianna, USA, Pelican Publishing, 1995).

Chadwick, E, *Report on the Sanitary Conditions of the Labouring Population of Great Britain* (London, W. Clowes and Sons, 1843).

Chadwick, E., *Report on the Sanitary Conditions of the Labouring Population of Great Britain* (W. Clowes and Sons, 1843).

Chamberlayne, J., *Of Vices and Punishments. The Present State of Great Britain, Part One, Book 3* (London, 1736).

Chapman, T., J. Hockey, *Social Change and the Experience of the Home* (London, Routledge, 1999).

'Character of the French', *Blackwood's Edinburgh Magazine*, Volume 26, Issue 156, 1829. (California, ABC-CLIO, 2003).

Charsley, S. R., *Wedding Cakes and Cultural History* (London, Taylor and Francis, 1992).

Cheeswright, R. J., *An historical essay on the livery companies of London, with a short history of the Worshipful company of cutlers of London, and combining an account of its charters, fundamental laws, bye-laws, estates, and charities* (Croydon, J. W. Ward, 1881).

Cheltenham Looker-On (Saturday 29 December 1900).

Clermont, B., *The professed cook; or, The modern art of cookery, pastry, & confectionary, made plain and easy* (London, T. Simpson, 1812).

Cobbett, P., *A ride of eight hundred miles in France* (London, Charles Clement, 1824).

Cobbett's Weekly Political Register (London, Clement, Saturday 14 July 1821).

Coff, C., 'The Taste for Ethics: An Ethic of Food Consumption', *The International Library of Environmental, Agricultural and Food Ethics* (2006).

Coffin, A. I., *A Botanic Guide to Health, and the Natural Pathology of Disease* (London, British Medio-Botanic Press, 1850).

Cole, G. E. H., *A Tour Through the Whole Island of Great Britain, Volume 1* (New York, Everyman's Library, 1962).

Collingham, L., *Curry: A Tale of Cooks and Conquerors* (New York, Oxford University Press, 2006).

Collins, E. J. T., 'Dietary Change and Cereal Consumption in Britain in the Nineteenth Century', *The Agricultural History Review* (1975).

Colquhoun, K., *Taste: The Story of Britain Through its Cooking* (London, Bloomsbury, 2007).

Croydon Corporation, General Purposes Committee Minute Book, January 1891 – January 1898. Electric Lighting Sub Committee, 10 December 1894.

Curwen, J. F. (ed.), *Supplementary Records: Troutbeck, Records relating to the Barony of Kendale: Volume 3* (IHR, 1926).

Dalgairns, Mrs, *The Practice of cookery: Adapted to the business of every day life* (Edinburgh, 1830).

Davidoff, L., 'Mastered for life: Servant and Wife in Victorian and Edwardian England', *Journal of Social History* (1974).

Davidson, A., *The Oxford Companion to Food* (Oxford, Oxford University Press, 2006).

Davis, R., 'English Foreign Trade, 1700–1774', *The Economic History Review* (1962).

Day, L. & I. McNeil (eds), *Biographical Dictionary of the History of Technology* (London, Routledge, 2013).

Day, I., *Cooking in Europe 1650–1850* (Westport, USA, Greenwood Press, 2008).

De Muralt, B. L., *Letters Concerning the English and French, Describing the Character and Customs of the English and French* (London, Edlin, 1726).

de Saussure, C., *A Foreign View of England in the Reigns of George I and George II* (Plymouth, Van Muyden).

Dean, D., A. Hann, M. Overton, J. Whittle, *Production and Consumption in English Households 1600–1750* (Routledge, 2004).

Deane, P. and W. A. Cole, *British Economic Growth, 1688–1959, Second Edition* (Cambridge, University of Cambridge, 1962).

DEFRA, *United Kingdom Slaughter Statistics, 2014* (London, DEFRA, 2014).

DeLacy, M., *Prison Reform in Lancashire, 1700–1850: A Study in Local Administration* (Manchester, Manchester Uni. Press, 1986).

Dennie, J., *The Port Folio* (Philadelphia, USA, 1812).

Dickens, C., *Dickens's Dictionary of London* (London, H. Baker Press, 1879).

Dictionary of National Biography, Volumes 1–20, 22 (London, Oxford University Press).

Directory, General and Commercial, of the Town & Borough of Leeds, for 1817, containing an alphabetical list of the merchants, manufacturers, tradesmen, and inhabitants in general ... to which is prefixed, a brief but comprehensive history of the borough ... (Edward Baines, Yorkshire, 1817).

Dodd, A., A. Smith, *The Gentlemen's Magazine, Volume 86, Part 1* (London, Nichols, Son and Bentley, 1816).

Dods, M., *The Cook and Housewife's manual: A Practical system of Modern Domestic Cookery and Family Management* (Edinburgh, Oliver and Boyd, 1829).

Dolby, R., *The Cook's Dictionary and House-keeper's Directory* (1830).

Dukes, C., *Work and overwork in relation to health in schools; an address delivered before the Teachers Guild of Great Britain and Ireland at its fifth general conference held in Oxford, April, 1803* (London, Percival & Co., London).

Dutton, H. I., *The Patent System and Inventive Activity During the Industrial Revolution 1750–1852* (Manchester, Manchester University Press, 1984).

Eadon, R., *History of the Company of cutlers in Hallamshire, in the county of York, by Leader* (Sheffield, Pawson & Brailsford, 1905–1906).

Earle, P., *The Making of the English Middle Class: Business, Society and Family life* (California, University of California Press, 1989).

Eden, F., *The state of the Poor: An History of the labouring classes in England, from the conquest to the present period* (London, J. Davis, 1797).

Eger, E., *Women, Writing and the Public Sphere, 1700–1830* (Cambridge, Cambridge University Press, 2001).

Engels, F., *The condition of the working class in England in 1844* (New York, Cosimo Inc., 2009).

Espriella, M. A., *Letters from England Volume One* (Edinburgh, James Ballantyne and Co., 1814).

Falvey, H. (ed.), *The Receipt Book of Baroness Elizabeth Dimsdale, c.1800* (Hertfordshire Record Society, 2013).

Farley, J., *The London Art of Cookery and Domestic Housekeeper's Complete Assistant* (London, Scatcherd and Letterman, 1811).

Feltham, J., *The Original Picture of London. A Correct Guide for the Stranger, as well as for the Inhabitant to the Metropolis of the British Empire* (London, Longman, Rees, Orme, Brown and Green, 1802).

Fitzgerald, R., *Rowntree and the Marketing Revolution, 1862–1969* (Cambridge, Cambridge University Press, 2007).

Francatelli, C. E., *A Plain Cookery Book for the Working Classes* (Gloucestershire, The History Press, 2010).

Franklin, B., *The Writings of Benjamin Franklin, Volume IV* (New York, Haskell House Publishers, 1907).

Franklin, L. C., *Kitchen Collectibles* (USA, Krause Publications, 1997).

Frenk, H. and R. Dar, 'A Critique of Nicotine Addiction', *Neurobiological Foundation of Aberrant Behaviours* (2000).

Gambier-Parry, E., *Annals of an Eton House: with some notes on the Evans family* (London, John Murray, 1907).

Gater, G. H. and E. P. Wheeler (eds), *Survey of London:Volume 16, St Martin-in-the-Fields, Charing Cross* (London, 1935).

Gendzier, S. J., 'The Corkscrew', *The Journal of Food and Culture* (2001).

Gibson, A. J. S. and T. C. Smout, *Prices, Food and Wages in Scotland, 1550–1780* (Cambridge, Cambridge University Press, 1995).

Gisborne, T., *An enquiry into the duties of men in the higher and middle classes of society in Great Britain, resulting from their respective stations, professions and employments* (London, B&J White, 1797).

Giuseppe, P., *Semi-serious observations of an Italian exile during his residence in England* (Philadelphia, Key and Biddle, 1833).

Glasse, H., *The Art of Cookery, Made Plain and Easy* (Strahan, Rivington and Hinton, 1774).

Griffiths, R. and G. E. Grifiths, *The Monthly Review, Or, Literary Journal, Volume, 76* (1787).

Griffiths, R., *The Monthly Review, Volume 31* (1800).

Griffiths, T., *Slicing the Silence: Voyaging to Antarctica* (USA, Harvard University Press, 2007).

Grivetti, L. and H. Y. Shapiro (eds), *Chocolate: History, Culture and Heritage* (New Jersey, USA, Wiley-Blackwell, 2009).

Gunter, W., *Gunter's Confectioner's Oracle* (London, Alfred Miller, 1830).

Harrison, W. (ed.), *New Monthly Magazine* (London, Chapman and Hall, 1847).

Hayward, A., *The Art of Dining, Gastronomy and Gastronomer's* (London, John Murray, 1852).

Hewitt, R., *Coffee Its History, Cultivation, and Uses* (New York, D. Appleton and Company, 1872).

Hickox, R., *All you wanted to know about 18th Century Royal Navy* (USA, Rex Publishing, 2007).

Hill, J., *A History of the Materia Medica* (London, T. Longman, C. Hitch and L. Hawes, 1751).

Hindle, G. B., *Provision for the Relief of the Poor in Manchester, 1754–1826* (Manchester, Manchester University Press, 1975).

Holland, M., *The Complete Economical Cook, and Frugal Housewife* (T. Tegg & Son, 1837).

Hone, W., *The Every-Day Book* (London, 1825).

Howard, A. T., *Seventeeth-Century English Recipe Books* (Hampshire, Ashgate Publishing Ltd, 2008).

Hussey, D. E., and M. Ponsonby, *Buying for the Home: Shopping for the Domestic from the Seventeenth Century to the Present* (Hampshire, Ashgate Publishing Ltd., 2008).

Inglis, L., *Georgian London: Into the Streets* (London, Viking, 2013).

Irving, W., *The Analectic Magazine, Volume 11* (Philadelphia, Moses Thomas, 1818).

Jeanes, W., *Gunter's Modern Confectioner* (London, Dean&Son, 1870).

Jeffries, F., *Gentleman's Magazine, Volume 57* (London, John Nichols, 1785).

Kelly's Directory of North & East Ridings of Yorkshire [Part 1: Places] (1893).

Kitchener, W., *The Cook's Oracle*, Fifth edition (New York, Evert Duyckinck, George Long, E. Bliss and E. White, 1825).

Kitchiner, W., *The Cook's Oracle: Wherein Especially the Art of Composing Soups, Sauces, and Flavouring Essences is Made So Clear and Easy ... Being Six Hundred Receipts, the Result of Actual Experiments Instituted in the Kitchen of a Physician, for the Purpose of Composing a Culinary Code for the Rational Epicure* (London, 1817).

Klooster, J. W., *Icons of invention: the makers of the modern world from Gutenberg to Gates* (USA, ABC-CLIO, 2009).

Koot, G. M., *Shops and Shopping in Britain: From Market Stalls to Chain Stores* (History Department, University of Massachusetts Dartmouth, 2011).

La Boone, J., *Around the World of Food: Adventures in Culinary History* (Lincoln, USA, iUniverse, 2006).

La Roche, S. (trans. C. Williams), *Sophie von. Sophie in London – 1786, Being the Diary of Sophie v. la Roche* (London, Jonathan Cape, 1933).

Langford, P., *Eighteenth-Century Britain: A Very Short Introduction* (Oxford, Oxford University Press, 2000).

Latham, R. (ed.), *The Diary of Samuel Pepys* (London, Penguin, 2003).

Lee, S., *Dictionary of National Biography, Volume 18* (London, Macmillan, 1889).

Leslie, E., *The Lady's receipt-book, A useful Companion for large or small families* (Philadelphia, Carey and Hunt, 1847).

Levy, M. (ed.), *Medicine and Healers through History* (The Rosen Publishing Group, 2011).

Limbard, J., *Arcana of Science and Art; Or, an Annual Register of Useful Inventions and Improvements, Discoveries and New Facts, in Mechanics, Chemistry, Natural History, and Social Economy* (London, J. Limbard, 1829).

Linnard, W., *John Perkins of Llantrithyd: The Diary of a Gentleman Farmer in the Vale of Glamorgan, 1788–1801* (The National Library of Wales, 1987).

Londonderry Corporation Minute Book, Volume 4 (1720–1736) (1915).

Londonderry Corporation Minutes, Volume 9 (1788–1793).

Louis, W. R., A. M. Low, N. P. Canny and P. J. Marshall (eds), *The Oxford History of the British Empire: The Eighteenth Century, Volume 2* (Oxford, Oxford University Press, 1998).

Mac Con Iomaire, M., 'Searching for Chefs, Waiters and Restauranteurs in Edwardian Dublin: A Culinary Historian's Experience of the 1911 Dublin Census online', *School of Culinary Arts and Food Technology* (2008).

Mac Con Iomaire, M., 'Public Dining in Dublin: the history and evolution of gastronomy and commercial dining, 1700–1900',

*International Journal of Contemporary Hospitality Management,
Volume 25, Issue 2* (1989).

Mackintosh, J., *An Essay on ways and means of enclosing* (Edinburgh,
1729).

Macky, J., *A Journey through England: In familiar letters from a
Gentleman here, to his friend Abroad, Volume 1* (London, J. Hooke,
1722).

Magazine of Domestic Economy and Family Review (London, W. S. Orr
& Co., 1838).

Manley, D. (ed), *Technology of Biscuits, Crackers and Cookies*
(Cambridge, Woodhead Publishing, 2011).

Mantoux, P., *The Industrial Revolution in the Eighteenth Century*
(Oxford, Routledge, 2013).

Marshall Cavendish, *Exploring Life Science: Lymphatic Systems –
Organisms* (Marshall Cavendish, 2000).

Martin, F., *The History of Lloyd's and of Marine Insurance in Great
Britain* (The Lawbrook Exchange Ltd, 1876).

Mason, L., *Food Culture in Great Britain* (Wetsport, USA Greenwood
Publishing, 2004).

Masson, M., *The Compleat Cook: or the secrets of a seventeenth-
century Housewife* (London, Routledge & Kegan Paul, 1974).

Matthews, C. J., *Duncombe's second, and only correct, edition. Mr.
Mathews 'At Home', etc.* (Duncombe, London, 1826).

May, R., *The Accomplisht Cook or The Art & Mystery of cookery*
(London, Obadiah Blagrave at the Bear and Star, 1685).

Mayhew, H., *London Labour and the London Poor; A Cyclopaedia of
the condition and earnings of those that will work, those that cannot
work and those that will not work, Volume 1* (London, G. Woodfall &
Son, 1851).

McKinley, D., 'The Tea Caddy' in *Article 128, The Early History of the
English Tea Caddy* (Association of Small Collectors of Antique
Silver, 2010).

Mechanics' Magazine and Journal of Public Improvement, Volume 1
(Boston, Samuel N. Dickinson, 1830).

Mennell, R. O., *Tea: An Historical Sketch* (London, E. Wilson, 1926).

Mennell, S., *All Manners of Food* (Illinois, University of Illinois Press,
1996).

Midgley, G., *University Life in Eighteenth-Century Oxford* (New Haven & London, Yale University Press, 1996).

Miller, A. E., *The Southern Review, Volume 5* (USA, Charleston, A. E. Miller, 1830).

Miller, J., *The Coffee-House, a dramatick piece, etc. By James Miller. With musical notes* (J. Miller, 1743 Miller).

Mitchell, J., *A Dictionary of Chemistry, Mineralogy, and Geology* (London, Sir Richard Phillips and Co., 1823).

Mitchell, S. I., *Urban Markets and Retail Distribution, 1730–1815, with Particular Reference to Macclesfield, Stockport, and Chester* (Oxford, Oxford University Thesis, 1974).

Murray, J., *The Quarterly Review, Volume 42 (*London, John Murray, 1830).

Nasrallah, N., *Annals of the Caliphs' Kitchens* (The Netherlands, BRILL, 2007).

Neild, J., *State of the prisons in England, Scotland and Wales* (London, John Nichols & Son, 1812).

Newton, W., *The London Journal of Arts and Sciences* (London, Sherwood, Gilbert and Piper, 1831).

Noble, M., J. Granger, *A biographical history of England, from the Revolution to the end of George I's reign* (London, W. Richardson, 1806).

Northcote, J., *Memoirs of Sir Joshua Reynolds ...: Comprising Original Anecdotes of Many Distinguished persons* (M Carey & Son, 1817).

Notes and Queries, Series 2, Volume 6 (London, Bell&Daldy, 1858).

Observations on the Utility of Patents (London, Ridgway, 1791).

Official Catalogue of the British Section (London, William Clowes and Sons, Ltd, 1893).

Olsen, K., *Daily Life in 18th Century England* (Westport, USA, Greenwood Publishing Group, 1999).

Owen, R., *Report to the County of Lanark: Of a Plan for Relieving Public Distress, and Removing Discontent, by Giving Permanent Productive Employment, to the Poor and Working Classes* (University Press for Wardlaw & Cunninghame, 1821).

Oxford, A., *English Cookery Books* (Germany, Unikum, 2012).

Panayi, P., *Sausages, Waiters and Bakers*, in S. Manz (ed.) et al, *Migration and Transfer from Germany to Britain, 1660–1914* (Germany, Walter de Gruyter, 2007).

Paris, J. A., *A Treatise on Diet* (London, Sherwood, Gilbert and Piper, 1837).

Parker, J. H. & J. Parker, *Our English Home* (London & Oxford, J. H. & Jas. Parker, 1861).

Parliamentary Papers, House of Commons and Command, Volume 24 (London, HM Stationery Office, 1836).

Pascoe, C. E., *London of To-day: an illustrated handbook for the Season* (London, Roberts, 1890).

Patent Office, *Subject-matter Index of Specifications of Patents By Great Britain.* (London, HM Stationery Office, 1857).

Pecchio, G., *Semi-serious observations of an Italian exile, during his residence in England* (London, Effingham Wilson, 1833).

Pelzer, J. D., 'The Coffee Houses of Augustan London', *History Today* (1982).

Perkins, J., *Every Woman Her Own House-keeper; Or, The Ladies' Library: Containing the Cheapest and Most Extensive System of Cookery Ever Offered to the Public. ... Also, The Family Physician; Or, A Complete Body of Domestic Medicine* (London, James Ridgway, 1796).

Picard, L., *Dr Johnson's London* (London, Phoenix Press, 2000).

Pigot's Directory of Cornwall (Pigot & Co., 1830).

Platzer, R., *Women Not in the Kitchen: A Look at Gender Equality in the Restaurant Industry* (California Polytechnic State University, 2011).

Radcliffe, J., *Pharmacopoeia Radcliffeana* (London, Charles Rivington, 1716).

Randall, G and A. Seth, *The Grocers: The Rise and Rise of Supermarket Chains* (London, Kogan Page, 2011).

Richards, S., *Eighteenth-century Ceramics: Products for a Civilised Society* (Manchester, Manchester University Press, 1999).

Richardson, A. E., *Georgian England* (Yorkshire, Jeremy Mills Publishing, 2008).

Roach, J., *Roach's London Pocket Pilot, or stranger's guide through the Metropolis* (J. Roach, London, 1796).

Robertson, J., *London or Interesting Memorials of its Rise, Progress and Present State* (London, T. Boys, 1824).

Robinson, H., *The Monthly Review, Volume 5* (London, Thomas Hurst, Edward Chance & Co., 1827).

Royal Commission on the Ancient and Historical Monuments of Scotland, ScotlandsPlaces, *Male servant tax rolls, Volume 06, 1785–1786* (Scotland, 2009).

Royal Commission on the Ancient and Historical Monuments of Scotland, ScotlandsPlaces, *Female Servant Tax Rolls, 1785–1792* (Scotland, 2009).

Royal Institution of Great Britain, *Royal Institution of Great Britain Journals Volume 1, Issues 1-8* (London, The Royal Institution of Great Britain, 1802).

Rundell, M., *A New System of Domestic Cookery* (London, John Murray, 1808).

Sala, G. A., *Paris Herself Again in 1878–9* (London, Remington and Co., 1879).

Salaman, A. D., M. Ghadiri, M. Houslow (eds), *Particle Breakage* (Amsterdam, Elsevier, 2007).

Scragg, T. W., *Chester City Council, Old and New* (Liverpool University Thesis, 1971).

Scully, T., *The Opera of Bartolomeo Scappi (1570): L'arte et prudenza d'un maestro Cuoco (The Art and Craft of a Master Cook)* (Toronto, University of Toronto Press, 2008).

Selfe, N., *Refrigeration and Refrigerating Machinery* (Chicago, H. S. Rich & Co., 1900).

Shackleford, S., *Blades Guides to Knives and their Values* (Iola, USA, Krause Publications, 2009).

Sheppard, F. H. W., *The Social Character of the Estate: A Survey of Householders in c. 1790, Survey of London: Volume 39: The Grosvenor Estate in Mayfair, Part 1, General History* (London, Athlone Press, 1977).

Skrabec, Q. R., *William McKinley, Apostle of Protectionism* (USA, Algora Publishing, 2008).

Smiles, S., *Thrift* (Chicago, Donohue Henneberry, 1800).

Smith, A. F., *Pure Ketchup: A History of America's National Condiment, with recipes* (USA, University of South Carolina Press, 1996).

Smith, A. F., *The Oxford Companion to American Food and Drink* (New York, Oxford University Press, 2007).

Smith, E., *The Household Companion* (Hertfordshire, Wordsworth Editions Limited, 2006).

Smith, T. C., *The Naval and Military Magazine, Volume three* (1828).

Society for Bettering the Condition and Increasing the Comforts of the Poor, fourth edition, Volume 1 (London, 1805).

Sokolov, R., *Why We Eat What We Eat* (New York, Simon and Schuster, 1993).

Some selected reports from the *St James's Chronicle – New Invented Patent Papier-Machee Tea-Trays and Caddys* (London, Thursday 30 March to Saturday 1 April 1775).

Soyer, A. B., *A Shilling cookery for the people* (London, Geo Routledge and Co., 1854).

Spang, R., *The Invention of the Restaurant* (USA, Harvard Uni Press, 2001).

Stead, J., *Food & Cooking in 18th Century Britain: History and Recipes* (London, English Heritage, 1985).

Stephen, T., *The Diaries of Dummer: Reminiscences of an Old Sportsman* (London, Unicorn Press, 1934).

Stobart, J., S*ugar and spice: grocers and groceries in provincial England, 1650–1830* (Oxford, Oxford University Press, 2013).

Strype, J., *A Survey of The Cities of London and Westminster, Ancient Housekeeping* (London, HRI, 2007).

Stuart, J., *Three Years in North America, Volume 1* (Edinburgh, Cadell. Robert, 1833).

Surrey, J., *The British Electricity Experiment: Privatization: The Record, the Issues, the Lessons* (London, Earthscan, 1996).

The Court and City Register (London, 1801).

The Court Journal, Court Circular & Fashionable Gazette, Volume. 5 (London, Alabaster, Pasemore & Sons ltd, 1833).

The Diary of a Farmer's Wife 1796–1797 (London, Penguin, 1981).

The Farmer's Magazine, Volume 20 (London, Rogerson and Tuxford, 1861).

The Monthly Magazine: Or, British Register, Volume 32 (London, J. Adland, 1811).

The Repertory of Arts, Manufactures, and Agriculture (London, Nichols & Son printers, 1820).

The Repertory of Patent Inventions And Other Discoveries and Improvements in Arts, Manufactures, and Agriculture (T. & G. Underwood, 1828).

The Repertory of Patent Inventions, and other Discoveries and improvements in Arts, Manufactures and Agriculture Volume 10 (London, G. and T. Wilkie, 1799).

The Repertory of Patent Inventions, and other Discoveries and improvements in Arts, Manufactures and Agriculture Volume 12 (T. & G. Underwood Publishers, 1800).

The Repertory of Patent Inventions: And Other Discoveries and Improvements in Arts, Manufactures and Agriculture; Being a Continuation, on an Enlarged Plan, of the Repertory of Arts & Manufactures (London, T. & G. Underwood, 1830).

The True Briton, Volume III (London, 1752).

Thornbury, W., *Old and New London, Volume 1* (London, 1878).

Tieken-Boon van Ostade, I., *An Introduction to Late Modern English* (Edinburgh, Edinburgh University Press, 2009).

Timbs, J., *Club Life of London, Volume II (of 2) With Anecdotes of the Clubs, Coffee-Houses and Taverns of the Metropolis During the 17th, 18th, and 19th Centuries* (London, Richard Bentley, 1866).

Travels of Cosmo the Third, grand duke of Tuscany, through England during the reign of King Charles the Second (1669) tr. from the Italian manuscript in the Laurentian Library at Florence. (London, Mawman, 1821).

Ubrey-Rees, J. S., *The Grocery Trade : Its History and Romance* (London, Duckworth & Co., 1910).

Ude, E., *The French Cook, Or, The Art of Cookery* (London, J. Ebers, 1815, 1822).

Vallejo, J. A., J. A. González, J. Ramón and J. Antonio, 'The use of head louse as a remedy for Jaundice in Spanish folk medicine: an overview', *Journal of Ethnobiology and Ethnomedicine (*2013).

Verrall, W., *Recipes from the White Hart Inn* (London, Penguin, 2011).

Walford, E., *Old and New London: Volume 4* (London, 1878).

Walker, H., *Cooks and other people* (Totnes, Prospect Books, 1996).

Wallis, T., *The Nic-nac: Or Literary Cabinet, Volume 2* (London, T. Wallis, 1824).

Webster, T. and Mrs Parkes, *An encyclopæaedia of domestic economy: comprising such subjects as are most immediately connected with housekeeping as, the construction of domestic edifices, with the modes of warming, ventilating, and lighting them ...* (New York, Harper and Brothers, 1815).

Weinberg, A. A. and B. K. Bealer, *The World of Caffeine: The Science and Culture of the World's Most Popular Drug* (London, Routledge, 2002).

Western and Midland Directory; or Merchant's and Tradesman's Useful Companion, for the year, 1783, Pigot's Directory of Hampshire, 1828, Pigot's Directory of Kent, 1824, Universal British Directory of Trade, Commerce & Manufacture, 1792–98. Hampshire extracts.

Wheatley, H. B. and P. Cunningham, *London Past and Present: Its History, Associations, and Traditions* (Cambridge, Cambridge University Press, 2011).

Wheaton, B. K., *Savoring the Past: The French Kitchen and Table from 1300 to 1789* (USA, Simon and Schuster, 2011).

White, J., *A Great and Monstrous Thing: London in the Eighteenth Century* (USA, Harvard University Press, 2013).

White, J., *London in the Nineteenth Century* (London, Bodley Head, 2011).

Wilan, A., *The Cookbook Library: Four Centuries of the Cooks, Writers, and Recipes that Made the Modern Cookbook* (University of California Press, 2012).

Wild, A., *The East India Company Book of Spices* (London, Harper Collins, 1995).

Wiley, M., *Romantic Migrations: Local, National, and Transnational Dispositions* (New York, Palgrave Macmillan, 2008).

Wilich, A. and J. Mease, *The Domestic Encyclopaedia: Or, A Dictionary of Facts and Useful Knowledge, Comprehending a Concise View of the Latest Discoveries, Inventions, and Improvements, Chiefly Applicable to Rural and Domestic Economy* (Philadelphia, W. Y. Birch and A. Small, 1803).

Willich, A. F. M., *The Domestic Encyclopaedia, Volume II* (London, Murray and Highle, 1802).

Wilmeth, D. and L. T. Miller (eds), *Cambridge Guide to American Theatre* (Cambridge, Cambridge Uni Press, 1996).

Wilson, P. H., *A Companion to Eighteenth-Century Europe* (USA and Oxford, Blackwell Publishing Ltd, 2009).

Wise, S., *Inconvenient People: Lunacy, Liberty and the Mad-Doctors in Victorian England* (London, Vintage, 2012).

Witzel, M., *Management History: Text and Cases* (London, Routledge, 2009).

Wood, H. T., *A History of the Royal Society of Arts* (London, John Murray, 1838).

Wohl, A. S., *Endangered Lives: Public Health in Victorian Britain* (Taylor and Francis, 1884).

Woods, J., *Letters of an Architect, from France, Italy, and Greece: In Two Volumes, Volume 1* (London, John and Arthur Arch, 1828).

Wright, J., *Mornings at Bow Street: A Selections of the Most Humorous and entertaining Reports which Have Appeared in the Morning Herald ...* (London, 1824).

Wyatt, J., *The Repertory of Arts, Manufactures, and Agriculture* (London, John Nichols and Son, 1811).

Yates, L. H., *The Model Kitchen* (New York, Longmans Green and Co., 1905).

Youmans, E., *Hand-Book of The National Training School For Cookery, South Kensington, London* (New York, D. Appleton & Company, 1879).

Young, E., *Poetical Works of the Rev. Dr. Edward Young* (London, printed for Benjamin Johnson, Jacob Johnson & Robert Johnson, 1805).

Web Resources

Ancestry.co.uk <www.Ancestry.co.uk>

British History Online <www.british-history.ac.uk>

British Library <www.bl.uk/>

British Museum Collection Online <www.britishmuseum.org/research/collection_online>

British Newspaper Archive <www.britishnewspaperarchive.co.uk>

Gwynedd Archives <www.gwynedd.gov.uk>

Humanities Research Institute <www.hrionline.ac.uk>

IHR <www.history.ac.uk/>

Lincolnshire Archives <www.lincolnshire.gov.uk>

Museum of London Collections <www.collections.museumoflondon.org.uk/Online/>

National Archives <www.nationalarchives.gov.uk>

National Library of Scotland <www.nls.uk/>

Nottinghamshire Archives <www.nottinghamshire.gov.uk>

Public Record Office of Northern Ireland <www.proni.gov.uk>

Science Museum Archives <www.sciencemuseum.org.uk/about_us/collections.aspx>

ScotlandsPlaces <www.scotlandsplaces.gov.uk>

Shropshire Archives <www.shropshire.gov.uk>

The National Library of Wales <www.llgc.org.uk>

The Proceedings of the Old Bailey <www.oldbaileyonline.org>

The Women's Library, London School of Economics <www.lse.ac.uk/library/collections/featuredCollections/womensLibrary>

University of Leicester, Special Collections Online <www.leicester.contentdm.oclc.org/cdm>

University of Portsmouth, Vision of Britain <www.visionofbritain.org.uk>

West Yorkshire Archives <www.archives.wyjs.org.uk>

York City Archives <www.york.gov.uk/libraries/>

List of Illustrations

Index

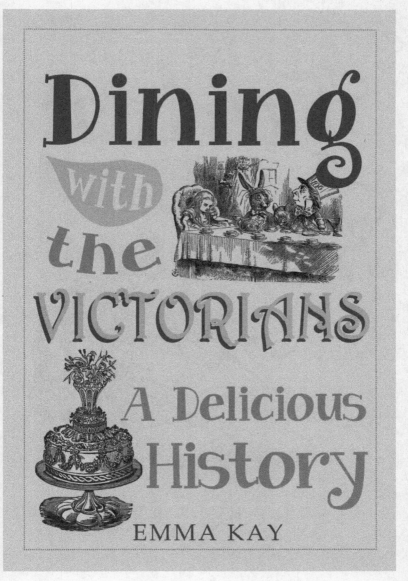

Dining
with
the
VICTORIANS

A Delicious
History

EMMA KAY

the Tudor

Kitchen

What the Tudors
ate & drank

TERRY BREVERTON

Also available from Amberley Publishing

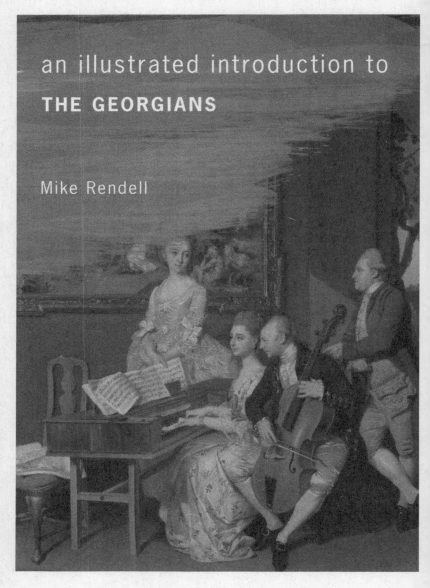

an illustrated introduction to
THE GEORGIANS

Mike Rendell